595-2000 UPS

Log (o)Ui
Log (o)ny 2390
fcU

Something Hidden

Something Hidden

by Louisa E. Rhine

McFarland & Company, Inc. Publishers

Jefferson, North Carolina, and London, 1983

Other books by Louisa E. Rhine
Hidden Channels of the Mind
ESP in Life and Lab
Mind over Matter
Psi, What Is It?
The Invisible Picture

Library of Congress Cataloguing-in-Publication Data

Rhine, Louisa E., 1891–1983
Something hidden.

Bibliography: p.
Includes index.
1. Rhine, J.B. (Joseph Banks), 1895–1980.
2. Psychical research — Biography. 3. Rhine, Louisa E.,
1891–1983. I. Title.
BF1027.R48R46 1983   133.8′092′4 [B]   83-42888
ISBN 0-89950-082-X

Manufactured in the United States of America.

Published by McFarland & Company, Inc., Box 611,
Jefferson, North Carolina 28640

Special thanks for inspiration,
criticism, typing, cooking to
Miriam Whaley
Sally Rhine Feather
Betsy Rhine

Contents

Foreword

Writing this book provided a real sense of purpose for Mother during the difficult period following JB's death in 1980. Often during that time while steadfastly plodding along on this story, she would tell folks, "I have to hurry before my brains run out." Near the end of the first year when she had gone through the diaries and journals which were her main resources, she admitted she felt stumped about how to end it. Then in February 1982 at age 90 she suffered a nearly fatal heart attack which left her with neither the energy nor the will to resume the book for almost a year. She would tell me, "Sally, you'll have to finish this book," and I was afraid I would.

But then, with the resiliency that was so much a part of her character, she managed to pull herself together to finish it, though limited in the creative ability or memory of her earlier years. It was a happy day on January 28, 1983, when she and I drove up to the snow-covered mountains of Ashe County to deliver the manuscript into the hands of the publisher.

Mother died on March 17, 1983, at the age of 91, within two months of completing the book. We who have edited it chose to leave it in her own words and phrasing as much as possible.

Sally Rhine Feather
August, 1983

Introduction

This book is not easily classifiable. It is not fiction. It is not history, although I have tried to make it historically accurate. It is not biography, although incidentally much biography is in it. My original hope and intention in writing it was to emphasize some elements of character and personality of my husband, J.B. Rhine, and the purpose that animated and directed his lifework.

In attempting to fulfill that intention, I began to realize I could not do it as impersonally as I had thought. Too much of *me* got into it and I seemed unable to get it out without crippling the main theme. The result, therefore, is not entirely his story, as I had intended, but rather our story. However, it will not include a detailed account of research on that controversial facet of human nature, the psychic, with which the name of J.B. Rhine has been associated. That record is available in the *Journal of Parapsychology*, which he founded, in his own books, in other parapsychological journals, and in scientific reports from the devoted workers in the field of parapsychology. Instead, this is a more personal, "behind the scenes" account of the origin and development of his ideas and thought, and consequently of his research in the field he named, parapsychology. As such, it covers mainly the twenty-year period of the 1930's and 1940's during which he established the experimental method of research in parapsychology.

The life of J.B. Rhine falls naturally into two main parts. In the first, a question arose and grew until it became all-engrossing. In barest outline, this question was, does the human being possess any inherent feature detectable by objective scientific method that is not physical and which could give a basis for religion? In essence, of course, this is the ancient question of mechanism versus vitalism which is still, under whatever name, the universal one that separates science from religion. The two disciplines answer it differently and arrive at their answers by quite different methods. It was only as the question took form and shape in JB's mind that the second part, the one that covered his lifework, could begin. In that lifework, he endeavored to answer the question not by faith and authority, the method of religion, but by the method of experimental science.

JB and I were married in 1920. That event, so important to us then, serves me now as a landmark to show the stage of development of his thinking, then, on the great question to which he devoted his adult life. I shared the question with him over the succeeding years, and to some extent, his effort to answer it. Consequently, the story resulting is as intimate as life to me. I have known it, thought it, and felt it, practically from the time JB first began to ask it. And although it is JB's story — or Banks', as his family and I, too, called him — and not mine directly, so much of mine is necessarily interwoven that it is only at the expense of considerable natural reticence that I can tell it.

Although we shared the question, Banks was the one who raised it. His mind was much more penetrating than mine, more serious, direct, and single-track. Even before I met him, I had had religious problems of my own, quite different from his, it is true; but I had evaded mine while he met his head on. Although we shared the question, we had different viewpoints. I can distinguish them now, and the stages through which we passed, not only from memory but from several recorded sources. These include not only diary entries and letters, but also a longer account which I wrote some years ago and which JB read and approved. It was written after he had made a considerable effort toward answering the question and after it occurred to us that, since the changes in our viewpoints over the years seemed significant to us, it might well be that in years to come, when our children arrived at comparable stages in their lives, they, too, would be interested to know about them.

Banks and I knew each other for about eight years before our marriage, and during most of that time we were influencing each other more than we realized then, but to an extent that is easy to recognize now. He was only about sixteen and still in high school when the Rhine family in Pennsylvania responded to an ad my father had placed in a farm paper, the *Rural New Yorker*, by renting and moving to our little truck farm in northern Ohio. I was nearly twenty then, had finished high school some years before, and was teaching in the village school.

This difference in our ages and stages was probably more significant to our relationship at that time than it ever was in later years, although I did not even think of it then. Neither did I suspect the effect it had on Banks until years later, when circumstances revealed, and made understandable, reactions of his that otherwise had seemed inexplicable to me.

The effect on me was to the good, for it meant that I was not constrained intellectually in his presence as I might have been had our ages been reversed, for, as I later realized, he was much more self-assured than I, freer of the self-doubt that has always been a part of my nature. But at that time I knew nothing of his nature, nor had I as yet figured out very clearly my own mental characteristics. It was only after years of acquaintance had passed that we began to be conscious of the effect each of us was having on the intellectual and philosophical outlook of the other.

As a class assignment in college two years after Banks and I were married, he wrote an autobiographical sketch. Its final paragraph (deeply touching to me) runs like this:

> But if I ever do anything of consequence or merit, if my life has aught of strength or happiness, and of the latter I already have two years of assurance, I shall attribute it entirely to the influence and help of this wonderful old Pal of mine. And my life shall be successful only in the measure in which it brings her happiness, and serves humanity.

To the entent that it "brings her happiness" I alone can testify: I believe that the objective was attained to as great a degree during our nearly sixty years of life together as any husband has ever succeeded. To the other objective he mentioned, "and serves humanity," I think the verdict is also that he succeeded. Because I think that, I shall first trace the origin of the question in the early part of his life, since only I can do that, and then record something of his attempt to answer it.

Louisa E. Rhine
Durham, North Carolina
January, 1983

Something hidden. Go and find it.
  Go and look behind the Ranges —
Something lost behind the Ranges.
  Lost and waiting for you. Go!

  — *The Explorer*, Rudyard Kipling, 1898

1

Childhood and Youth

It was almost night at the end of a gloomy February day in 1911. The train would not arrive until late, and Banks knew it was very uncertain what they would find at the end of the long trip. It might be a lot better than the place they had left, or it might be a lot worse, for this was not the first time that his father had made such a gamble. This move was only the latest of a dozen or so the family had made that Banks could remember. Each one had meant leaving all the companions he had come to know, and facing a crowd of strangers. This one was taking them farther from the familiar Pennsylvania hills than any of the other moves, and so it was all the more questionable. Even his father had never seen this place. He had never even been in this state. All the rest of the moves, except the one to New Jersey, had been on home territory, as it were. But now — Ohio. Almost "out West," it seemed.

Banks had no idea, really, of what it would be like there. He knew that the country was almost flat — a few little hills, but nothing like the familiar Pennsylvania mountains. The picture the man had sent was not reassuring either. Even the girls looked unattractive. The only bright spot in the situation was the horses. The man had said there were three horses. Banks had never had much opportunity for horseback riding. Now he could look forward to that, at least.

In February 1911, I was teaching the primary grade in the village school and living at home. But now all that was changing. Everything was torn up, only the furniture left for the new people. All of my own family, except my father, had already gone to my mother's childhood home in western New York state where he was to take over the operation of her aging father's farm. He would leave, too, in a few days, after the new family arrived. Then I would be alone, for sure, because of course I had to stay and finish out the school year. I knew I'd die of loneliness.

My few personal effects were stacked in disorder about the room. I had worked hard, cleaning up the old house where we had lived for the new people who would occupy it and who were coming in on the late train. I was too tired and dispirited to try to arrange things. I flung myself into a chair by the window of my aunt's upstairs back bedroom, the only place that now would be my own, and looked across the valley to the cluster of trees and buildings that had always been home, but was so no longer. Worse than the feeling of desolation of a stranger in a strange land came over me. A stranger in a strange land could never be as desolate and lonely as a stranger in a familiar land. To be hundreds of miles away from home would be bad enough to anyone young and unused to separation as I was, but to be away from home and yet in sight of the old place, trampled over now by strangers, was ten times more unendurable.

As I sat, moody and half-resentful, the daylight faded and the light of a lantern began to glimmer around the old place on the hill beyond. Papa was still finishing up over there and later would have to drive to the station to meet the new people.

It was hard telling what they'd be like. We didn't know anything about them, really, except that their name, Rhine, was German like ours, Weckesser, and that the man wrote intelligently and took the same farm paper we did, something of a recommendation. There were children, too, but unfortunately mostly boys. However, they had one girl, only a little younger than I. Perhaps she might be interesting. But unhappy as I was that night, I felt I wouldn't be surprised if she were as impossible as most of the girls in the neighborhood. She'd be silly and boy-struck and the pack of small boys would trample the big flower bed beside the house that I had worked on so long. I'd have to walk past every day and see the weeds grow up in my perennial phlox border, and they'd probably put chicken coops in the front yard...and no knowing what they'd be like — they might be...

They turned out to be Americans, at least, but awfully poor I thought, though I couldn't hold that against them, considering our own situation. The parents seemed all right, just kindly, ordinary people. Soon I was invited to the Rhine's for dinner. I met Myra and her flock of four black-haired young brothers, who, of course, were quite inconsequential — just children to me then. But Myra was nice, and I thought I would like her. Along with that observation, my chief memory of the occasion is Mrs. Rhine's delicious homemade whole wheat bread.

I remember an account Banks himself gave me later of his expectation of the situation that he and his family would meet in Ohio. It seems my father had sent a snapshot of our family, which must have been a poor one even for 1911, for it showed my sisters and me as if so badly freckled (which we weren't) that any interest a sixteen-year-old boy might have had in us was dampened at once. But my father had mentioned that we had several horses; that, to Banks and his brothers, raised happy hopes of horseback rides to come. Fortunately or unfortunately, my father had not sent pictures of those poor old farm animals!

Something of the background of the Rhine family was described by Banks himself in an autobiographical sketch he wrote many years later for a college course, I think in 1922. It begins

> I was a plain son of the hills, born in a log house in the mountains of
> central Pennsylvania. For five years I had no playmates except my sister,
> two years older, for we had no near neighbors. As a consequence, I was
> shyer than a wild turkey and about as ignorant of the world. But I learned
> to love the big blue mountains, the rich dark woods and great bald brown
> hills. Even to this day I feel that I belong more to them than to the
> crowded cities and lighted boulevards.

That observation about himself and his attraction to the out-of-doors is one that I'm sure would be supported by all who ever came to know him well. I recognized it long before I knew it was an attitude dating back to his childhood, before, in fact, I knew much about his background at all. But eventually it became very clear both from his own description and from a trip we took many years later in which we retraced scenes from his early childhood and saw again the log house where he was born and where his parents and theirs before them had lived.

There, surrounded by the hills that were almost mountains, and far from the noise and stir of civilization, all his ancestors for generations had dwelt. One of them, a great-great-grandfather, I think, came from Germany—the Rhine valley—at some forgotten time, and he supplied the name. The origins of the rest are unknown to me, although family names still remembered, as well as some of the features and characteristics of those yet living, speak loudly for England and whisper some of Scotland and Ireland.

But no matter when or whence they came, there in the mountains they had dwelt, simple people, perhaps unambitious and at any rate unmindful or unknowing of the wide world beyond their narrow horizon. Mostly farmers, they were content to wear away their lives in the hard, unproductive labor of cultivating the steep and rocky fields, few feeling any aspiration except to do as their fathers and mothers had done. Many of them hardly left their native cove or valley in their lifetimes.

As Banks' account says, the mountain child's heritage—the hills and the forest—were his. Nature also gave him the kindly, honest virtues of the mountain people, and one other, less common characteristic. That one precious gift was a spirit of inquiry and the concomitant energy of initiation. In his father, it was this spirit that in time led the little family out of the hills and into the world outside. In Banks himself it was a tireless impulse that urged him on from the closely confining limitations of traditional belief and lines of thought to the wider, freer regions of mental endeavor that lie beyond. In a material sense in the father, in a mental sense in the son, the effort that was involved was terrific. In both, the struggle was marked by many a heartache, but there was no turning back.

Thus it was, that in Banks' infancy and early childhood the family lived on in the quiet and sheltered little spot at the head of "Rhine Valley." When his father, Ellis Rhine, became discontented with farming, he applied for and got a job teaching in the district school. Then for a year or two he was satisfied to teach during the winter and to farm in the summer. This contentment was short-lived, but while it lasted the family stayed on the old farm and life went on as usual, except that the two older children, Myra and Banks, went to school. Though Banks was scarcely four years old, he went to the schoolhouse with his father to relieve his busy mother at home. A four-year-old perhaps couldn't learn much, but somehow he must have learned to sit in his seat and make little trouble for his father, thus freeing his mother for the multiplex duties that were hers.

Mountain women of that generation and probably many still today seldom get full credit for the marvels of management and achievement they accomplish. By their husbands, their "men," they are rarely accorded any particular credit for what they do. They stay in or near the house and do "cool and easy" work, while the husbands do the hard work in the fields, run the farm, plow and cultivate and harvest the grain, buy the stock and machinery, handle the money, and take the credit. Their wives take care of the house, get the meals, bear the children and care for them, help out in the fields occasionally at busy seasons, plant and cultivate the garden, care for the hens, raise the chicks, feed the calves and milk the cows. In return "the wife" gets the "egg money" and the "butter money" and buys most of the household necessities with it.

Banks' mother was no exception to the rule. She did not know that she worked hard or managed skillfully since she never could do either one well *enough*. She bore her children, five little two-year-stair-steps, fed and clothed them, tried to keep their clothes mended. Teasing small boys, as Banks remembered, usually got their "apple butter piece" with dispatch so they would clear out of her way the quicker. And so after the daily chores she had little time or energy left for the less tangible aspects of motherhood. If her baby of four could go to school she counted it no misfortune. The baby of two and the one that was coming gave her occupation enough. No doubt she was thankful, rather, that with their father as the teacher she was free from responsibility for the two older ones on school days.

Banks' account of his own memories of his childhood continues:

> My father was a dreamer. He was always sure that "over the hill lay better pastures." He was a country school teacher as well as farmer and had gone off to business college, coming back with dreams far beyond his opportunity and training.

The business college venture apparently was the result of a dream, a wild-eyed one that stayed with him into daylight. The business college was in far-off Harrisburg. A break more unusual or unexpected in a discontented mountain farmer, married and with a family, could hardly be imagined. It must have been an unheard-of venture and the neighbors must have talked.

But nothing stopped Ellis Rhine. Away to the city he went, while his wife and family waited hopefully for him to finish the course, get a job, and send for them. But this was during the depression of the late 1890's and the school was unable to help its graduates get jobs. While he waited, hopeful, hating to go back with only a diploma to show for his effort, he got a job as a conductor on a streetcar. For a short time he continued, but finally he went back to the hills, disappointed but not daunted. I wonder what the folks back there said then. They surely must have looked their "I told you so's," whether or not they put them into words.

I doubt if Ellis Rhine or any of his acquaintances ever understood the real victory of this apparently unsuccessful trip out into the world. But in later years when Banks looked back over the forces of environment that affected his father's and his own life, he gave full credit to that venture, the first definite break with the situation that bound Ellis Rhine, and to the spirit that prompted it, as the impetus for his own early exodus from the hill country to the larger world beyond. To that spirit, too, Banks owed the unrest and initiative that made him press on against the forces in his life that could have been limiting. I'm sure that whenever he saw his father's huge old framed diploma hanging in the "best room" back home, he knew that he himself must ever push back the obstacles that became his problems, just as his father had pushed back his.

Banks' own account, interrupted above, then continues with his father's story:

> But being a hard worker and ambitious he [Ellis Rhine] left the farm when I was five years old. During the next ten years we moved from place to place in Pennsylvania, then in New Jersey and finally back to Pennsylvania, each time trying out a new venture with the same result, a mere living or little better. Finally, ill health drove him back to farming and soon after we moved to Ohio.

> As I look back over those ten years of our family life they seem to represent the "rapids" of our stream of existence, for a toiling turbulent life we lived. Tossed about by this current and that, we came frightfully near perishing on the rocks of financial ruin. My mother's jokes about the poor house always had a note of anxiety in them.

> Once a disastrous fire destroyed all our worldly goods and forced us to seek shelter with relatives. In another town father was tricked into

practical bankruptcy by a justice of the peace and the man from whom he bought the store. In still another place, a competitor through his lodge, circulated a falsehood about my father...

These troubles and many more which I cannot relate to this space would embitter the soul of an angel and father was a very human person. He became irritable, quarrelsome and indeed very unkind to mother, especially in money matters. They were never well mated in temperament and during these years of turmoil they grew further apart until at length family quarrels became painfully common. Every one I ever heard was burned deep in my memory. They seared my childish soul like hot brands on flesh. I couldn't understand why father had to talk so roughly to mother, why she should say she would have to leave, or why there should be any such scenes in our home at all, since we all thought a lot of each other. I cried over these quarrels many times and usually we children were so badly frightened that we would cause a disturbance to end by the fright we expressed.

But as we grew to understand what lay back of these troubles we had only sympathy for both parents and a desire to relieve their difficulties. My sister and I both helped out financially while quite young and desired to do so long before we were able. We have never blamed either parent and only hoped their future would compensate for the unkind past. She [his sister] has always been the biggest factor working to bring them peace and happiness.

The influence of home contacts during these years would take a volume to tell about. But, in brief, they drew me to my parents in affection much more than a smooth colorless life could have done; they taught me to consider circumstances before judging; they warned me of the danger of unhappy and unsuitable matings; and they made me resolve never to make anyone whom I should marry as unhappy as my parents did each other, during those hardest years. It is a wholesome influence and even by contrast alone will teach me to enjoy my own home the more for having lived in that one.

Much more normal, more pleasant, but of less influence on my future were my social experiences of this same period. The only handicap I had was that shyness I got in the mountains. My father moved so frequently that I scarcely had time to become well acquainted in one town until we moved to another strange place and I was about as shy as ever. There is no doubt that this "backwardness," as my mother called it, did lead me to try to "shine" in school work. I wanted very much to be recognized and to make an impression, and being too bashful to do it in other ways I did it in class. As an aid in this too, I had the encouragement of my father. He himself had started my education in my fifth year, and continually encouraged both me and my sister. He helped us with our spelling and arithmetic, even in some of his busiest times. He was always pleased with every hundred we showed him. He encouraged and helped me in public speaking, in music, and in the reading of good literature. In fact, he wanted us to have the things he saw he had missed and believed that I was due to become something unusual in later years. He would say to me, "If you keep right on, you'll make your mark in the world." Of course, it was only parental indulgence but it was a powerful stimulus to me. It is even yet, for I know every little success means much more to those simple-hearted old folks who love me than it does to me. They believe in me yet [ca. 1922] and I still want to fulfill their expectations.

Because of these incentives I did pretty well in my schoolwork in the eleven different schools I attended before entering high school. Anyone ought to finish the eight grades in ten years with some degree of success. But outside the classroom I wasn't always so successful. As the "strange boy" in a strange town I was continually picked on for teasing, and my shyness made me even a better candidate. I wouldn't take much of this and so scrapping began. It began while I was quite young and my initiation into every new crowd of boys consisted of a number of encounters with them. Then we would become acquainted and live in comparative peace unless someone abused my little brothers. That was my own special privilege and anyone else had to fight me before he could mistreat them.

Though I didn't always win, I stood up for my rights as I conceived them, and that is good training for a boy. I soon learned, however, to do things I am less proud of than my quarrels. At about the age of ten, I landed in a larger town, in New Jersey, and in this village occurred a critical point in my life. Owing to the fact that we lived there two years, a long time for us, I became better acquainted with the town boys and girls. Being fairly good at swimming and baseball and such boys' sports, I soon had my cronies, and also, for the first time in my life it was just one "amour" after another. The shy mountain lad became a brazen young lady-killer all at once. I walked boldly up and down the street with my affinities, took them to the little social functions of the town, and got most of my practice in English composition in writing notes to them. About five years of this, with a new girl every few months, showed my awakening sense what a fool I was. I turned abruptly and resolved never to go to see a girl I wasn't perfectly willing and actually wanting to marry. I didn't, as it happened. But now I must go back to that town, to the boy at the age of ten to twelve.

As I said previously, I entered into the life of this village intimately. Now, due to the fact that I had lived mostly in the clean mountain towns of Pennsylvania up to this time, I was a very innocent sort of boy when I arrived there. But in that little modern Sodom I became as wicked in a year's time as I ever knew a boy to be. I became a sort of leader in much of the village vice and did it for effect mostly, for I was very much ashamed at times, especially in Sunday School, which I was obliged to attend. Awakening instinct, curiosity, and a desire to startle others led me to outdo the evildoers among my companions. When I reached the age of twelve there was no doubt but that I had "gone over to the devil, soul and body," as one old saint there put it. And I probably would not be writing this sketch tonight had it not been for one circumstance at this point — a book. And now begins a new epoch.

Four years before, while I was spending some months at the home of a devout aunt, she had read to me stories from the Bible, written in a big illustrated volume. I had been begging my father for four years for one of these books, and about the time I speak of, just before my twelfth birthday, came a big illustrated Hurlbut's *Story of the Bible*. I plunged into it at once, for my interest had increased through those years of wanting it. The book gripped me. I read and re-read it, then re-read it again. In the simple, beautiful touch of the author, the characters of Joseph, David and Paul became real personalities. Jesus became a living man, a friend that one can see when he shuts his eyes. I was deeply affected, and decided that I would be like Jesus. It challenged me, this clean brave life I read of and absorbed. A little later the big Methodist camp-meetings were held at Vineland, New Jersey, near our town. I was there just looking on one day when my old Sunday School teacher came up to me and told me that Jesus wanted me to follow Him, to try to be like Him. Somehow, that appealed to me. She told me to come up to the altar, stand up and say I would live for Jesus, and pray. I did. However, no fundamental change came over me at all, as she led me to expect. Yet I hadn't done anything I regretted. I really did try to do just as Jesus would do in everything, thought I found it difficult, and often impossible.

Since I was very imaginative the personality of Christ became quite real to me. I felt as if I were constantly in His presence. This affected me profoundly and I felt chosen to do some great thing for Him. I wanted to preach about Him, and pursued my studies with renewed vigor with that end in view. I decided to go to high school (my father encouraged me) and then to college. I wanted to become a great preacher like Bishop McConnell whom I heard at Vineland, or Moody or Talmadge, whose books father had.

I shall not go any further into my religious experiences. They came with the age when one's *feelings* predominate; they often cease when one's thinking or *reasoning* begins to gain sway. However, the loving personality of Jesus, be it only an imagination, tided me over the most treacherous shoals of my young life after rescuing me from certain ruin. But I never got any further than my book took me. I sought after the elusive sanctification and holiness, or some evidence that I was saved. None was given me.

Meanwhile I was going through high school, studying hard and reading voraciously. I took every opportunity to speak from a platform. I practically left girls alone, following the idea that it was wrong for a boy and girl to waste time in the mere enjoyment of each other's society, and I had no other excuse than enjoyment to offer. I worked hard during vacation, on the farm, canvassing, doing odd jobs. One summer I sold Hurlbut's *Story of the Bible*, my favorite book when a boy, and because of my enthusiasm for the book succeeded very well at it. Part of the money I gave to my father and part of it I saved to go to school. As far as the mere events of the next few years are concerned, I went to a summer school following my completion of the three-year high school course. The following winter I taught a country school, the next summer returned to the summer school, and in the autumn set out to work my way through a small college in Northern Ohio, at Ada.

But the events enumerated take me beyond the beginning of a new period in my life, what may be termed my "age of reason." So we must go back to high school days, to introduce what was probably the biggest factor in my life — a girl. Then she was a truck grower's daughter, transplanting cabbage plants in Ohio. Now she will soon be taking a Ph.D. from the University of Chicago. I met her when my father moved to her father's farm. I was attracted by her mind alone, I made myself believe. (This was the period when I was blind to feminine charms.) She had finished high school long before me, and wanted to go to college. But she gave many years of service to her parents who needed her badly, putting off her college work. I caught up with her. We went to summer school at the same time [and place, Wooster College, the nearest and therefore the most inexpensive] and as it happened we started to college the same year.

We had been friends from the start. She loaned me books and we discussed them. Our discussions soon got into religion and centered there. She could not share my passionate sort of religion. She by her reason as well as personality made my point of view seem overdone.

Here I need to interrupt Banks' story and insert something of my own. It is true, as he says, that when the Rhine family first arrived in Ohio, I was often, evenings and weekends, "transplanting cabbage plants" in my father's greenhouse, although by the time the Rhines arrived, as I said above, I had begun to teach school in the village, with the ambition to go to college as soon as possible. But I did give priority to my family's need, for my father was perennially hard pressed financially. And so, although it is incidental here, I taught school for five years before a change in home circumstances made me feel free enough from the parental strain to dare to stop earning for my father and go off to college at last, to earn my way there as best I could.

But the Rhine interlude on my father's farm barely lasted out the season. Our fathers were soon disenchanted with each other, and the Rhines moved to another farm down the road from ours. The next season, although I was still teaching in the winter, my younger sister, Esther, and I "ran the farm better than the Rhines did," I confided to my diary. And by the following season my father, no more able to please his father-in-law in New York State than the Rhines had been able to please him in Ohio, moved our family back to the Ohio farm again.

Since Banks and other neighborhood boys and girls who lived farther down the road walked past our house to school, it soon developed that our front yard became a convenient stopping place for them, particularly on the way home from any evening entertainment in the village which we all had attended.

It was on one of those evenings that Banks and I first became aware of each other. I remember that it was interesting to find a young person in the community who read books. But Banks was then a tall, quiet, serious boy so much different from the others of his age that to me he hardly seemed a boy at all.

He had become affiliated with the church in the village very soon after the family arrived and it wasn't long before the minister was urging him on in religious participation. Long before this, as I later learned, because of his parents' and his own wish, it had been decided that he would become a minister, and so although only a high school student still, he was called upon to speak at prayer meetings and other such gatherings. He was serious and enthusiastic. He read not only the Bible but the old religious books and tracts that came his way, with an earnest piety and sincere belief that was never clouded by a doubt. He liked to get into religious discussions then and test out the strength of his own "sword of righteousness." And this I found out on what may have been our first but in any case a continuing argument.

Before radio, before television, in an area far from a library and in which only one of the families in the neighborhood besides my own even took a newspaper, active young intellects had to develop their own topics of interest. In my case the most flaming one then was women's rights, although this was at a time when the audacious idea of women's suffrage had not yet been taken very seriously. But I had already felt the sting of discrimination. Even in teaching, men were preferred to women and drew higher salaries at the same schools. I resented this. And then came this neighbor boy, a mere high school student, who defended it. Why? How could he in conscience tolerate such inequality?

Other neighbor boys and girls were present too during these discussions. None of them was sufficiently active-minded to take up the challenge. But Banks did so at once; because of the Bible, he said. He could find no support for women's rights in the Bible. And for this presumptuous high school student, as I then found out, the Bible was the supreme authority. It was or should have been the final authority for me as well; my Mennonite parents did not question it. But I had not read it through as Banks had done, not once, he said, but several times. And so, although I could not counter his argument, I could challenge it and did so with heat and fury.

After all, I reminded him and the assorted listeners, even while feeling vaguely sacrilegious for saying so, the Bible was ancient history. In the modern world it needed readjustment and reinterpretation. But all I said just opened the floodgates of argument and centered the discussion more and more intensely on religion itself. At first some of the others joined in a bit, but they soon dropped out and Banks and I had the field to ourselves. One evening in our front yard one of the girls fell asleep and tumbled off the bench on which she was sitting, as she waited for the argument to end. But Banks and I did not drop it. We continued it on ensuing occasions, neither one winning, neither one losing, and the determination to convince the other never waning.

And he read everything he could lay hands on, and especially everything of a religious nature, and that he accepted without a question. I remember the feeling of respect for his sincerity but pity for his credulity, when I accepted from him once a religious tract he had just read and thought very stimulating. He had read with interest the few books of mine I had to loan, like Cooper's *Oak Openings, Oliver Twist, The Prince of the House of David*, and so I could not tell him of my repugnance for anything like his tract. So I took it, gingerly, for to me it was not only without interest or possible value but even quite likely an actual work of the devil. To me, there were no religious writings that had any value except the Bible itself, the *Martyr's Mirror*, the writings of Menno Simon, and a few other dull and dusty leather-covered volumes on the bottom shelf of the bookcase at home. Though I never read any of them I knew they were the only ones that did not promulgate "false doctrines." After all, though I was not a Mennonite yet as my parents were, I had absorbed their belief that "fashionable churches" preached a "false doctrine," and of course their preachers were the purveyors of that doctrine. Naturally, then, this young man needed to be set straight; and when I learned that he hoped to be a Methodist minister I had to show him how duped he was. And so, in time, as he said, I made his "point of view seem overdone."

But I could find no way to make this earnest young religious enthusiast see this all at once. Little by little over the next few years as opportunity presented itself and as we became better acquainted I did what I could to open his eyes. I could not succeed, however. The inconsistencies and superficiality of "worldly" people he could see as well as I, but their shortcomings did not disgust him with their religion as they did me. Instead, they seemed only to quicken his eagerness to become a leader and help in the glorious work of awakening the sleeping world to the Great Cause. For it was a Great Cause that he, Banks Rhine, was more and more wholeheartedly enlisted in as he grew older, while the usual interests of young persons his age appealed to him less and less.

Meanwhile my own criticisms of the religions of the neighborhood in time led me to criticize my own, or rather that of my parents. I began to notice the shortcomings of some within the Mennonite church and to feel the narrowness and restrictions that creed imposed upon its followers. At twenty, and before, I was ready to join the church as soon as I could become humble enough. A few years later I was sure I didn't believe any of the other creeds, but not sure I held with this one either. In short, I knew which ones were not right, but I hadn't found one I was sure was right, "right" being a very definite concrete thing.

By this time I was getting some enjoyment out of being a heretic. I shocked Banks by telling him that I believed that "man descended from monkeys." He turned to the Bible and could find no evidence for evolution there and therefore he didn't believe it. We went over the first chapter of Genesis and I showed him the evolution of the world through seven *periods*, not 24-hour days. I was triumphant. But then he showed me the story of Eve created out of Adam's rib. I was beaten on that, and have been ever since. But in the New Testament he found no justification for war or self-defense or capital punishment; and on that, he came over with me, and believed theoretically in nonresistance.

Eventually, however, his attitude changed a little, although I did not know if our arguments had had any part in it. After several years he became less regular and enthusiastic at church, although his interest in the fundamentals was as strong as ever. But he decided that most of the other young people went to church merely because it was the thing to do and because it was a place to show off new clothes and get dates. In time, he began to stay away from evening services for, he told me, he had no clothes to show off, no girl to get, and he would rather stay at home and read.

About this time we were both away at summer school and, as it happened, at the same one, nearby Wooster College. To us both, so fresh from the country, so inexperienced, so eager for life and development, those weeks there were wonderful adventures. We happened to take the same courses in Browning, and it was taught by an emotional, erratic and highly unorthodox teacher. After each session, he left us quivering and trembling with questions. A strange, half-fanatic, versatile character, this teacher stimulated, enlightened, and daily amazed the high school students and schoolteachers who crowded his classroom. It mattered little whether he taught Browning or General Methods of Teaching, for his subject matter was simply his point of departure. His quick, independent mind, like zig-zag lightning, struck first here, then there. He told us why to buy corner lots to build upon, why he favored early marriages, what to do until the doctor comes, discussed the pros and cons of Catholicism, pointed out a local view that suggested the Italian town of Fiesole, and gave us snatches of opera on his Victrola. That particularly touched the sensitive music-loving soul of Banks who realized for the first time he had never heard any real music before. At the time, just the knowledge that music like that existed and that he could come to know it was an inspiration and a revelation to him.

Just how a man like this teacher ever got into this Presbyterian college is a mystery to me now, but he managed to preach the un-dogmatic religion of Browning—or whether or not he preached it, he opened new vistas for us and excited us to think about issues we had never dared approach before. After a summer of this, with Banks' orthodox, devoted views and my serious, freelance ones considerably widened, we were good friends, but nowhere near agreement.

I had never like the idea of Banks' (or anyone's) going into the ministry. I had no reverence for ministers. I put them all in one of two classes. Either they were insincere sinners, however smug and pious they might appear to be on the surface, or they were sincere but misguided and preached a false doctrine, as my parents thought. Neither kind was of any real service in the world. I was afraid Banks would fall in the second class. As a young minister he would become so abnormally "good" that he would never get the understanding it seemed to me a man ought to have before he became a saver of souls.

And so it was, as he says in his sketch, that, over time, I made his "point of view seem overdone." Although I didn't know it then, apparently my arguments had had some effect, for he says

I began to study over my situation, my creed, critically for the first time. In fact, until I began to talk about it with this wide-awake, thinking girl (Louise, we'll call her) I had never actually *thought* on the subject. I simply *felt*, trusted.

His overestimate of my "wide awake" and "thinking" ability was, as I know now, partly the result of our age difference (almost four years), although, as I later learned, only a part of it. Another factor was that because of my own unorthodox background, different from that of my high school classmates, none of whom came from Mennonite homes, I had early been forced into religious thought and questioning.

This was about the state in which we both were when we started off to college. Both of us were honest, earnest, and eager, and wanted only Truth, if we could find it. If each of us had been asked to name his most interesting acquaintance, then, I think each would have named the other. The difference in age had probably made it possible, for me at least, so that we could discuss these mental and spiritual problems without the self-consciousness of sex intruding.

In the fall of 1914, we both were able to start to college, Banks to Ohio Northern at Ada, Ohio, where he was able to get a job waiting tables in the college dining room, and I to familiar Wooster College. Although Wooster was a church college, the religious aspect had nothing to do with my going there. I went for the practical reason that since it was only about twenty miles from home, I could bring along most of the provisions I would need in order to "board myself" and so reduce expenses.

Banks, like myself, was working hard to earn his way and also was carrying full college work. And because of his intention to enter the ministry, he chose his courses, as far as possible, in Bible and elocution. Ohio Northern was not a school of religion, however, and the Bible teaching was not fervent and uncritical. Consequently, questions and perplexities poured in upon the young freshman almost as soon as his classes began.

My schedule that first year was devoted mainly to making up requirements of language and mathematics, so that in the way of ideas it offered little intellectually new or exciting. I was too absorbed in the pure joy of being in college at last, after years of almost hopeless anticipation, to find any fault with the life there as I was experiencing it.

Banks and I did not correspond, not only because we were too busy but also because, after all, to each of us then the other was only one of a number of old acquaintances from the home neighborhood and, as such, not particularly significant in this interesting time of making new contacts.

But Banks' experience in those early weeks was different from mine, as I realized when less than two months after the term began, I did receive a letter from him. He was too earnest to ignore or let pass by unheeded the criticisms and doubts that were raised in his Bible class about the Bible stories he had believed unhesitatingly. In meeting them in straightforward manner, he had the greatest jolt of his life. I quoted from his letter in a diary entry of mine dated October 31, 1914:

> Would you mind telling me why you came to college? I doubt sometimes whether a college education will pay. I realize I am undergoing a change, but the question is, do I want to change from my ideals now to what the crowd thinks. I see how one loses his religion when he goes to college.

I have no recollection of my answer to that. Of course, in my ignorance I had little idea of what the letter really meant or how deeply the situation was affecting him. Banks' next letter came in January, and it filled me with consternation. In the old days back home, I had wanted to see his complacent faith jolted. I had feared the danger of his becoming what, to me, would have seemed a good, orthodox, ordinary, uninteresting minister; but I never thought anyone ever could lose faith entirely, and I certainly had never, never supposed or even imagined he would. I had heard a tale floating around the campus about a brilliant student who "lost his faith" while in college and who never regained it. Terrible tale! I didn't want to see anything like that happen to my old companion in discussion and opponent in argument. But this second letter sounded pretty dreadful, for in it the story of his religious troubles went on to what seemed to me then to be a climax, but which time showed to be but a stage along the way. In this letter, he said he had burned one he wrote to me earlier because it was devoted almost entirely to his troubles in religion (as was this one, too, although he didn't seem to realize it). Then he went on to say

> You see it was and is a fight between Christian and Apollyon as the result of a clash between the modern criticism and "the old time religion." I knew it would come. I had tried for three years to hold it off and if I had stayed away from college maybe I could have succeeded, but now I have thrown down the bridge to Doubt and the fight is hand to hand.
>
> Sometimes I feel the old spirit and strength rise within me and I drive the enemy back across the moat by sheer force of will. But my armor of faith seems thin and I cannot find the famous "Sword of the Spirit."

My shield, belief in the divine efficacy of prayer, has been pierced through and through. The outer works, the Prophecies, stories of God and His people of course were carried easily. Then a mighty tower fell undermined by Doubt, God's interference with natural law, i.e. the Miracles. I began to despair. Then fell into the hands of the enemy one of the two main towers, belief in the story of Christ. I thought it impregnable, but it is captured. (I sometimes have hopes of regaining it. It is not destroyed, just captured.) Now I am virtually a prisoner of Doubt, shut up in the only remaining tower, Divine Power, with the surrounding turrets of Immortality, Clean Living, etc.

Ultimate Reality! Pah! That's fine consolation to the consuming driving passion that I have sometimes felt. Alas, they have taken away my Lord and I know not where they have laid him. Poor Mary Magdalen, I know how she felt.

I think and think and think till I come around to the same place and I feel like a derelict about to give up. But there are just about seven people that make me fight it out. [Banks' family numbered six including himself. I wondered who that seventh was.]

Then he referred to another teacher in Wooster summer school, a Mr. Donnelly, the son of missionary parents, whom we both had had although in different classes, mine in Virgil. Banks must have talked to him personally, for he says

I wish I could talk to Mr. D. I think I know now why he decided to teach instead of preach. One does not like preaching this new and cold scientific religion. My life work (momentarily, I hope) is lost to me. I grope in the dark. "Lead, Kindly Light." (I should have a black-rimmed envelope for this.)

The ache evident in that letter touched my imagination, or rather, my conscience. For wasn't I in part responsible? I had urged Banks to go to college and I was the one who had dragged — or at least tried to push — him up to the brink of religious doubt. If, now, he had fallen in, and fallen so much farther and more painfully than I had ever intended, was it not pretty largely my fault? And so must I not do everything I could to help him out again?

My reply, then, though I have no copy of it, was an attempt to neutralize those forces that were driving him out of the orthodox pathway. I, who had been the heretic, must now try to be the devout guide and point the way back to the path from which he had deviated.

And so I showed him the beauty and strength of the Christian religion. I assured him of my belief in most of the things he doubted. I tried to conceal my crowning consternation over his loss of his "main tower, belief in the story of Christ," by telling him that that couldn't be real, that no one who once had had that belief could actually lose it, although it might for a time be obscured.

I talked the situation over with several of my girl friends, none of whom had ever harbored such doubts, nor even any as mild as mine. And with their assurances I felt I could tell Banks that I had no doubt that his original faith would triumph, that these questionings along the way were but tests set up for his strengthening, and this whole stage but one necessary for him to pass through for his hardening, purification, or whatever, for the great responsibility of his life work.

From his reply a few weeks later, I thought maybe my logic had gone home. I felt somewhat relieved because his letter seemed to mark the climax of his struggle to adjust the old — which meant to him, then, the right, the established, the normal — to the new, the unknown, the hopeless. The struggle was not over, but the poignancy seemed to have passed, for in his next letter he said

> I have a few minutes before Bible class. In it they haggle around trying to show how the ten plagues, etc. were only normal events — you know how it is done — until I am thoroughly disgusted.

> ...Thank goodness I am not depending on that [professor's] class for my religion though I pity some blind followers of his. They come to class, shut their eyes, open their mouths and swallow it all and go away empty. I "close up" and go away empty. However, I am convalescent, I shall know better where I am as I grow stronger.

> I do not believe any more than when I wrote you last but since then I have felt things and needs that I believe will be something to depend on. I feel that there should be an answer to prayer. I somehow feel that the story of the Bible and its teachings are true. I cannot explain why but I find myself believing, or rather holding on to the "old time religion" unconsciously, but it seems that its strongest support was not fact or reason.

> I hate the word "mechanistic." If God does not, has not, and will not perform anything out of the natural order of things, if He does not answer prayer, if Christ did not perform the miracles, *real miracles*, come from God and ascend to heaven; if there is no "love of Jesus" to preach, I may as well be an Ebonite, a fatalist, a cynic. *But I believe they are true and I am going to prove to my reason the things that I feel.*

Yes, I'm going to fight it out. If I were to stop now it would take a miracle to change me later and I would never be satisfied without my life work as I first conceived it. Since I have read *An Uncrowned King* by Wright I have sort of worshipped Truth. I have where I can see it many times a day, "The Law of the Pilgrimate, the Price and the Why?" I have felt its influence. I would like to talk to Professor D. but I find myself depending too much on others. I must work out my own, etc. though I don't tremble enough.

And so, for the rest of that school year an occasional letter passed between us. His determination to "fight it out," to "work out my own" seemed to imply that he still had a hope that he could vindicate his "life work as I first conceived it." But it was a hope that must slowly have flickered out, for his letters continued to show the struggle, sometimes winning but more often losing.

My replies, I know, were constantly full of a dutiful attempt to be the righteous guide, to be an "influence for good," by constantly championing the very devout and orthodox faith I had earlier presumed to scoff at. As I remember, that hope of his was never expressed again, nor do I find it in any of the sources available to me now. He speaks for himself, though in abbreviated form, in his autobiographical sketch:

This rupture of my faith and shattering of my ideals and ambition has completely broken my mental equilibrium. I am left with no definite purpose.

Then I thought that a year at Wooster might help him regain a basic faith. Since the criticism he had heard at Ohio Northern had so upset him and since I had constantly praised my college, its strong religious atmosphere, its idealistic president, I thought it might offer just the antidote he needed, and apparently he did, too. I was much pleased and relieved to learn, near the end of the summer, that he was going to transfer and would be at Wooster in the fall.

That summer, I managed to get to summer school again, and I took a beginning course in biology. It was based on the evolutionary principle. The evidence put before me in that class of the life and development of organisms opened my eyes to a new view of the world. As the class passed from the study of single cell to multicellular forms, as we saw with our own eyes the change from the rudimentary organization of nerve and circulatory systems of repulsive old Lumbricus, the common earthworm, to the more complex systems of the vertebrates, evolution began to assume a new meaning for me in the scheme of things. It no longer meant only that "man descended from monkeys."

I wished that Banks knew about this evidence for evolution, for although I wasn't certain if it bore on his or my own side of the big question, I knew that he respected data, hard, indisputable facts like these biological ones which showed so strongly that the universe was a lawful and systematic one, whether or not it was because of a Planner behind it all, as I preferred to think. But I had no opportunity, then, to pass on to him my newly acquired knowledge, and nothing in his own experience had yet influenced him to look firsthand at scientific findings for any clue they might offer in his quest for the truth of things. However, Banks was not in school that summer. He was busily and successfully selling Wear-Ever aluminum kitchen utensils, the great stopgap occupation at that time for many college students. Both of us had to earn enough to make the next year possible.

I had had a month between summer school and college, and that month as scullery maid (washer of kettles and pans, lower in status even than washer of dishes) at a sanitarium had yielded me exactly twenty dollars. Fifteen of that I still had; that, and good health and the determination to earn what I needed as I went were my assurance for the coming year.

The new school year, then, saw us on the same old Wooster campus. We had not seen each other all summer and had not had time for correspondence; but after our first talk that fall, I realized that Banks' fight to get back his lost faith was not yet successful. The things he said bothered me, as did the hopeless tone in which he said them. I thought, of course, that the state he was in was quite unnecessary, his doubts groundless. Of course the world had a point and purpose, as Christianity teaches. It was a great pity that anyone had to suffer through the uncertainty of doubts like his.

In a diary reminiscence written some years later (May 1923), I recalled that at that time

> When we walked and talked together he startled me by the lengths of disbelief of all my old accepted religious concepts to which he would go. And it was neither bravado nor any wish to surprise or jar me which drove him on. It was simply the innate necessity of an active mind to struggle with the barriers of conventional dogma in the attempt to free itself for larger concepts. His mind was strong and fearless. I came to think he had to go to the utter limit of hopelessness.

I could not believe that his viewpoint was the correct one, and it was not possible for his clearer, keener, more penetrating line of thinking to be satisfied by my happier but less reasoned and more emotional one. Hour after hour of our occasional meetings that fall, we spent trying to thrash it out. The more he talked, the more I knew that he needed to be rescued, and the more tenaciously I clung to my belief that the old-time basic religious faith could be vindicated, but at the same time, the more I became aware of my inability to do so. All the way out to Highland Park, a mile or so from the campus, where we walked one Sunday afternoon I remember especially, we talked and argued earnestly and got nowhere. He simply could not accept the old dogmas. And some of the doubts and questions he raised bothered me continually and refused to be dismissed.

We were both honest and earnest, and this territory we were traversing was as new and untrodden to us in our ignorance and inexperience as if we had been the first persons ever to travel it. Then in the following days and weeks, I slowly began to think that I would have to accept such a cold and barren universe as he pictured if I could be convinced that it was the true one. One would be cowardly, indeed, if he were afraid to face the facts. Even to myself I could not stand being so branded. No, I would face the facts if only I could find out for sure just what they were.

Banks, I knew, was unafraid. He had taken the cold and fearsome side and clung to it. It was the Truth he wanted, simple, unsugarcoated, uncolored; and he would permit no tricks of emotion or desire to influence him. I often thought that in his earnest attempt not to be influenced by such tricks, he was like the man who, to avoid becoming stooped, stood up so straight that he leaned backward. I knew that Banks felt safer from the danger of believing "pleasant things," when he went to the utter limits of disbelief, than when he gave his driven spirit a little bit of comfortable, hopeful faith to cling to.

Since I understood how much Banks' early belief and ministerial ambition had meant to him, I was fully able to credit his strength and fearlessness now in staying on the side so far removed from them. He need not have pushed the problem so far when he suspected that it would lead him into unpleasant territory. He could have evaded, he could have turned back. No one but himself would have known or thought that it would have meant not victory but defeat.

But this was not for Banks. Started on the journey, he could not turn back. It was a type of native honesty, I think; that, and another nameless Something in his nature. It was that Something that drove his father out of the hills and now made easy acceptance and stagnation impossible for the son.

And so, on our occasional Sunday afternoon walks, he would have a fresh supply of information and ideas, and each time he would startle me again by the extent of his disbelief. By then we both knew he must go on. We both wanted to arrive at the bare, cold Truth uncolored by our feelings, hopes, desires, or our "previous conditions of servitude," if it was the *right* side. I never felt quite certain that I hadn't been holding to my own because I liked it better than Banks' colorless, more hopeless one, and not because I had any way of knowing it was the nearer right.

The Right, of course, was a very definite thing to us then. To me it existed as a purely arbitrary, absolute, indivisible, and uncompromisable concept. Either things were right or they were wrong. There was no middle ground, no dulling of the fine edge of distinction between the two. And so we wanted to know the answer, clear-cut, yes or no, no matter what the bitter cost.

In time, it came to be that he led, I followed. In the coming weeks Banks would go to the library to explore new fields, always seeking something to turn back the course of his thinking, and always failing. And then at our next meeting he would tell me about it, listening carefully to such determinedly hopeful suggestions as I still tried to offer, but he always found them unconvincing.

And so he stumbled on during those college days, more interested and absorbed, by far, in this painful problem than by any of his formal classwork. He spent hours in the library. He was an explorer, a path-breaker, who never tired of hunting for the Far Country whose vision he had seen and lost. And I was not an eager but a conscientious follower, always hoping that he would find the proof he needed, even while I could not discount the weight of negative evidence he was accumulating.

I hated that negative evidence, hated it and feared it, but I respected it and had to face it. For I could follow, at least. And I would not for worlds, not for any kind of peace of mind, have given up my chance to come along on this amazing journey. Oh, we knew, of course, that others before us had had religious doubts and questions, but we didn't know it well enough to make it a reality. And so, to us, we were the original one-and-only set of pioneers.

All this was very secret. I never breathed a word of it to anyone, for I knew, of course, that none of the other students had ever gone pioneering into territory such as this. I knew they had never even started. Most of them would have been horror-stricken by a serious question even as trivial as whether or not one should go regularly to church. They simply would not have tolerated a doubt. They knew that doubts were wicked; and moreover, such wicked doubts held for them no fascination. They had neither restless, inquisitive brains, I thought, nor any spirit for pioneering in this area.

I knew, too, that my classmates in that summer biology course believed consequently in evolution, but they also knew how to keep their religion. Our good old biology professor had handed around to the class, almost literally with the worms and fishes to be dissected, his leaflet, "The Reconciliation of Church and Evolution."

But even to these liberals I dared say little, that fall, about the wild scramble I was having on what must have seemed to them very ordinary Sunday afternoon dates. Those afternoons were no more dates to me than they were tame and commonplace walks into the country. They were fascinating, thrilling and disturbing adventures; my girl friends, had they known what they were, would have thought Banks a terrible and wicked young man and me a weakling being led astray by him. I very well knew that even the more liberal ones who believed in evolution were not pioneer stuff. Nor were the boys I knew, even those who had been in the biology class, much more daring. I heard one of them say that the "Rubaiyat" was his Bible, and another admitted to me once in the laboratory that he thought it possible that animals have souls. But in none of them did I find any tendency to cut loose fearlessly from the old landmarks.

Wooster had then an atmosphere of the most devout religion. It was a religious school, whether in the full sense of the word or not, and budding ministers and missionaries found their very hotbed there. Religious meetings of every kind, on Sundays at least, almost crowded out other activities. Every student had to attend daily chapel and church on Sunday. Religious meetings called to the student from every quarter, from one weekend to another. Some of the girls complained that they didn't have a chance to take off their hats from the time they went to Sunday School in the morning until they got home from church or prayer meeting at night.

The professors were chosen by the trustees to fit the place. They saw to it that no wolf got in among the sheep. They even eventually blacklisted the old summer school teacher who had first set Banks and me to thinking.

And so, the very atmosphere of the place, so pious, so devout, so orthodox, seemed to dominate everybody and everything. Everyone was good, good, good. There was no escaping it. In time it became a little smothering even to me and, of course, much more so to Banks:

I could not endure it and so (at the end of that semester) I left school with the question still unsettled. I toured the country, working here and there, trying to be a common working man with a job and no problems.

After a few months I thought I had found my job, forestry, an old boyhood interest, and I planned on a course at Michigan Agricultural School. But just then (1917) the war broke out [in the United States; in Europe it had been raging since 1914]. And then I joined the Marines.

Before leaving for Parris Island I saw Louise at my sister's wedding and in the five mile drive that evening our friendship almost outgrew the name but didn't quite.

Little did he guess how nearly I missed that wedding and our meeting there for one last time in years.

I still counted Myra about my best girl friend back home. I heard from her occasionally though I had never a line from Banks. But I learned from her that after leaving college, he had "gone out to see the world," that he had been at Cincinnati, Indianapolis, Chicago, various places where fancy carried him, working awhile at each, then drifting on aimlessly, it seemed, as far as either his folks at home or I could gather.

I knew that his family knew little of the unrest and struggle within him, and they were not disturbed as I was by his present wanderings. They saw them as a sign of youth's restlessness, as it were, and as it looked from the exterior. But because of what I knew from the inside, I was more worried about him than they.

Then one day toward spring came a letter from Myra in which she said she was engaged and was to be married May 26th. She wanted me to come to the wedding. I was the only person outside of the family she was asking, and she didn't want me to refuse. She said that Banks was coming home then too and would be there for the wedding. But then he was leaving to enlist in the Marines.

That letter came at mealtime. The food that had seemed so appetizing just before suddenly lost its attraction. I could hardly eat. Banks was leaving. He was enlisting in the Marines! That, for him so mentally at sea, could be fatal! He probably would just throw his life away. The ordinary attractions of living that would restrain other young men, had no appeal for him I knew. And even if he did survive physically, how would it affect him morally? I could only tremble to think of it. So young, so rash, so eager and so earnest — but so unballasted! What would happen to him? And guilt still for my part in it overwhelmed me again. I had even been going along with his thinking, had considered myself a pioneer!

I was then living with the kindly Painter family, working there to earn my board and room. It was at their table that I read Myra's letter. One of them noticed that I was not eating and wondered if I had had bad news.

"No, not really, a friend of mine is going to be married. She wants me to come to her wedding." And, I added carefully, as if an afterthought, "Her brother is going to enlist, she says." I didn't want them to suspect that I had any interest in that brother, did I? For of course I didn't have, not the way they might think. I was sure that it couldn't be on his account that I couldn't eat my dinner and had to be excused with a sudden headache. No, it was just because of — of course I couldn't go to that wedding. He would think I'd come on purpose to see him. As if I'd go to see him, when he'd never sent me a line in all this time and after all our discussions and everything!

Just like a girl, I'd gone and let myself be carried away by all the problems my contact with him had brought. I would have supposed, I did suppose, that he'd have had enough interest in me at least to remember me after all our talks. But he didn't. He was a man and that's the way men are! I had had one or two other experiences to show me that personal contacts very often don't mean as much to men as they do to women.

Well, I'd *show* him and myself too! I wouldn't go near him — I'd even miss Myra's wedding and not see him at all even though he was going off to war, for of course he would never think of coming to see me. If he wouldn't write, much less would he actually come to say goodbye to me. I'd never in the world — not even if it were the last chance I'd ever have to see him again, I'd never, *never* go to that wedding!

And so I sent Myra my regrets. I had to work that Saturday and I was behind in my lessons too. I was sorry to hear that Banks was going to war — and then I drowned that under inconsequentials about all the fine young college boys who were getting ready for training camp and how sad we all were to think that they were going. I decided that even if he should read that letter he'd not get any idea of the shock I'd had when I heard of his enlistment.

Then came the morning of the wedding day. Myra had said that she and her fiancé would come to Wooster that morning to get their marriage license (Wooster was the county seat) and I must go along back home with them. They would stop and pick me up. But I had refused the invitation. I thought of it all — even the ride that lovely May morning would have been a treat (automobile rides themselves were a considerable treat in those days), to say nothing of the wedding and seeing Banks, if only I could have gone with a good conscience!

But it couldn't be. At least I had pride even if I didn't have enough sense to keep from getting more interested in men than they were in me!

I had decided all that as I began a big ironing job I was to do for the Painter family. But just then someone was calling for me, and there out in front was an automobile with Myra and her fiancé. "You just must come," she said. Mrs. Painter heard it all. As soon as she understood, my excuse about the ironing was no good — the girls would do that she said, and I surely should go to the wedding. And so, no matter how I tried to refuse, I had to go.

Almost before I realized it, we were starting out on the country lane (few roads were paved in those days) for Myra's home — and Banks. Before I was really out of my daze we were there. The usual arrival — meet this one, meet that one, and all the family whom I already knew. It's all vague now but one item isn't. There in the corner back of the rest was the tall dark-eyed figure I knew so well. The minute his hand touched mine and I looked into his eyes, heard the ring in his voice when he said he was so glad I had come, I knew it was all right; that he had never meant to slight me, probably never thought that I'd expect a letter, never would have guessed that I'd tried to stay away to avoid meeting him or would have thought I came in order to see him if I had accepted the invitation at once. All that was "girl stuff," the intricacies of which this man who was still a boy, after all, could never hope to understand.

The wedding happened as weddings do; it was over in a minute, it seemed. Then came the big country dinner. I found myself at the long table between Banks and his mother and from each side food being urged upon me that I couldn't eat. I could hardly swallow, I couldn't even taste, it seemed. I let my plate be heaped, and so it stayed.

Banks' mother thought I didn't like the chicken because she had roasted it in an aluminum pan. I don't know how I eased her mind. Anyway, the meal to me afterward was a blur of chicken wings and drumsticks and pie and cake and forty things — while beside me, Banks, maybe for the last time. "Tomorrow he goes to Cleveland to enlist."

Something wrong with my throat. Somehow I just can't swallow. I haven't any appetite at all. Maybe I'm excited because this is a wedding. I guess it's the first one I've ever attended.

Then before I realized it the bridal couple left for the afternoon train. They were gone, everybody. Only the old parents left and the younger children and Banks and I. Consternation struck me then as I realized I must leave too! In the unexpectedness of getting there and in the swirl of things after getting there, I had not even thought of plans for leaving. But it would never do for me to linger. That would look as if — more "girl stuff"...

The parents invited me to stay at least until the next day. After all, we were old acquaintances since long before any of us were sensitive to the proprieties and they were probably still insensitive, knowing little if anything about the tension Banks and I were under. They urged me to stay. Now with Myra gone, it would be so lonely, his mother said. But no, I couldn't possibly. Finally a compromise was suggested. If I'd wait until evening Banks would take me to the next town. I could stay the night there with relatives and in the morning take the early train back to Wooster.

The rest of the afternoon and evenings was still ahead. Banks and I could have one more good talk. He said he had seen a white sparrow down in the orchard. He thought it would interest me. And so I started out with him, never thinking of the fact that I was interrupting his parents' last afternoon with their son who was going off to war. In fact, I couldn't remember afterward whether we ever even thought of the white sparrow when we got to the orchard. (Many years later when we recalled that afternoon's walk I remarked to Banks that we forgot about the white sparrow. "Oh, no, we didn't," he corrected me, "We found it, only it wasn't as white as I had thought." I suppose the fact that he remembered and I forgot that little extraneous episode was not entirely a difference in ability to recall, but another sign of "girl stuff.")

Even before we got to the orchard down below the house, we had picked up the old discussion again. First of all, I had to know why he was enlisting.

"No, Louie, nothing had changed. Life is empty, hopeless as far as anything except the present matters." He could see no future, no here-after, nothing. "All the world just kids itself along. I can't. I must get out where there is action, life. Something to take my mind off these things!"

I tried to credit him with much patriotism in so early rushing off to the war. "There is going to be a draft. Why not wait for that? What's the big hurry?" But no! It wasn't patriotism. He'd never stay and wait for the draft. If he was going, he was going. He would enlist in the Marines, "That's where you get action, adventure, the life I need."

And so we wandered down among the apple trees to the woods beyond, in intervals in our so serious discussion stopping to pick some wild flowers so he could ask me, the botany student, their scientific names as well as their common homemade ones, and hear my answers. He said if he hadn't decided to enlist he would have gone to Michigan Agricultural School and taken up forestry. He wanted to know plants too. He already knew the names of many of the trees. He liked that sort of thing.

Then he told me of the months since he left college, of the spirit of unrest and adventure that had taken him from city to city, trying to see every kind of "life" he could find. And now, after all those months, those experiences seemed so tame in comparison to the Big Adventure, *war*! He hoped he could quickly get into action. It was rumored that United States troops were to be rushed to France very soon. Maybe he could get in line! He hoped he could avoid being sidetracked off to some "desert island" somewhere. (This is essentially what did happen — an island, though not desert.) And then he said it was action he wanted. Action so thick and fast that thought would be crowded out.

The same old feeling of hopelessness and fear for him when he left Wooster came back but now intensified a hundred times as for an instant we stood side by side poised on an old log, as we were picking our way through a marshy part of the woods. Here he was today, so close I could touch him with my shoulder; tomorrow, perhaps forever, far beyond my reach. A feeling of yearning and tenderness that moment came over me which, though I didn't forget, I never suspected for what it was until a long time after.

After a time we were back at the farmhouse, then again I was trying to eat a meal which again I could neither taste nor swallow. I remember his mother's comment that I ate no more than a bird. She wondered how I could stay so plump and healthy. And then we were starting out on the five or six-mile "buggy ride" to the town where I would spend the night. It truly seemed "The Last Ride Together," every moment important, a crisis, an epoch. But again I've forgotten what we said. I only know that I was trying to encourage him and to fan to life in him any embers not of rational thought but of a satisfying faith that might still exist.

I had only the vaguest idea of what enlisted life might be like, but I feared and dreaded it, and the action to which it certainly would lead. Forgetting all the brave days of pioneering, I felt that Banks needed strong armor but had none at all. I thought that even a man settled in a reliable religious conviction would find army life a tax on his moral strength. Small wonder I suffered with concern and fear for this young man who, as I well knew, had little of orthodox tangible belief to guide him.

I worshipped purity in men as well as women. I knew this young man had it now. I was sure of that, but how could he keep it? It seemed so hopeless for him to go, as it seemed to me, entirely at the mercy of an uncaring world. But even in my desperation I could do nothing to help him be forearmed against a danger the existence of which he didn't even seem to recognize. And no one else but me had the opportunity to do so. I tried to say what I could to turn his mind to his parents, to what he owed them, to the letters he should write them, for I thought that the only guiding force left in his life would be his family.

My last effort as we parted was a sorry failure as I almost knew it would be. It was only desperation that made me ask for a promise as a last favor. Would he read the Bible once again? I knew he had ceased long ago but would he give it one more try? We might have been wrong to doubt it so — even read a little daily — and at any rate read it all again?

A considerable pause, then, "No, Louie, I can't. And it wouldn't make any difference if I did. I'm past that stage now, hopelessly."

"Oh, you don't really know. Nothing is ever hopeless," I cried. "Do it Banks! Promise me you will!"

He sat silent for some moments. Then with all too evident pain in his voice, he said low and sadly, "No, Louie, not even for your sake can I promise that."

It was about to end. I took his hand. He waved back at me, as I could just see in the summer darkness. Then the horse trotted off, and I was alone. I went to the house, hardly conscious enough to explain to my surprised relatives how I came to be at their door so unexpectedly.

I have often realized what a saving provision of Providence it is that makes it possible to appear calm and natural to the world when under that exterior the crisis of a lifetime may be breaking. "Yes, it's fine weather — a little warmer. It may rain — ".

"How is your rheumatism?"

"That's too bad. I hope it will be better soon. Tell me about May. Is she moving? We heard she was..."

The next morning I was back at Wooster. Life was entirely empty, nothing to do. Oh, there was the work at Professor Painter's and a lot of class assignments and final exams ahead. But it all was so meaningless. What did any of it really matter — nothing was *real* and never would be, any more in all the world. The only thing to hope for now was that the war would end before any of the boys got out of training camp. But many more of them were leaving college every day.

Banks was gone! And there was no one to whom I could talk about it, for everyone, if they knew I was worried about a man in training camp, would think it was a love affair. I certainly couldn't have that, because it wasn't a love affair. I was only interested in Banks because he stimulated me mentally and because, as I thought, he needed me so badly.

But people never understand such things. They always rush to the conclusion that if a girl is interested in a man at all, it's a love affair. They can't understand how much more serious such a relationship can be, with maybe even a soul depending on it. And Banks was such an earnest and kindly young man. It would be like playing cards in church or mixing jazz (a horrible new kind of music) and a symphony concert to have to stand a lot of teasing about him by those who could have no appreciation of the delicacy of our relationship. I had to keep it hidden.

Some of my girl friends, I'm sure, suspected, but they didn't dare to venture any comment. Long after, my roommate said I asked her to go for a walk "to talk something over," but then we walked great stretches and I never said a word. She said later she was sure it had to do with Banks' enlistment, but I wouldn't volunteer anything so all she could do was guess.

Anyway, I struggled on alone in the gloomy period that followed when all the country was darkly shadowed by the war cloud. That alone made life dull and the future dreaded. The only possible hope it seemed would be religion if I could still fan it to a cheering blaze as I had tried to do for Banks. But those attempts too had ever poor results.

My diary was my only confidant, and confidances to it were only half what they would have been had I not been afraid that someday they might be read by someone if through some mistake on my part I might let the diary lie unprotected. I find entries in it such as this:

> I'm at a standstill. I don't seem to have much conscience or anything. Not that I do bad things. I just don't do anything. I need a stimulus I guess.

I even started to read the Bible through, but I think I got only as far as "Numbers." I was glad when the end of the term came, for college had lost its interest because of what was happening overseas and in all the training camps. It absorbed not only my attention but everyone's.

Then soon I had a note from Banks. He was in training camp down in South Carolina. I was overjoyed that this time he wanted to write to me, glad for the chance I might therefore have to be part of the thread that still linked him to his earlier life. But his letter created in me a great agitation and turmoil. I find in my diary:

> Had a short letter from Banks last week. I didn't suppose his going to war or anywhere could affect me like it has. It seems as if I can't get over it. It will be a long while before I find any other person to whom I can talk as freely on subjects that are interesting as I could to him. Oh, this terrible war! If it would only end soon! Banks has only nine weeks in training camp, he says, and then he goes into active service. And poor Frances is expecting daily the call that will take her new husband to France. It will be terrible to think of even a friend in constant danger, never knowing for sure if he is living or dead.

(I thought my real meaning was pretty well camouflaged there if anyone else ever read it.)

My attitude toward life in general was reflected in the rest of that entry:

> Mabel came home with me last Sunday, and that night we had dates with Jim and Harold. They took us to Barberton after church. I think she had a pretty good time. Better than I did, I guess. But somehow I don't care enough about being sociable to bother my brains to talk to and try to entertain anyone like Harold who just naturally doesn't excite me a bit.

That summer my Wooster roommate and I stayed in Kenmore, a nearby town, selling Wear-Ever. It was the way Banks had earned enough to make his time in college possible. We thought we would try it too. And it worked, up to a point. Each of us made about half as much as he had. I think I sold about $2,000 worth. With the percentages I earned from that I managed to get back to college again that fall.

My diary entries for that summer reflected, above all, the worry, necessary or unnecessary, of those at home with relatives or friends who had "gone to war."

Had a letter from Myra today. She's so worried about Banks. I'm sorry for her but I'm worried too. It's queer we don't hear from him — it's been over two weeks. If I have his correct address he must be sick or isn't allowed to correspond freely. I often wonder if the boys in training camp might be sent out into active service before their training period is over and the fact be kept secret.

Anyway, I'd give anything if this awful war would only be over and this dreadful suspense ended. I see now how work that absorbs one's whole mind is a good thing. Today is Sunday and I've had more time to think than any day since I've been here. And I've been more lonesome and worried than I've had time to be all the days of the week together. And yet with Banks only a casual friend, it seems as if I have small cause for it compared to some.

I wish I dared to write all that is on my mind tonight but since the girls found and read my earlier diary I have to remember that they may someday read this. I'm going to get an iron box with a combination lock that no one knows but me and then I'll really express the things that have never been expressed and there I'll put my treasures and only those that I value most of all shall be in it! [I never got it.]

Another beautiful morning, birds singing, sun shining. How can such a terrible war be raging? "All of nature pleases and only man is vile," seems really true right now.

If prayers can help to end the struggle, then from the millions of breaking hearts everywhere, enough of them must soon have ascended to usher in the dreamed-of peace. But every passing day brings closer the time when anxiety worse than ever must begin. That short period in training camp is passing so rapidly, and after that, what?

Blanche and I went to a movie last night and saw 'The Scarlet Letter.' It was good enough. But amusements nowadays are like cake without flavor. We went on a fishing trip on the Fourth to Rocky River and I did enjoy it a lot, when I could keep my mind only on that one day and not let it stray into the future.

... Today is the fateful draft day. Blanche is worried for fear her brother may be drafted. I hear the same thing everywhere. But I can't say a word about my own worries though I think I have more about which to worry than those whose friends have not yet even gone to training camp. No wonder I was nearly sick Monday after I had time to think all day Sunday and therefore I knew, though no one else did, why I was "all in" Monday. The rest thought it was loss of sleep and overwork, but I knew better and why I couldn't even get an audience that day, much less make a sale. I've made up my mind to control my thoughts better and make myself worry less. It's the only sensible way — only I hate being sensible! I've already missed too much of living by being sensible.

In these diary entries of that summer I can also see the reflection of the letters I was getting from training camp. Brief and pencilled notes they were — oh those letters! I hardly need a diary to keep my memory of them fresh. I wrote

Will prayers help? Is all creation merely the acting out of set and definite rules with no free will anywhere? Can't I help being and doing what I am and do? Doesn't it matter what I believe? Why should a sensitive, feeling creation be tortured for no purpose whatever? If the choice is between two guesses, it's surely wise to take the most likely and the most reasonable according to one's best judgment. That's what I think I'm doing in still trying to stick to the old beliefs.

But what about Banks in training camp?

2

The Marines and Marriage

To try to follow Banks to training camp I can only rely on the fragmentary letters he wrote me at such intervals as he was able. But they afford a general picture which is not too difficult to visualize.

In his first letter to me, and in that one only, he was still enthusiastic about the novelty and adventure of his new life. But that changed very soon and something of the discomforts, monotony, and small injustices of the life showed through the lines, although he apparently tried to temper it somewhat. In a few weeks he wrote

We have been drilling and working for about three weeks now and are about half through with the training. It is hard and hot but I can't say that I'm sorry I came even though there are things I never expected in the way of treatment at the hands of drill officers. I'm still glad I came. But I wouldn't urge a friend to do likewise.

The talk is all about going to France, even among the officers and chaplains. There seems to be a certainty of that but most seem to be quite indifferent to the dangers of modern warfare.

One changes quickly here. There is nothing to make one realize or philosophize. One becomes a stoic in his attitude toward duty and danger and trials. But he also becomes Epicurean in his habits if he has no restraints. He learns to bow many of his instincts before military rule and order but the full force of the dammed stream is turned into that narrowed channel. The recruit must swallow his pride, his spirit of revenge, his sense of right when an officer pushes and cusses him around. And then with nine-tenths of the men in his tent he indulges in the most shocking language until it becomes the custom.

But living here in the ocean breezes, the live oaks and salt palms, covered with wavy hanging moss, swamp thick with impenetrable masses of shining green bushes, seeing the sun rise and set in splendor grander than I have ever seen before and listening to the everchanging notes of America's feathered songster, the Southern Mocking Bird, lying in our tents in the cool evenings and looking out at the "forget-me-nots of the angels" and hearing the sweet notes of the last call of the bugle floating through the night — Well, I forget the coarseness of the crowd and I always have the same simple thought, I wish you were here to see, hear and like it too.

I suppose I would hardly dare say that, were I not in my present situation when it is as indifferent to me whether I live or die, as whether I pray to God or Buddha or Mohammed. [Obviously he was just as indifferent to, or unaware of, the turmoil his words would produce in me!]

And then his next letter:

It was a most welcome bit of light you threw from your big world to me. I could appreciate nothing more at this time and situation than the little volume of Tennyson you sent me. [Little did he guess with what feeling of uncertainty as to what it would betray or imply about me, I had sent it. And little did I know then how insipid he actually thought Tennyson.]

Yes, I do like Tennyson, I think because he believed and felt the things I wish most to believe and feel. I like to follow him along his beautiful paths, though they are all well-beaten and he never wanders off into strange and untrodden ways, except in "In Memoriam" and then he soon finds his way again.

I'm glad you like the "Five Great Philosophies of Life"...[did he give it to me? I think I bought it] although I am quite certain that not one of the five will satisfy you, although they are great, each one.

This is the way I figure it out: naturally we all seek happiness, not consciously, perhaps, but surely. Even the most faithful in religion strive for happiness. Well, the things that will give pleasure to one are determined in a general way by Nature in the process of evolution. You know that happiness is reached through the gratification of certain instincts. The more powerful the instinct the greater the happiness if it is given play. And the fixing of our instincts is a matter over which we have no control. Therefore we have no control over happiness seeking. We delude ourselves by thinking that we deliberately grind out happiness with our little machines. Instead, we simply live, have our existence; our bodies and minds have been so fixed and constituted that certain actions, thoughts, sensations, surrounding circumstances give us a feeling which we wish to have repeated, from the basest pleasure to the purest and the greatest. Some pleasures are simple — like that of the cup. Others are not so obvious or easily recognized, like that of losing one's self in some great cause. Then too it may be simply the gratification of an abnormal desire to sympathize, to help as some reformers do, and gain pleasure thereby. In religion there is pleasure in gratifying the instinct to worship and to sacrifice.

But in all happiness of the mind or pleasure of the body there is a price. The price is what determines the good and the bad. "Take what you will," say the gods, "but pay for it." Not even heaven is free. Lowell says, "Heaven alone may be had for the asking," but the asking is a heavy price.

So don't you see that we have no issue here at all? It is of no avail that I have a Philosophy of Life to guide me, a purpose for my life when those things can be of no service to me, when my life will go just the same anyway, when I am only a part of the vast mechanism? Their only value is that they are delusions without which I cannot pass as a natural normal person.

You invite me into your big world. You urge me to cease resisting your persuasion and to accept the ideas that will make me happy. But I guess it does make me happy, somewhat happy at least, to find out the "bitter truths," though I may react otherwise sometimes. I have an abnormal instinct to take hypotheses in their most impossible way and work them out, in order to be certain. Well, of course, I get happiness from indulging that tendency, even though often it has given me unhappiness by countering some other instinct.

Say, I didn't realize I was so prosy and sleepy. You don't imagine what kind of a place this is. Here we are, several thousands of us with nothing to keep us in touch with the world except letters (although they help wonderfully). Not even civilians allowed on the island except an occasional visitor. No reading matter except some old secondhand magazines, a monotonous routine without enough variation to give our sleepy minds a surprise, depression of spirit caused by strictures of officers. Nothing to think of except our daily work, a merciless sun that makes one's blood thicken and even drives all bird life into the depths of the swamp, all except an occasional flock of buzzards that sail lazily and easily around over their carrion, or a chance butcher bird that sits grimly on a lone palm and watches sleepily for an unwary victim.

Then through the sweltering heat stirring up clouds of burning dust and sand comes a long column of Marines. As they fall out before the bunkhouse they drop wearily to their beds and lie there until mess call. They don't care for anything for they have no reason to. Few Marines build on the future; they live only in the present and so they fall into a sort of stupor, mentally, that seals their intellects with the rust of disuse.

Or another letter:

I'm sitting down under our big old live oak tree, writing on my knee. Over in the northeast the big dark clouds are rolling up from the sea. The sun is lighting up the marsh grass in a million shades of green and brown. And away out over the big green salt marshes little sailboats and fishing vessels are sailing swiftly up the Sound before the strong wind that is rising. They tack this way and that, a little streak of white follows each on its briny way.

A preliminary flash of lightning and roll of distant thunder has hushed the bird life. The pair of mocking birds that had been playing around the dead tree nearby have disappeared, a little warbler in the depths of the big oak has been silenced, half a dozen black and white curlews went sailing over the depths of the swamp. Now not even a buzzard is in sight. The mud hens have ceased their harsh calls and not a rail is running along the sands where there were dozens.

But apparently defying the storm, flying swiftly with the wind out to sea, high up, almost in the clouds is a pair of white gulls. And now the beautiful pair comes out from the shadow of a cloud — the light of the sun strikes them — and they are gone.

I wish you could see all this. The tide is very high, the storm is about to break. The breeze is cool and strong. Now I can say, "How good is man's life, the mere living."

(I am inside now.) Haven't you often wanted to get out in a big rain and just let it rain on you as hard as it wanted to? Well, I was out in a small cloudburst the other day. The rain isn't very cold when it shoots down through this hot air. It was better than a shower bath by a mile.

I'm going to tour this country, the whole South someday, whether as a well-padded tourist or as a hobo, I don't know. But I like the scenery. The South is the land for a poet to visit if the heat doesn't make his mind stagnate. It's a land worth fighting for, at least.

Well, I enjoy this work and life. We're in good health and brown as our khaki trousers and don't care a snap for anybody or anything. In fact, we're all ready for France when we get our ten days off from Quantico, which our coach says we will get.

After that came a break of a week or two during which time I lived in constant dread of hearing that his company had been ordered to move. Even the anticipation of a preliminary furlough home wasn't enough to make me less afraid to hear of his going. And then from Myra came the word that he was ill and detained from his company, which was leaving for France. The next to me was this:

Why should I think? By thinking we grow old. So I say, let's cut the gloomy stuff and "can" the philosophy and religion. Why, do you know, I'm just so superlatively happy and everything is so cheerful and bright around here that I can hardly contain myself. I'm *so* happy because the rest of my teeth don't ache — we have the dearest darling of a dentist — so gentle and considerate you wouldn't believe it, why he leaves you escape alive right before his eyes!

Ye gods! What's the world coming to? It's only by continued whistling that I can reduce the pressure of surplus mirth (?) within me when I contemplate the good fortune in having my limbs free from anything whatsoever annoying (other than that trifling abscess on the elbow of my "shooting arm") and I must pause to chuckle, the great benefit my dear young surgeon got from the daily incisions and probings he found occasion to do.

Well it did my heart good to be able to contribute my bit to the cause of surgery and medicine — don't you know?

And then, for some weeks in which Banks swallowed as best he could the disappointment at being transferred to another company just as his own was ordered to leave for France, his letters were fragmentary, detached, poignant, half-incomprehensible, filled mostly with strange (to me) contradictions showing the heights and depths of the life and experiences through which he was passing.

My heart was wrung by pity and sympathy for him in the stress and strain of all I thought I read on the lines and between, and then lifted high by the half-vague references that came more and more frequently, of his need for me and of what I meant to him.

Could I be in love with him, or near it? With Banks Rhine, a neighbor boy — the same old one I had known so long? Oh, no. Not that. My feeling certainly was based entirely on impersonal interest in his welfare, I was sure of it. I only felt for him more keenly than for other boys from home (with several of whom also I had correspondence, however desultory) because of that strange, active questioning mind of his. He had made himself unhappy and therefore he needed any help I could give, more than did any of the others. More than that, he was the only one who commanded my respect for his mental strength and honesty. All that was more than adequate reason for the feeling I had for him, as I told myself; and if I was made so unbelievably happy by the knowledge that I did mean something to him, that was only because I as well as his homefolks could be an influence, maybe an anchor to him at a time when the abnormality of camp life threatened a man with losing himself.

But soon this stage seemed to cool down to a different duller one, and one which filled me with foreboding. Came this:

Should I resist change? This army life is affecting all who live it. It hardens them, makes them "set" in their ideas, tends to make them eliminate their emotional life and sentimental tendencies. And its isolation from civilization and its monotony makes them fall back on certain fundamental feelings and leave fine theories and philosophies alone. They become almost stoical. The only way these changes can be prevented is by a very close and continued contact with those outside.

The question is raised very strongly when one gets to looking himself over and seeing in what respects he is different from what he was when he enlisted. (You notice I assume in the question the possibility of a person controlling the changes in his life. I don't believe that but it is best to assume it, that is all.)

So shall I keep on trying to follow the same course regardless, or go with the wind and the current? Shall I try to keep alive in my mind the thoughts of home and friends? (Try not to be shocked — though I suppose you are more moved to laughter being somewhat used to my mental wanderings.) [Little did he know how much nearer tears than laughter I would be as I read!]

Shall I try to keep hewing through the swamps and mountains I seem to scare up in front of me? Shall I go on building plans for the future, looking on my present surroundings only in the light of their effect on the future I am planning? Shall I continue trying to find a philosophy of life and a philosophy of the universe that will sleep in the same bunk with a religion that I need?

Or shall I go the easy natural way, living intensely in the present and leaving the future to unravel itself as law decrees, allow the changes to take place that are expected when one of my age leaves home and become more or less indifferent to affections that once were strong?

You may have felt it, felt that you were losing something you treasured, a "heart feeling" or something — I don't know what to call it, but should I let it go? Shall I let my mind drift in its natural currents and not try to hew out new channels for it? Shall I fall back on the mere instincts for a religion and a guide to live by?

Won't you answer me? In the latter I shall come out a normal man possibly with a simple view of life and my individuality. Yet in the other is the fight and the striving, the stimulating ideals and the high plans for the future. Please don't make the mistake of classing this problem with the impractical theorizing I usually do — this is very practical and vital to me.

My attitude toward you is changing slowly and as I change. I can't tell how and I am sure it is a change beyond my control — it is circumstance. I don't know whether to rejoice or lament it and I don't know whether to resist it if I should wish to. I don't understand you—or only a little. You have always puzzled me in many ways. Just now I am thinking in particular of your statement, "I have always had a desire to try my hand at engineering social parties." [I am as puzzled now as he was then to think I ever said that.]

You enjoy the society of people, you are interested in society and social problems. You are charitably inclined, but tell me now is there not an untamed spirit within you that revels in the wildness of nature—in rocks and rivers, forest and fields, that soars among snowy mountains and over billowy oceans?

Would you not be drawn by the big free out-of-doors? Will your life not have to be something unusual? Forget your modesty, and tell me, will it not have to be exciting, full of variety such as is not found in the confines of society and its problems? Or will the varnish of education and civilization outlast the natural color? Both show up beautifully on such a grain but which will prevail?

No wonder I was puzzled. Didn't he know me at all, even after those college walks into the country? But I guess his mind then was too filled with his personal unrest to notice and I think now he was in a way describing himself and had no idea that he was leaving me guessing as to what his attitude toward me had been, or to what it was now changing.

Well, do you laugh, or do you worry for fear the squirrels will get me? I am on the range again. You must not work too hard—my old company is on its way to Quantico and I am marooned here!

Then sometime later, "I am still here!" and then he goes on not realizing, I'm sure, that what he says about me now conflicts with what he said before:

It is strange how well I think I know you. I have your answers to a number of things I never asked you. I think I know what you would think of most of the things I do and many you wouldn't think much of. What you would think is a sort of compass or chart or both.

Then he went off on a tangent:

Now I've hit the circle again, that old melancholy, pessimistic circle.

Haven't you found out yet that I am by nature gloomy, that nothing short of a miracle could make me a bright, optimistic chap, going up and down the world spreading joy? No, I am naturally a doubter, a skeptic. Will that miracle happen? [Well, he was right about that characterization!]

Now for instance, I think this war was, will be a blessing to humanity. Isn't that the limit? I'll tell you why when I get my furlough. [He never got the furlough and I never found out why he thought the war a blessing.]

You see, I seem to enjoy perversity, to revel in bitter truths, that is, my inner nature does — Are you sure you have considered that characteristic when you hope I will become a believer in the better ways of living and thinking? Now that my habits of thought are becoming fixed I am pretty sure of becoming settled into my present tendencies and conclusions.

I know I assured you of my intention to fight my way through, at any rate. But I can't make a fight out of it anymore. I find the other party missing. My conclusions are taking their places on the shelf as habitual thoughts and are part of me.

I must tell you of my good fortune. I won my first medal and a $3.00 a month extra pay by making sharpshooter on the rifle range.

And then obviously in reference to something I had written him:

You think too much of the horrors of war. They make war look pretty bad in "The Birth of a Nation," I remember. War is not "hell," not horrible. It's but a natural scene with many elements of human nature that are good as well as the other.

The training and actual service will be a benefit to those who survive, much as they seem like trial and tribulation now. There is nothing really horrible about any of it. The killing, wounding, gas, bombs — the horror of them is mostly to those back home, to those who care, and sometimes to the soldier in anticipation but seldom to him in action. We can only have one emotion at a time so fear has to step out when eagerness to kill steps in. It may seem horrible to want to kill, but it is instinctive. It is instinct that makes us fight. I am sure you would rather see men fight and kill than to turn yellow. I know you hated Arnold just as I did, that your blood tingled when you read of the great charges at Fredricksburg, Gettysburg, Marathon in Greece, of old Leonides at Thermopylae — Oh,

I know you'd clench your fists and wish you could go out and fight for your country and die bravely — you must be thrilled by patriotism at times.

And another time apparently after my answer:

To be sure I'm skeptical enough to say "Rot" once in awhile, but all the same it's there, the patriotic urge — don't you feel the same? The urges that make men willing to die in battle are as great blessings to the human race as those that make them die as martyrs. I am sure they are.

You have by far the worst part of it. You suffer many times in imagination and anticipation, while we can but once. But now give yourself relief. Just think of it in its natural way — I have several ways of looking at war as a benefactor of the human race that do me good to think about.

No, I do not desire to go to school at Wooster anymore. I shall never be able to shake off the memory of that stifling atmosphere of Faith, Orthodoxy, Ancient Custom in thought, and all. I'm afraid I would insult that old Bible teacher if he should ever mention "the Church" to me again. I feel toward the place like I would to a person who sits in an unventilated room all day through faith in old fogy ideas and who resists enlightenment.

No, I'll not go off in secret — I shall let you know as soon as I know we are going to leave and I'll write you from the new place. I expect we'll soon leave this island but I don't know when. I am very eager to leave. I have been here about three months now, and expect my furlough as soon as I get to the new place. And now to bed. We had a hard day's work today, Sunday, so I will enjoy the night. That's the reward.

Excuse this letter. It is finger-marked and poorly written because of the variety of times and places in which it was written.

I still long for the woods and mountains and rivers. I care little for the society of men for mere society's sake. I have so few ties to civilization that I think I shall always feel closest to the wilds of nature.

As I glance over the next letter, even now, I think small wonder I was nearly distracted, small wonder I thought the pain and hopelessness of it would almost drive me crazy. With nothing I could do, no way of help, no one to tell, and my vivid imagination to add ever fresh fuel to that his lines supplied, the situation was slow torture to me.

Dearest Friend, — I am drifting away — away from you and all the associations I treasured most — away from the beautiful "big world" you live in — away from the beautiful Isle of Faith in all things that I have been gazing upon since I first beheld it. With my helm hard aport I have tried hard to land but the tides and currents and winds have swept me away and now it is too late. Now I have gone far past and know I shall never return. Your Isle was a fancy, a dream of mine. I always looked forward to "dwelling" there, always gave it every beauty that my heart could desire. It would have been heaven without dying for it, and you, spiritual and material, were in the center of it.

You beckoned me, you believed in me, hoped for me. But even as Ulysses of old opened the bag of evil winds through curiosity, so I opened the bag of skepticism and with an angry roar it swept me far out on the troubled ocean — Now I would rather be an expert with the bayonet than with the pen. I would rather know how to save men's lives than their "souls," my own of course included. I would rather be in a lumber camp or on the quarter deck of a vessel than in a church, school or social gathering. You see there is a revolutionary streak in me that breaks through in every case. It means *change* for me, continual and lifelong.

The spirit of the Wandering Jew has been reincarnated in me I guess. It's "Go! Go! Go! Stay not!" that has been burning itself into my mind since two generations ago. Social restraints have acted in the past, but cannot always. I may yet become a hopeless wanderer.

Of course, I don't care what I shall become for I don't need to. The laws of the mind are kind enough to give equal pleasure no matter what develops, a life of self-sacrifice or one of indulgence. And as for one's friends those who understand him understand his changes and development. Those who don't he disregards.

... No, I have no desire for religion anymore, no more than I have to fall in love or to become a good industrious model young man. All are good and all right but — I don't have a taste for them anymore.

Some little time after that came a card written on board the transport which took him and his company, so suddenly that the long expected furlough was denied them, to Santo Domingo (later, the Dominican Republic). Only from a report from Myra did I learn how bitterly disappointed he was to have to leave the country without even the promised few days to see the homefolks one more time.

I, too, was keenly disappointed, for I had hardly realized how much I had been anticipating even a few hours with him. I only then acknowledged to myself that my new waist and skirt had been chosen for his eye entirely. But I was especially sorry to have him leave without the opportunity of renewing home ties — those he had admitted were growing less real to him.

How eagerly I waited for a letter then! The papers were full of submarine atrocities and even though the destination, Santo Domingo, was safer than the one in France would have been, I never knew, in the vague ignorance that those of us back home were in, where the danger was or where it wasn't. Consequently, it was everywhere off the U.S. coast.

I was not alone in my worry and uncertainty. One day a long-distance call came to me (no common happening then, at least to ordinary people). It was from Banks' mother. She knew that Banks corresponded with me and she wanted to know if I had heard from him recently. She had waited until she was nearly ill with worry. But her last word from him, and mine, were dated the same day, so neither of us found any comfort in the news from the other.

At last, however, a letter came from Santo Domingo. He told of the interesting ocean trip. His delight in the change from the monotonous camp life was obvious. He described the island, the natives, the outlook for the life of a Marine there.

> We have liberty here every evening, and enjoy it. But the town is full of rum and beer and a good many fellows get in the "brig" for things done while drunk.

> I cannot get my mind awake in this sleepy town and hot sun. I have written almost mechanically so far. Maybe I shall awake in San Marquisa where I with others am to go soon. Be sure and write soon. I am sending you some views from Parris Island. I shall send you some from here too.

And then — that was the end!

I waited eagerly, and as time went on desperately, but no further word came from Banks. Every day for me was hope twice deferred, once at noon when I hastened home from class to look for a letter, once at night as I literally ran up the hill from the job I had gotten downtown (making paper roses, believe it or not!) in expectation of the letter that I was always sure would be there at last. But it never was. All the bogeys of a lively and war-scared imagination were before me hourly.

How I got my lessons and attended lectures, was a mystery to me then, as it still is. Again, this time not for a period of hours but for months, some second brain center seemed somehow to serve for the first, which was always so far away from Wooster and from the actual practical living of life.

He had asked me to write, even in that last letter from San Marquisa, not once but often. He had said he would write from San Marquisa, he would even send pictures, and then—nothing! I could think of no explanation, except that some contingency of the war was preventing it. Or maybe the mail was intercepted, although my letters to him were not returned. He might be ill. He might be hurt. Maybe he had been sent on to France. Maybe he had been taken prisoner on the ocean. Maybe the heat in such a tropical place had overcome him. Maybe his mind was gone. Maybe—maybe—a thousand maybes! For two months I lived this agony, then at Thanksgiving I heard from his parents—he was well and still in Santo Domingo!

That news put a different construction on the situation, the only "maybe" I had not considered. Nothing was preventing him from writing to me. If his letters home got through, letters to me would too. He *could* write, but he didn't! Incomprehensible as it was, it meant that he didn't want to. For some reason he no longer wanted the correspondence.

And to think, in the face of that, I had continued writing to him! How many letters had I written during that frantic period when I so feared for his safety? Why I had just written and written with complete loss of the reticence I ordinarily would have had in writing to a man. I had written just as often as I could snatch the time and just as freely as a mother or sister or sweetheart, hoping as I did that even if he were suffering, physically, mentally, whatever—maybe some part of all I was caring, hoping, could get across the ocean and help a little bit. Only a little bit. The only solace I had in those days, as I remember now, was the hope that I might be able to help, if just a little bit.

Toward the end of that period of uncertainty when I doubted if I had his correct address, I had written still but saved the letters, and now had a box full of them I had hoped that I might get to him for Christmas.

By imagining myself in his place, I thought the most welcome Christmas present would be lots of letters. And so I had gone on in my simple foolishness. Well, thank goodness, they hadn't been mailed. Even without them I had sent enough to take years of silence from me to atone for. Fool that I was ever to let a man "get one on me" like that! Nothing but the abnormal and incomprehensible terror of war could so utterly have shattered my good sense and good training and modesty and everything!

I hardly knew what to call the mood that then possessed me. Anger was in it, at him, at me. Disgust, deep and bitter, with my own foolish girl self. "I will pluck it from my bosom though my heart be at the root." "But this isn't Locksley Hall. My heart isn't at the root. I haven't any heart—and I can't pluck it from my bosom," I found myself crying alone up in my own attic.

The attic, that term was literal. It had in it my bed and dresser along with the usual cobwebby shadows and the decrepit refuse of all attics. But it was mine, my castle. I earned it by taking care of the furnace, and when I was in it I was alone. Here I could be myself. Downstairs with the other girls in this small rooming house I held up my "false front" unflinchingly. I even earned the reputation of being the most lighthearted and jolly one of the crowd. But the crowd would not have known me in the attic. There, I told my poor old diary,

> I could cry my eyes out—but I can't. I can't talk about it, nor write about it except indirectly nor could I have avoided it, I suppose. I'm not really to blame, either, and yet I suffer blindly. The shame of failure I think makes the sting worse. Oh, I *wanted* to be a friend! Why should I have presumed to—I've always failed before. I might have known I would again. In other cases it mattered to me chiefly—in this case—if I could be sure of that, it would be a comfort!—Oh, life's so little, so horribly little. Personality is so little, so tiresome! I want to be someone else. I'm deathly tired of being *me*—fickle, fluctuating, pleasure-loving, too deep for the shallow, too shallow for the deep, too wise to be silly, too silly to be wise —a misfit!

After a few weeks, my mood calmed somewhat, at least on the surface. I wrote

> I just read over my last "spasm" for the first time. I went home that night and went to the school fair thinking I would "drown my troubles in drink," in a way of speaking, and not stay at home and think. I had a pretty good time. Time does lots. If sore spots didn't heal we'd all be ready for the grave internally as well as externally in much less than three score years and ten.

> I still can't see why I should care so much. For whole days I'm sure I don't. And then for a time I'm intensely sure I do. Just now I'm trying very hard to be as selfish as I can. Why should I worry? I'm not suffering and even if I were, no one else would be the better. If only there were no Sundays and no nights when I can't sleep I'd have myself hoodwinked— or imbued with common sense, maybe is better—in no time."

And so, the best I could do was to put it all down to another attempt at friendship gone bad. Several other incipient attempts, with college girls, for instance, had died a natural death when after we separated I heard from those persons no more. Those persons, I decided, had not formed the letter-writing habit like I had, and so it meant the old cliché — out of sight, out of mind.

With Banks, however, that explanation didn't seem to fit very well. He could write, he had written, but now he didn't. But I had given him a lot more of thought and interest than any of those others. It was just because of that, I told myself, that my disappointment now was so much greater than in any of the other cases. But, after all, he was just a neighbor boy, certainly nothing more. It was only because I had thought we were friends, too, that the disappointment now was so painful.

And so I struggled on, none too successfully, trying to put it all out of mind. For *two whole years* I struggled, little suspecting that here our age difference was affecting him and making him think that my interest in him was just the kindly one of an older school teacher toward a pupil, and that therefore it did not occur to him that his silence would affect me deeply if at all.

Later in a diary entry I wrote

> Botany (my major) is getting interesting. And that, I'm glad to say, is an interest that is direct, not caused by the influence of any other. I'm interested too in Philosophy. Only I know that that's half from his influence and the other half from religion and my natural and acquired skepticism...

> If I could only know for *sure* why I don't hear from Banks! If I only knew it was any reason except that he just doesn't want to hear from me anymore — any quixotic idea of his I'd dispel it in a hurry. But under the conditions and in light of the facts I'll just make my reason sit real hard on my sympathy and wait to know.

As time passed and I began to get my bearings, I decided that what I missed most was the mental stimulation I had gotten from Banks. Only when it was definitely removed did I realize to what extent I had depended on him and how little actual thinking I could do unstimulated. My brain, it appeared, wasn't the self-starting kind, or at least it was badly in the habit of depending on him for a start.

My pride rose up in rebellion at this idea and subsequently one deep-laid, seldom-expressed but never forgotten determination of mine was to acquire mental independence. Whether or not Banks ever came back into my life again in any way, I would be my own mistress, his mental equal and always independent. Never again, I vowed, would I let myself be so dependent on anyone as I had become dependent on him for my mental stimulation.

I can hardly say now whether this effort could ever have been called successful. But at least the consciousness of it gave to me a certain self-respect. That and a kind of moral stamina that standing alone seemed to give became soon my strongest internal satisfactions. It was one thing in myself I didn't have to be ashamed of, as I was of those weaker womanish times when my high standard would lower and I would let myself "sit with tears in my eyes, and that same old awful pain within," or when I suddenly addressed and mailed the package of Christmas letters I had vowed I'd never send him. I did it in the hopeless hope that he might like them in spite of himself.

As the school term passed and I clung determinedly to my purpose to make myself think, to stand up straight and independent, I began to feel increased interest in my study of botany. A love of plants was almost literally born in me, and the years at home in the greenhouse and garden had fostered it well. And so I found an almost instinctive interest even in the unplantlike course called botany. And the best part of it was that it had nothing to do with my recently past bitter experience. It seemed clearer, fresher, more desirable, on that account. I couldn't have respected myself if I had developed the interest because it had been Banks'. And now the farther away I could get from anything that suggested him and all of our old lines of thought, the better.

Religion as such began to slip from my mind. I still did the prescribed weekly church and Sunday School duties and the daily chapel, but none of it left a trace. Those times were only occasions to sit and think of, or to try to keep from thinking of, the things I could not help but think of.

My absorption in the botany class continued to grow as in my mind I gave it every possible advantage of attitude, for I wanted it to grow. I was bound to get some sort of interest to fill the still aching void inside of me. The professor, luckily, was one whose personality was for me something of a restorative. He was a man still young, but old enough that I knew the trials and struggles of living could hardly have passed too lightly by. Yet he, unlike myself, still had enthusiasm. He still seemed to find the world good. He was still cheerful, happy and engrossed in his work. I watched him closely in class and tried to analyze him in forty ways that I'll wager he never thought any student was doing.

In the course of a conversation developing from a question of mine that I asked him after class, and in which he seemed to be as interested as I, I must have led him up to the brink of some of my old questionings about the reality of matter and the nature of the universe; those which had been left in my mind with their sharp raw edges sticking up where my discussions with Banks had left them.

The professor was sympathetic, said he'd been through just such a state of mind as I apparently was in. Then he told me about his own viewpoint, talked kindly and earnestly, and quickly passed on to me something of his own optimistic, cheerful philosophy so that I walked home oblivious of clouds or clods. I talked to him several other times, always getting a full measure of idealism that did much to make my days less morbid.

But I told myself at once, "No more leaning. Get a little inspiration from him but don't forget that you're walking alone now." And I did remember.

But I still didn't succeed in keeping the old mystery of Banks' silence out of my mind at all times. My knowledge of Banks' sincere, kindly nature and his lack of lightness, caprice, or fickleness made it very hard to keep believing that he deliberately meant to "cut" me or that I might have become too forward in writing to him so freely. It was almost impossible to think that any of that had anything to do with the silence. I still had spells of turmoil and constant unrest and indecision to overcome. I find such ravings as this in my diary:

> Fool human nature! At least fool my part of it. I lay awake half the night trying to decide whether to throw up everything, cut loose and join the Red Cross and begin something entirely new, or whether to plod on and someday emerge from the portal of experience plus agricultural college, a perfectly capable mannish emotionless apple-orchard superintendent, with blue denim dress [no slacks, those days] and straw hat, thirteen orphans [a longtime dream—the orphans, not necessarily the thirteen] and an intolerable self-disgust, a deep-seated sense of failure and a grim determination to make the best of it!

> Then I work all morning helping at home and get back here at Wooster so disconnected from all the previous existence that it takes all evening to get back in line. And then when I realize that I've let myself dream that a letter might be waiting for me and have to admit how badly it hurts when there isn't one, I say "Fool Human Nature," all over again. I'm not actually disappointed. I wasn't actually expecting one. Neither am I angry. I'm disgusted with myself. "Woman's passion, woman's pain." Aye, verily. Tennyson knew something about woman's nature all right.

> Now I find a sort of philosophy growing up in me, yet hardly that, either.

Just a blind questioning, ever and ever around in a circle. Why should one have to suffer on and on? Why is a creation made like that? What's the answer? What's the end? Is this a squirrel cage, then, after all? I speak of "the lottery of life," in which I tried so long not to believe. But if circumstances which I can in no possible way control, develop in one way—if all my thought and interest in Banks, for instance, had turned out to be for some good, then I would praise myself for insight; if they develop in the other way, I'm a bigger fool than my common sense even now tells me I am. We all do the best we can with the light we have, and so whose fault is it if the result is good or bad?

My own reactions are beside the story in which I intended to show Banks' development, rather than mine. But for the rest of that year and all of the next, his reaction was so utterly a mystery to me, and mine all too much a reality, that it seems incomplete to omit mine in tracing his. Besides, when the time comes that the two lines run on together, they soon become so inextricably tangled, that one is the other, almost.

On my own side, the short of it is that I grew on as best I could, never entirely being able to forget, but ever trying to, and always struggling for more mental strength with which to build up for myself some kind of acceptable life philosophy to settle the unrest that still was within me.

When the opportunity came to live and earn my keep in the home of my botany teacher, Professor Strausbaugh (or Strasy as everyone called him), the one whose enthusiasm for his field had stood out above that of all others of my professors, I accepted it at once. I was glad for the chance it gave me to repay him for the help he had unwittingly given me by being what he was. Although much work and distraction that winter was involved in helping his family as best I could, through the various illnesses and misfortunes that beset them, and though I left an easier (though not quite as inexpensive) berth (and my attic) to do it, I felt that I was amply repaid.

Then in the spring, by which time my own boredom with the college had mounted almost to the quitting point, there came an opportunity from this same kindly professor to continue to work with his family and to go along with them to the University of Chicago for the following year, my senior year, while he worked there for a higher degree.

The next year therefore saw me at the University of Chicago. Between my contact with Strasy and my roommate, Ella, another student from Wooster who was also influenced by him, I was exposed full-time to what they called Idealistic Monism. Before very long, I was glad to find myself affected by it, partly because of its almost diametric opposition to the materialistic philosophy that had captured Banks and hovered like a grim spector just beyond my own horizon.

Many and many a night, as Ella and I lay awake talking and arguing, I would hear myself urging Banks' old objections to idealistic ways of thinking, with the satisfaction, however, of not realizing nor recognizing them as his until I heard myself stating them. This always gave me a bit of pleasure, since it seemed as if my mind was of its own accord traveling over ground his had.

But Banks' lingering influence on my thinking (little as he had ever seen evidence of it, I suppose) is reflected in some diary entries of mine of that time. For all I remember now, the first of these may only have marked a temporary spell of disillusionment when on February 1, 1919, I wrote, "There's nothing! I'm nothing! The god I've come to pray to is no god. Where is the one I used to know?" Then on February 9:

> I only begin to see how thoroughly I'll have to rebuild my house if I'm to be anything but a materialist. It seems to be in the very fiber of my thinking. Of course, I think it's only the result of experience and environment. It doesn't bother my roommate whether the Miraculous Birth was fact or fiction! Maybe I'm just trying to hang onto the rag doll of my childhood, but a Bible built on a fake assumption can be no Bible to me.

Again, April 3, 1919:

> One cannot wholly govern his ideas and we must respond to the strongest stimulus. I surely can't see any answer to the determinism question but the "will to believe."

In time, however, my separation from Banks and his doubts and questions had its effect, even while I continued to counter this idealism I was hearing, by the old mechanistic arguments and even though I hated myself for not being a more independent thinker. In time, I found myself being affected by the idealism of my friends. For them, the material world was just the summation of "little whorls of energy." The materialist viewpoint had no support whatever in their Idealistic Monism.

I had listened eagerly to their arguments even while I debated them. This was what I wanted to hear. It was the answer I really wanted and which I would have tried to explain to Banks if he had still been in my world. If I should ever meet him again, or any other such materialist, now I could demolish him for sure, because as I urged every objection I could think of, Ella and Strasy were able to vindicate their viewpoint, and more and more I found myself accepting it.

Finally, from them and from Snowdon's *The World a Spiritual System* the Universe seemed to take a new shape for me. Its outline was something like this: Everything is spirit. We are tiny sparks of God who is everything. Our souls are spirit and all material is but the sign in our consciousness of a thought of God. A tree, a stone, our bodies are thoughts of God. Our duty is to stay in harmony with the Universe. Then all is well. If we don't, then all the troubles and disasters of the world are to pay.

I didn't quite know what being "in harmony" meant, but Ella seemed to know and strangely enough in her life I could see what it meant, but it didn't seem to fit in mine. It didn't make sense. For she thought she got out of harmony if she planned and strove for or wanted some special thing too strongly. Her greatest opportunities had come when she planned and struggled least as when she gave up struggling to get the money to go to college and a scholarship dropped from the very skies.

But in my life it was quite different; I only got what I struggled for. After three or four years in college when I knew where every penny I spent came from before I spent it, and when I knew I'd never have gotten to college if I hadn't made a desperate effort to get there, I couldn't see how not planning or struggling would have been better. Yet I knew that something had gone wrong, that somehow I had "jammed the works"; and if that was being "out of harmony," I must be one screeching discord in the universe.

Still in time I came to think of myself as a pretty good Monistic Idealist, since science was now resolving Matter back and back into the Nothing from which it springs. Even molecules are now broken up into atoms and electrons. And electrons—why, they are only "whorls of energy" revolving around whorls of energy. Where was any *material*, any hard solid *stuff* in that?

In November came the Armistice! To me, at least, it was sudden (no TV then or even radio). It was the END of the War! No words now can capture what it meant for the world. Such feelings are soon forgotten, lost in the pages of history. But for me it was such a relief, such joy, it seemed beyond belief. Of course, the world *looked* just the same, yet it seemed that the very character of the daylight must be different! How could one really comprehend that the dull leaden feeling could go now?

My brothers and other friends in training camps would now be safe. They would never get sent overseas. And Banks was still living, still in Santo Domingo from all I knew from Myra's occasional letters. Once when visiting her I had seen among other pictures Banks had sent home, a picture of a cute little Spanish girl and a pencilled note on the back saying that he was studying Spanish with her. The fierce hard stab

I got at that made me wonder about my feeling for him which I had tried so hard to think was impersonal. Maybe I was half in love with him in spite of myself. But awful thought! In love with Banks Rhine who wouldn't even write to me. That would not dare be. Kill it! Kill it! Then I began to try to do just that with all the fury, determination, will and weapons I could muster. To be in love with a man who didn't love me, and who even as a friend had neglected me as he had, was an ignominy I could not endure while I retained a shred of self-respect! I rejoiced then that I had kept my contact with him a secret from all of my acquaintances. None of them would know how I had been "stung." I could say nonchalantly to any question about him, "Banks Rhine? No, I have not heard from him," just as I would do with any of the other boys of my early acquaintance.

As that college year wore on, lonely, hard and with problems at my rooming place, I was at last getting my bachelor of science degree and that was a great satisfaction. I struggled to build stronger my idealistic outlook and always to kill anything of passion there might be in my feelings for Banks.

I realized that just wanting not to be in love didn't put one out of it. I realized it in the long night hours when sometimes I tried desperately to sleep but couldn't. I ceased then having much doubt that I had fallen in love. I never ceased being ashamed of my weakness and I kept trying to keep my thoughts from wandering off over the ocean instead of staying put on Bryophytes and enzyme action as they should.

So much for my own story during this uncertain time. And now let Banks tell his in his autobiographical sketch, which, after his remark already quoted about one last meeting at Myra's wedding, continues

I had entered the service as a man dying of thirst enters a lake to drink. I wanted French service, but got sent down to little old romantic San Domingo. Here the troubles that had harrassed my mind almost to madness melted out under the vertical rays of the tropical sun. What I would do in the future, what I had lost in the past, became insignificant beside the great living present in the sunny, lazy, pleasant old island of Haiti. I enjoyed life there, learning the language, visiting the agreeable and hospitable people, swimming by palm-covered beaches, hiking over the island, exploring caves, scenery and vegetation and wondering at the most ancient architecture in America, built by Spanish explorers.

When in 1919, the U.S.M.C. cast me out into the cold northern world again, I was as carefree as any man that ever got his discharge. My mind was even free from plans for the future. I wanted to do something, and here it seems that I began a new stage. I seemed to be starting an age of doing things, of achievement. But I needed a stimulus. I wanted forestry in a vague sort of way, but I had no special immediate incentive.

Now, I had not corresponded with anyone except my parents during those years in the service, thinking thus to hasten the forgetting of my past philosophical problems. This was hard to do with Louie, but it was with her I felt it to be most necessary. Consequently, when I was mustered out, I knew not what to expect her to be like. Two and a half years can make great changes. I simply knew she had gone away to college, and no more.

As for me, I graduated that spring and went back home to Ohio again, almost convinced that the old worries would trouble me no more. The war was over. I had my degree, although as yet no particular aim nor work to which to turn. I spent some time trying to find out what to do with this college education now that I had it, and I enjoyed being home, and the light round of social activities of the little town. I enjoyed them with abandon. No one talked religion or philosophy, and my tired mind was glad they didn't. I even found the old ache at the thought of Banks wearing off. I almost felt like shouting one day after working in the garden, I realized that I had not thought of him once "or any of that old stuff" for an hour or so. It was the first really encouraging sign I had had that I could ultimately gain control. I knew then that one could gain such control, at least if no fresh fuel was added. That had been one advantage I had had, certainly, no fresh fuel!

But a young college graduate couldn't loll around at the parental home very long, especially not when a $300 debt to Wooster College was due. The manager of the local grocery store needed a clerk. I responded. But at the rate of pay it seemed I'd be working there forever, and so after a few weeks I ventured further. The Goodrich Rubber Company twenty miles away in Akron was hiring help and carpools made transportation reasonable. I got a job along with many other women (few men; the pay wasn't good enough for them, another practical experience with sex discrimination). It was an easy job just like cutting cookies all day long. These cookies, however, were not edible. They were war-related, valves for gas masks, cut from thin sheets of rubber.

I continued on this job all that winter. All that remains today, however, to remind me of that uninspiring time is a fragment I find written one day while on the job, but in an interval when apparently the "cookies" were all cut and even the monotony of factory work interrupted. The fragment says:

Today it takes all my self control to sit in this noisy grimy old office and tabulate, when every stray breeze that gets lost and wanders in here where soot and rubber smells predominate, speaks of a fresh outdoors where the world is thrilling with interest and where material to study and stimuli to think are abundant — where one can find out about reality and perhaps sometime push back the veil of ignorance one little notch further.

I've just got to go out into that world. If I let other things choke out this fundamental impulse, I can be content, perhaps nine-tenths of the time, but the other tenth will be discontent, acute enough to overbalance the rest. I'll lose a certain basic self respect that I don't dare lose.

I feel so bewildered now. I must find myself. *I will, too.* In this as in other things I will find my own way. That same old tendency to wait for a guide is bothering me. How I long for one, either an old one or new one. But I can't have one. If I get one later, it will be after the crux of need has passed. I will either have hopelessly fallen — or I will have learned self-dependence. I believe I can make it be the latter.

There's a pure cold brilliance to a diamond. A warm ruddy liveness to a ruby. Both are beautiful, both right. But even if a diamond should turn into a ruby, need it lose all of its former quality?

Shall it be for me, ecology or genetics? Ecology, I believe. Make me *stick* to it! Maybe I haven't brains enough. But anyway let me keep *the will* to try.

By spring, however, a respite from that drudgery came, another job, this one back in my old college town, Wooster, Ohio, one where monotony, while not ended, was much reduced. It was a clerical job at the Agricultural Experiment Station there. Even though that job had little to do with plants or plant life, at least a bit of botanical flavor was there. The job at B.F. Goodrich I then left with no regret; but now, these long years afterward, I realize that it had been educational in at least one way. Now I knew from unforgettable personal experience something of the way factory workers must feel. Now I can read about "labor problems" with a degree of sympathy for workers, for those who for no fault of their own must be condemned to uninspired and uninspiring monotonous daily jobs of making the wherewithal of industrial culture. I would hardly have felt this so keenly otherwise.

One day that summer at home, and out of a blue sky, as the saying has it, a letter came from Banks. It was as sudden and as unexpected as the Armistice had been, or rather, more unexpected. I always knew the

Armistice would have to come someday. But by then I had no idea that any further word from Banks to me would ever come. Of course, I had thought of it many times. I had imagined such a letter with so many different contents that it is really queer that the one which did come was different from any of them. But it was.

I was at the stove in the kitchen at home, helping to get supper, when one of my sisters came in from the post office waving a letter at me and calling out teasingly, "Oh, Louie, Louie, he wrote." To explain that, I should say that neither she nor any of the folks at home knew of anything special in my relation to Banks Rhine, but they did know that I did not customarily get letters from boys, even old acquaintances. Although by this stage of family life my young sisters were having boyfriends and dates, I never had any and was already pretty generally marked down, I knew, as an "old maid."

With calmness, complete and deceptive, I took that letter knowing with absolute certainty before I actually saw the inscription, from whom it came. I knew, hadn't I always known, there'd have to be a letter? And here it was at last. I dropped it nonchalantly into my apron pocket. (We always wore aprons then.) But now I needed to get away out of the world where no outside distraction could ever penetrate and claim one iota of my attention.

Somehow I did slip away, long enough later that they would all have forgotten about the letter. I went out the back door, but the back yard was not far enough. No calls to supper must interrupt me now. Down over the hill I went, not breathing freely until I was out of sight. Then I ran on flying feet on and on into the darkening woods below. Finally I found a grassy spot behind a big tree and there I flung myself down and tore open the envelope with trembling fingers.

Dear Louie: It is over. I now stand detached from your "big bright world," or rather, my world in which you were the center. For that purpose I enlisted, hoping my duties would solve the problem, and though not as I expected, they did. I left the tropics, changed. I now want to do as other men, to work, play, laugh, love, marry, etc. But Louie, can you understand my silence? Can you pardon my apparent ingratitude? I want to atone for it now but no other course was open for me then. You represented my other world—I had to leave it. But may we be friends? Will you write me once more? Sincerely.

Again, again I read it, trembling, puzzled, in ecstasy and out of it, as I tried in vain to comprehend, first that I had this letter at all, that after almost two years it really was word from Banks direct to me and second, what it meant. I'd think I understood and then I'd be sure I didn't.

Anyway, he wants to be friends again, wants to hear from me. Will I write him? Oh, I must. I can't do otherwise. I ought at least to wait a week or so — but I knew I couldn't wait. A dozen answers were already composing themselves in my mind. I knew I couldn't choke them back for long. And so I compromised — and was lost.

I decided to write an answer at once "to see how it sounded," but I wouldn't mail it until my better judgment said "go!" I wrote it that night. With infinite care I picked a few noncommittal (I hoped) sentences out of the English language and finally decided they'd do. I dared to say I was glad to hear from him again and to know that he had gotten safely through the war. I would say that much to any of the boys I knew. I could also say I'd be interested to hear from him and details of army life, etc. He needn't know *how* glad or *how* interested I would be.

For once I was glad, too, that paper and pen are as noncommittal as they can be. The thousand warm and happy nothings that clamored for expression I ruthlessly and sensibly ruled out. No use thinking of sleep that night, and for once I was happy to stay awake. The night passed quickly as I thought over the brief lines of my reply, as I tried to squeeze something more explanatory from between his lines, as I tried to know what he could mean, "now detached from the world in which you (I) had been the center," to comprehend that he still wanted my friendship and to renew correspondence, as I wondered what he had changed to and realized that he really was a stranger to me now.

In the morning I managed to keep my determination not to post the letter, but by afternoon my eagerness to hasten the hour when I would hear further from him overcame my good sense and I mailed it.

In a story, I suppose his next letter would have been all that I expected. He would have written at length and given a full explanation for the long break. He'd have filled out the half-hinted outlines of his first letter and emphasized and dwelt upon his desire to make up for his apparent neglect. He'd have shown he realized that he had something for which to ask pardon. And he would have made me understand the changes that the life in a strange land had brought about in him.

But in real life and with real men, things often don't go the way a girl might expect. And this one didn't. The next letter came quickly and its thickness promised well, but the contents to me with storybook expectations were worse than a disappointment. They were a slap in the face, a dash of cold water, and the letter left me with a deep and furious anger, and I hoped I could keep it forever. My mother said I must be angry about something for I worked about the house so fast and hard that I did two days' work in one.

The letter was long and told about his life on the rifle team — never a word of explanation! He was in New England training for the

National Rifle Matches. He had been to Boston and he wrote a page or so to make what really was a good and interesting description of that city, though I didn't notice that then when Boston was the last of my interests. Another page or two went to congratulate me for having finished college and "reached the heights while I have slid to the foot." And that was all.

Is it any wonder I was disappointed, even angry? How was I in my inexperience to know that men are like that? I didn't know then that they are simply made so that the emotional side is only a compartment of the mind, while it is the very center of a woman's. I didn't know then that the best man in the world could go to sleep while I told him something that should be to him a very heartthrob and it would not be because he wasn't interested, but just because he was sleepy.

No, I didn't know then that the letter he wrote me was really a good one and from his point of view a very friendly and proper one. It takes years to understand things like that. I'm beginning to think I do now, and that whether I do or not, it's no use getting angry and making life miserable or even uncomfortable if a man acts "just like a man." He can't help it because men are made so. It's dyed in the blood, whatever that means. We women can't really blame them. We just live with them and smile to ourselves when once again they react just like a man.

But that day I was angry, "mad" clear through for as much as a day. Then I cooled off and decided to make what I could of the contact with him and not to expect more than I'd get. And so we struck up a fairly even correspondence. In it we learned about the exterior changes that the intervening years had brought. Or at least, he learned that of me; I didn't feel that I learned as much of him. In his only reference to the past, he spoke of his "old lamentations in his hair-tearing brain-contorting days." But he never dipped beneath the surface, told nothing about the real man I had known, nothing intimate, nothing personal. And I had to be content to wait and wonder. As for being in love with him, that had vanished from my consciousness. It was someone else, Banks as I remembered him, the earnest, kindly, grave old friend that I had, in a way, fought and bled for, with whom I had fallen in love. But I could not guess if any of that man still lived in this new person he had come to be. He loved chess and swimming, he said. That far we had developed alike, but that was about all I did know. Any real explanation, or any kind of apology for his long neglect, I did not get; and my only slightly cooled resentment still burned within me.

Before long came another note. In this one he said that he, Banks Rhine, had won the President's Rifle Match! It was the yearly national match for which he had been practicing so many weary weeks and the winning of which was the greatest individual distinction that any

Marine could win. Although I did know which was the shooting end of a firearm, my interest in them went no further, and yet I was probably as thrilled, excited, exhilarated by his news as his mother. I didn't even stop to question why this success of his should so affect me. But I did know that this win was the mark, the end, the culmination of all his months of striving. Somehow I was taking his success as if it were my own.

Then I began to expect word that he was home, back to his parents' home, now some fifty miles or so from mine. The last letter I had had from Quantico said he expected to be discharged immediately. I felt sure he would come to see me before many days, and it was with the most interested expectation that I looked forward to that. What would he be like? How had he changed? Would I care for him at all? Would he for me? What kind of a mental attitude would he have?

He had said that the Marine Corps was a "nut and bolt factory." How much had the life in it, plus the lethargy of the tropics, affected him and how permanent would that effect be? Questions, of course, but gone was that old tormenting unrest and aching wondering. This was expectant, eager, happy. It was going to be interesting, this knitting together of the old and the new. Even the superficial correspondence we had had recently showed me that whatever of a stranger this young man might be to me now, he was still an interesting one, and one with whom I wanted to get reacquainted.

It is queer how suddenly something can finally happen even if one has waited two years for it. If the time is ripe, it only takes an instant. One afternoon a few weeks later, as I bent over my typewriter on my new job at the Wooster Agricultural Experiment Station (I was making a list of the Leguminosae) I heard, "Miss Weckesser, someone to see you." Before I could stir, there he stood—Banks! I arose as soon as I could. I don't know what I said, something stiff and formal, I guess, as I fought for composure. I must have succeeded at least somewhat for the thought ran through my mind, "I'm no more ill at ease than he is, anyway." The worst of the stiffness soon wore off, and I was able to notice how slim and straight he was in his tight-fitting khaki uniform with his medals on his chest. We talked briefly and arranged to meet outside when my afternoon's work was done.

After he went out, I certainly did not earn the salary I was supposed to get. I was in a different world. A coma or stupor of some kind came over me. I couldn't really think. I was just "not there." Stunned, I guess. The war and all it meant was over. Banks was back. I had seen him and would again!

Somehow even in those few short, strained moments with him, I knew, as I reflected, that he was still at heart the same pure, clean person I had known before. He had come through the trials of army life, even without the guiding rules of Christianity I had thought so necessary. Maybe, no matter what he might have become, I would have thought that. Maybe it was not woman's intuition but just woman's foolishness, believing what she wants to believe. However that may be to a skeptic, to me I *knew* and nothing could have changed my conviction unless it had been negative evidence written on his clear, open countenance. And such was never written there.

After awhile I "came to" sufficiently to wonder how I looked, whether my hair was combed, my dress OK. I had not thought of any of that in the complete absorption of those minutes with him; and that I had even forgotten my hair in that day before "bobs," and for me at least before hairdressers, tells a "mouthful."

When a little more consciousness returned, I remembered that I was being paid to work that afternoon and that I was expected to finish the list of Leguminosae as soon as possible. I was, I guess at No. 435 when Banks appeared. I went back to the typewriter and worked the rest of the hour. Later when I looked over the numbers on that sheet they ran something like this: 436, 438, 435. It was hard to believe that a college graduate could get to a stage like that and still pass for normal. But sanity eventually did return.

We spent the whole of that long evening together, hunting each other, so to speak, finding fragments, trying to hark back to the discussions of the past but finding them much less gripping than before.

I tried to explain a little bit of idealism to him. He neither agreed or disagreed very much. He was not in a thinking mood. Civilian life was still too new. His mind, after a long vacation, was still inactive. He said he had let himself drift entirely, lived in the moment, studied Spanish and adapted to the country, and now his mind was creaking with disuse and he hadn't yet felt enough of Northern stir and challenge to drive it on.

The next day was Saturday and a half-holiday for me, and he said that he would stay on and meet me for the afternoon. When it came, I hardly realized at first that he was not as conscious as I was of all that lay between the past and now. But I had thought too much, suffered too keenly, wondered too deeply about him to be satisfied long with no chance to get beneath the surface, to get a real understanding of or an explanation of the past. Yet I was so fully conscious of what I had to hide that I dared make no advance into that hidden territory.

I couldn't tell him of what in the time past had so much concerned me. I dared not say a word about that or even lead him near the subject; and yet as every fresh wave of realization that this was really Banks again broke over me, it was the only topic I could think of.

And so the hours passed. I had brought Gray's *Manual* along, and I tried to show him how to analyze a flower, and he seemed interested. But in my mind fresh revolt was rising. If this was the way he was — so utterly oblivious to all I felt — I wouldn't go through another time in purgatory on his account. He'd leave casually tonight, expecting probably to see me again sometime, to write when it pleased him.

I'd have to stop it short. I couldn't afford the price it would take from me, for his presence and thinking of him afterward would affect me too deeply. I knew I could not take it casually. If he would stay away, completely out of my life, as he did before, I knew I could recover — with time. I could find myself again. Hadn't I almost done it once? If he'd stay away, I could manage. But empty letters, pleasant but empty visits like this would just unnerve me forever. Underneath the pleasantries of the surface, I knew I'd have to stop it all. If he asked to return I'd have to say, "No." If he wrote, I wouldn't answer. In fairness to myself I could not do otherwise.

At length toward evening we paused in a little wooded glade, between the pleasant cultivated Experiment Station fields. A little stream trickled by. I had brought along some sandwiches so we could avoid a public restaurant. On a suitable spot beside the stream, I sat and opened the lunch and asked him to sit beside me. But he was absorbed, apparently, with throwing rocks into the water.

No, he said to my invitation, he wouldn't think of depriving me of my supper. And nothing I could say would persuade him. In frustration, at length, I tossed the sandwiches into the creek. We watched them float down stream. He said the sight would haunt him forever. I said I hoped it would!

As darkness fell, and for the last few hours still remaining — and in my mind, the last few hours of all our evenings — we walked back up past the college and out into the country beyond. It was a lovely, starry, moonlit night. Somehow as we walked we seemed to draw a little nearer each other. Maybe it was the old recollections the campus stirred to life in him as we passed it, maybe just the moonlight. Anyway, for the first time we seemed to find a real and natural theme for conversation. The campus aroused recollections of the old struggles and the ideals of those days before the war.

He outlined again the belief, or rather the lack of belief he now felt; how the world still seemed wholly material, wholly mechanistic to him, how altruism is but a snare and a deception; how the hard, material facts of life predominate always over thought and idea; how the brain and anything of soul that might be dies, therefore, when the body dies; how useless and senseless it is to expect an eternity, an on-going of spirit; and how possible it is to live content and happy even after an understanding of these things. He said it was only the idea that was frightening, and had frightened, worried and half-crazed him, sometimes, in the old days when the faith his reason could not support slipped from him.

But he said after he had thought it through and adjusted to it, he had come to feel at ease with the new viewpoint because he knew it was true, and he knew that through no weak desire was he deceiving himself into an easy philosophy.

"This life is enough in itself," he said. "Why should I want more? The only reason I did was because I had been taught it. Isn't this life worthwhile without reward or prolonged continuation? Those months down on the island were paid for just as I lived them, just the easy, quiet, uneventful life was worthwhile in itself. Don't you understand, Louie, why Browning said, 'How good is man's life, the mere living?'"

"But, Banks," I interrupted, "You are, we both are, too young, too inexperienced to decide like that. We've never had any trouble. Pleasant life may be worth the living but what about unhappiness? What about those whose lives have not been cast in such pleasant places? And what about ourselves when death comes to us, when our loved ones leave us? How can we tell now how we will feel then? We've never had a bereavement, we're not in a position to know how it will be, and especially not if we believe as you do that when someone we love is dead, that he is gone, annihilated? It's then it seems to me that your outlook, right or wrong, is inadequate. That's the time when it would be hard to say, 'The game is worth the candle.'"

But no. He couldn't see it. Surely the death of those we love would be hard, hard in any event, but no harder under his philosophy than any other.

And then eagerly, earnestly I told him that no matter what his outlook was, no matter what cold hard philosophy held his mind, I knew and knew beyond all doubt that he didn't himself live by the philosophy he thought he held. I knew that he was better than it was, "For Banks," I said, "You went to war—I know what that did to many boys—didn't you tell me yourself of the drink that ruined one of the best of the young chaps you knew in service? Didn't I hear a lot about the loose relationships with women—with native girls—all that?"

"And through it all with no motive to guide you, no idea that it mattered if you went straight or crooked, you came out, Banks, as clean morally as when you went in—No, you didn't say so, but I know—I know even the crap games, the gambling—Why I know you haven't even smoked—and that all the vile language you've had to listen to is still as foreign to you as ever. Banks, I know all that—But I don't know how you did it on the principles you profess. There's nothing in them that I can see to help a man through the hard places. Something more worked in you, but got no credit."

In my mind this something really was the unrecognized shadow of his early training and ideals, and I still think this was so even though the answer he gave then, and the one I know he believed, was that it was, "Just you, Louie."

The rest of that hour never may go on paper — But we found each other, the real, living, feeling selves underneath. All the restraints and constraints were gone forever, as I found him all I'd dreamed and learned that all the "changes" were but bugaboos that need frighten me no longer. I also found the love I'd tried so long to kill, spring up full grown, and stronger far than ever. I dared to recognize it, as he told me again and again all that I had meant to him over the years since he first realized that of all the girls he knew, I was the one he needed and cared about. As I told him, how through realest suffering I had come to realize my love for him, as I dared confess at last all the precious aching longings I had suppressed so long, he listened in astonishment.

"Why, Louie, I never knew, never had the slightest guess that you would ever think twice of me. You were kind, interested, and your letters down in training camp meant everything to me. But you were older than I. You seemed much older then. Once in my boyhood I had a teacher, twice as old as I or more she was, who took a warm personal interest in me. I told myself your interest was of the same sort. It was kindly, pitying maybe, but never anything more. You never gave me any reason to think otherwise, you know. You hardly let me come to see you back at Wooster. You never would even go to a football game with me. How could I guess, Louie, that you cared? And how awful that I didn't. How those days down there would have been changed if I had had even the slightest hope."

"Couldn't you read between the lines in my letters?" I asked. "I'm sure it was there so plainly it worried me many a time for fear it was too plain, too evident."

"No, I couldn't. I didn't read between the lines. Perhaps I didn't fully credit all that was on the lines. I couldn't imagine that 'Dearest Friend,' from you was literal. It was too much beyond my expectations."

And then he explained how after he got to Santo Domingo, the lazy ease of that tropical place, coupled with his desire to see what "stopping thinking" would do to him led him to decide to drop all correspondence except that to his parents, which he continued for their sake rather than his own. They were the only ones, he thought, who would be really affected by his silence. He wanted just to sink into the life cut out for him, let everything drift, and see what time and mere living would do.

I never will understand how he could have failed to read the almost heartbreaking anxiety some of my last letters must have shown. I can only put it down to the curious and un-understandable ways of "men" again. No woman could ever miss plain signs like those!

But then when he came north again on the rifle team, just as his short first letter indicated, he felt that the experiment was over, and he never realized that I hadn't known that one was on, or that the brief message of that one note had not explained it adequately. The experiment over, coming back to the free civilian life in the U.S.A. brought the old associations back with more reality to his mind. And then he wrote to see if I would renew the correspondence. He had never thought that I had written him too often. He was glad for all the letters I sent, but had no idea of my reaction when they went unanswered.

He knew nothing of "girl stuff," of course, that girls have pride, or should have. All such signs had passed him by as scatheless as lightning does the ocean. But when he realized something of the way I had cared and suffered, it hurt him through and through.

But to me, now that it was all over, it seemed as if it was a relief to remember it and to recognize it as but a stronger proof of my affection, a proof that in my mind carried not the slightest reproof to him. To him, however, it was painful just to realize that, however unintentionally, he had caused me unhappiness. Not for worlds would he have done so if he had known. And now he valiantly and earnestly pledged himself to the cause of making me happy.

But curiously enough my hand trembling with pleasure and excitement in my letter complimenting him because he won the rifle match, he said, revealed to him the fact that I must be somewhat interested in him, though perhaps unconscious of it.

I had finished college and was strong for botany, he knew. He had thought that he would go to Michigan or Cornell and take a forestry course. That would give us something of a common ground. If I did have a spark of feeling for him, he thought it would only grow slowly and through some small point of interest, like our mutual love of nature. Then maybe — years hence perhaps — he would dare to ask me to share his life with him. With this idea, his visit to me there at the Experiment Station was just the first of numberless visits with which sometime in the dim future he would entrap me for a final surrender.

We trembled then, when it was all explained, to think how narrow the margin had been: that at the very eleventh hour, without further years of waiting, we had found each other; that it was just because he had read meaning in the quiver of my pen when I congratulated him for winning the President's Rifle Match and then of my voice when I asked him what it was that had helped him through the war years — and that I would have refused his future visits. To the delicate shyness of his hopes, that refusal perhaps would have been all that was needed to tell him what he was presuming, that it was after all only elderly school teacher regard I had for him. And I would have gone on again struggling to kill my feeling for him.

But now, after all the words I've found it takes to tell this story, I turn to these few from him in his autobiographical sketch:

> Our first meeting was another milestone in my career. Our growing together had been by such imperceptible gradations through the eight or nine years of our acquaintance, that we never knew what our real relation was until long absence defined it for us. We had our work, our recreation and our interests in common. These increased during the war. She turned to botanical science and I to forestry; they are essentially the same. Her religion and philosophical experiences paralleled mine, except that she was finer and better balanced than I. Her games and sports were mine from swimming to chess. We thought essentially along the same lines, and the convergence of our lives seems to have been inevitable, given the contact we had. This convergence came at that first meeting, and came abruptly. I cannot tell about it — how it affected me to find her the same little charming girl she had been in my dreams in Haiti; how she gave herself away by a little quaver of her voice that gave me the nerve to claim her. There is where the beauty of my life began, and where it took on color.
>
> She is a challenge, a stimulus to me. I want to achieve things for her and for humanity for her sake. The stages through which I have grown have left their impress upon me, but in this present stage the desire to *achieve* something, dominates everything. I am becoming more practical and more sensible. Even philosophy, which has taken a place of secondary importance, must be pragmatic to satisfy me. I am feeling more of responsibility and am looking farther into the future with definite, concrete plans. I am ambitious and enthusiastic, and I believe I can attain heights that will more than satisfy the predictions of my father. I hope so for his sake.

The third and last paragraph of this sketch I have quoted in the Introduction on page xiii with his emphasis, "and serves humanity."

Sometime after Banks left me at my door that night and I had regained a bit of consciousness, I smiled to myself as I pictured him on his way back to his night's lodging. Although the realization that we had found each other and that the future was rosier than any dream was new and astonishing to me, I thought it must have been ten times more so to him. Here he was, still in his early twenties, fresh from two years of tropical army life, with no money, no trade or profession, college scarcely begun, suddenly finding himself engaged to be married, without having had any intention to do so for years and years.

Even if he was half intoxicated emotionally with the reality, as he must have been, the practical aspects of the situation when he "came to" would surely have been arresting enough to make a prudent and responsible young man wonder what he had gotten himself into. For me, however, that question raised no problem. One doesn't question a rainbow or look for the pot of gold at the end of it.

A week later we met again, this time as planned, at the little railroad station near my home at which from our different directions we arrived the same afternoon — and Banks had a surprise for me. Pausing by the shady margin of the little wayside lake on our walk to my home, he placed a diamond ring on my finger! No matter how tiny the diamond, its meaning could not have been greater.

The fact that all of Banks' scant army savings had gone to purchase that diamond, even had I known it then, would not have affected my appreciation, not of the diamond as such but of the reality it signified. "We have no money? Well then we'll earn some," would have been my own blithe equivalent of, "We have no bread? Well, then we'll eat cake." Practical considerations were of supreme unimportance, now the the war, the uncertainty, the silence, were over and our mutual love was fast between us.

Banks' reaction to the awkward fact that he had no ready-made resource was voiced in the first of the letters that came in quick succession.

> It makes me ashamed, Louie, to have this best moment of my life see me so poorly prepared. I'm going to begin work next week on something. What do you say to a month on a hay-baler? — that month I had intended to idle away at home? Tommy [his brother] says I could get a hundred a month. I've also been looking over the old Wear-Ever question. I believe I could do pretty well at that again. I'll talk it over with you on Saturday. That day comes awfully slowly, doesn't it, Louie?

It is easy to see from that the situation in which Banks found himself, confronted with the unexpected responsibility ahead, was the best possible one for him. He was as eager as I to hasten the time when we could be together. In fact, his aspirations were aroused and caused him to snap out of his army lassitude much more quickly than he would otherwise have been likely to do. It set an immediate and definite goal for him. Later in that first letter, as he enlarged on the effect on him of his attitude toward me, the attitude of which I had once been so painfully unaware, he wrote

> I saw you in the great green world, the breeze took and brought the message—but I could see you only inviting me to share your *intellectual* world, and I wanted to share your heart, Louie. —I felt there was no hope. And then, too, I was doubting everything and it was hard to have faith in anything, especially hard to believe you would ever care for me as more than a friend.

> I know I never expressed anything of this—it is my fault, but I was afraid I would lose my best friend by doing so. And then I would tell myself that maybe we would just "grow" together. But my skepticism easily robbed me of that, and as I lost faith in God I seemed to lose hope. Then I just longed to get to the front lines! I expected to, Louie, I may as well tell you now. I expected to so much at one time that I thought there was no use in having my dental work done—needless bother!

> But now—I know the Big Truth, and as I look back I pity my blindness. Once or twice the thought has come to me that I might lose you again through doubts—might philosophize you away, but it just "can't be did." I've got you and we're bound a thousand times by the big old dogma, love.

And so, after only a few days at home with his family, Banks started on the first job that presented itself. He baled hay and worked his unaccustomed muscles to the limit, glad for even this opportunity to measure his determination and to prove to himself and others that he could be equal to the situation even in a material sense.

Perhaps it isn't strange that this new change in his life should have exerted an influence even on his very deep-seated skepticism. Not that it changed it radically, for that it didn't do. At the time neither of us was aware that it was having any effect on that at all, absorbed as we were in our new relationship itself and the enchanting future opening before us. But now, looking back, it is easier to see that it was one large factor in the continuing growth and development within him—in me, too, I suppose—of his philosophical attitude toward life.

Even as we had talked eagerly and excitedly that unforgettable night of Banks' visit at Wooster, I realized that his mechanistic view of the universe had only become more ingrained and habitual and, he thought, satisfying. He had thought it was good enough to help him even through bereavement, should that come. But now he admitted that he did not know if it would suffice for the great joy that had come to him. He could contemplate death, annihilation in the abstract, for himself, unflinchingly. But now we both felt that our relationship and comradeship should be, must somehow be, eternal. We felt it was so wholly good that a lifetime could be but a beginning. To cover that, he admitted, called for a bigger philosophy.

Of course, I mentioned idealism, but it never seemed to penetrate, then or later. In this first letter to me, however, he recognized the effect on him of some of our early contacts, and wrote

> I used to wonder if your path and mine would converge somewhere in the future. Later I began to wish they might. And now when I see all the various circumstances that furthered that convergence, the books I read, the meetings, the separations, etc. that were all part of it, it would not be so hard to put a Planner behind it all, would it?

In his short and necessarily infrequent visits (because before long he went to sell Wear-Ever in a town in southern Ohio) while much of our attention was devoted to our intimate and personal plans and feelings of the present and the future, we were continually slipping onto philosophical ground. As Banks' mind began more and more to throw off its army lethargy, its old activity returned. As I expressed it,

> Although his outlook no longer satisfied him as much as it had, he could find nothing to make him change it and it stayed with him just as it had of old, except that now a little of the extreme youthful fervor was gone. It was possible now to be happy in the daily rounds of this life even though he still didn't know the secrets of the next or whether or not there was a next.

As we talked it over at various times, I think we each came to be more or less influenced by the viewpoint of the other. I too had changed a lot. The flickering remnants of a formal religion had slipped gradually and more or less completely from my mind. I had a strong position toward an idealistic viewpoint. I thought that mind *should* be supreme in the universe and matter somehow an attribute or expression of it. I felt that there should be a God, though my idea of that too had undergone much change and probably would no longer fit an orthodox definition. In fact, it meant to me now all the mystery in which the origin of earth and man and natural law could be summed up.

By maybe feeble logic, I argued that whatever personality may be, since man has it, it does not seem rational to suppose that an element which makes up so distinctive a part of humankind should be lacking entirely in the supernatural. Simply this: I am a personality, therefore God must be one, too. At least personality must be one of his attributes. Believing in God, I naturally believed in a future existence or continued life of some sort, although I did not attempt to limit or define it. So far I thought I saw my way easily enough.

But at Christianity my certainty stopped, influenced obviously by the old questions Banks had asked. I would have agreed that it is a great and wonderful religion, only it was *a* religion. I too had looked behind the mirror. I could no longer persuade myself that it was more.

Along with my loss of belief in formal Christianity I lost also my old time goody-goody attitude that those on that side are on the *right* side. There was no longer a *right* side or wrong side to it. Banks was no more wrong or right than I. We both were right in our desire to arrive at the best and truest for us. The difference in our viewpoints was easily explained by our differences in heredity, early training, and subsequent experiences. There was nothing on either side by which one or the other could be praised or blamed.

As we talked, then and later, Banks' first objection always was to my placing a God so unquestioningly at the back of the Universe. "Don't you see, Louie, it's just a name? I prefer to use the word Law instead. It doesn't connote so much. True, I can't say how Law originated but neither can you say how God originated." And he couldn't see any evidence for making mind supreme over matter, and in truth neither of us was any more able than the other to find a real explanation to back up his position. In fact, it is plain now that the only possible explanation for our difference was one of circumstance and not one bound up in the merits of the argument at all. And the thing that bothered both of us more and more was our ignorance. I had accepted the dictum that an atom is a "whorl of energy," and built Idealism on it. Banks wanted to know if that concept was literally true first, before he allowed it to influence his thinking. We wanted to know the latest developments of science in various fields, and in physics especially. We saw ever more plainly that we must get more knowledge, more facts, before trying to go farther on the question. Sooner or later, we would have to go back to the university.

And so over succeeding months, even my Monistic Idealism somehow evaporated in the intensity of our exchanges. The low level of success I achieved in my attempt to press it on Banks is shown implicitly, I think, in his autobiographical sketch covering this period, for in it no reference whatever to idealistic thinking is even hinted at. And there is no sign that he felt any need to look beyond the mechanistic interpretation of the Universe. But we tacitly agreed that we could live in that Universe, and with each other, even though our beliefs about that Universe were not the same. The difference thus did not divide us emotionally but it became instead a kind of stimulus from which both of us, I think, gained considerable mental development, as we continually attempted, never quite successfully, to harmonize our differences.

After our engagement, we both went back to work, Banks back to selling aluminumware and I, after the short summer job in Wooster, to an office job at the B.F. Goodrich Rubber Company in Akron, and I lived there in the company dormitory. There, one night, I put on paper my "day-dream," and I kept a copy of it. It went like this:

Jan. 9, 1920   B.F. Goodrich Dormitory

Day dreams? Oh, I had a splendid bunch of them today. I tabulated for an hour. Mrs. Fries read the numbers to me, I punched the keys, and we never made a mistake. [Quite different from my performance with the Leguminosae at the Experiment Station at Wooster.] My real mind wasn't at B.F.G. ten minutes in all that time. It was out at the University of Chicago with Banks and me at college. I was taking a lot of botany and geology. Being a graduate, I had a little room in the botany building, where Banks and I were studying together as we ate our lunch. I don't think we had pimiento sandwiches, either. [In my frugal senior year there, I had found them to be the cheapest possible lunch.] And I heard Dr. Fuller [one of my former University of Chicago professors] call me Mrs. —— I can't write it yet.

A little later, we were standing out at Lake Michigan. I don't know what we were thinking, but somehow all the vastness, the magnificance of the natural world almost choked me, there in my dream.

And I saw the time passing, saw us grow more absorbed in our work; saw, especially, my darling finding himself, saw his work increase, mine adapting to his, supplementing it. Then I saw opportunity, vague and vast and pleasing, come to him, to us.

After that, it still went on, the dream. Then we were no longer only two, but there were others who added still to his, our, life plan, even life work, for they seemed to unite us soul to soul even as we had not before been united. And I thought I was still the pal of my husband, growing on with him, all of us, not stagnating, not standing still.

How much of my dream, I wonder, will we realize? The spirit of it all, I'm sure. And that's the essence.

Oh, Wonderful Planner of All, I'm only beginning to get my lines. I'm only growing slowly into a concept of what the future can mean — of what you intended when the Whole you Planned.

Oh, may I not the beauty mar
May I not the music jar.

To fulfill that dream, I needed, first of all, to pay off the few hundred dollars I still owed to Wooster College for the tuition I had borrowed. By then, Banks and I both were hoping that next year we would be able to go as a married couple to the University of Chicago.

By careful saving, I managed by spring to pay the debt and to buy my modest wedding clothes. Banks, too, by almost miraculous industry and success in canvassing, had a neat little sum saved up.

Then Banks' continual plea of loneliness and our mutual eagerness for more time for companionship which necessarily had been limited by the distance, time, and money that were involved in his visits to me, hurried our plans that had been for a summer wedding. By early April, just about seven months after he had come back to civilian life, we were married at my home and "stepped out into that new world which is the old."

We went to Zanesville, the town where Banks had been working all winter. There I so gladly, so eagerly and proudly, hoped to prove to him that the inspiration to him of my presence would earn us more dollars than the wages I might otherwise have earned.

We arrived at the town in the late evening of our wedding day. Although nearly tired out by the sustained emotion and excitement of that day, neither of us could have been happier or more filled with enthusiasm for the life beginning then and there and stretching on and on into the unknown and untried vistas ahead of us. As we passed the peaceful and silent little park of the town lying serene and deserted in the moonlight, my new husband led me over to a little pond and rustic bridge under some big basswood trees, and there where the world was all our own and all pristine and new, we stood, silent, reverent, thanking whatever gods there be for the great glory that had come into our lives. As a little ray of moonlight filtering down between the budding twigs fell on his face and I saw it lighted by the deepest earnestness and grave and strong in the thought and purpose stamped upon it, I knew then, and even more strongly than before, that "no wind shall blow our bark astray," and that, hand in hand, life for us should be good and great and rich no matter how humble it might be. "If springs are pure the waters too are pure that from them rise." And so, when lives are blessed, blessing must rise from them.

After the few days of honeymoon which were all that we allowed ourselves, Banks started out again on his business of selling pots and pans to the inhabitants of the town, having special success with young brides. He apparently imbued them with the same enthusiasm for the life before them he felt so strongly for his own, and evidently he convinced them that they needed just the culinary aids he offered. He could do it, I think, because he was himself convinced.

As he started out each morning, lingeringly and reluctantly but determinedly, carrying a big suitcase of samples in either hand, I watched him from the window until a blur of happy tears cut off my view. Why was I so blessed? I know that many and many a girl had loved as deeply as I and her love had gone unfulfilled with no more blame and as much deserving as I. Why had fate so singled me out to receive her richest blessing?

Neither then nor since have I been able to find an answer to that question. But in those happy evenings when he returned successful and I had practiced my very rudimentary kitchen skills on him, we came to our working hypothesis. If there is a Planner, he obviously has some special work for us which we can only do together. Our joy must strengthen us for it. And even if nothing but blind fate or chance is responsible, even if our union only "happened," the least we can do is to return to the world, to the society in which we live, joy for joy, help for help, and to try to give of our plenty to those to whom fate has been less kind and to whom will never come this supreme gift that now is ours.

A few weeks later, April 27, in a diary I wrote

> I can't decide whether this is really life or only playing at it. My time here is too pleasant, too easy. But then a little of that maybe I deserve? And I know I'll soon get my feet back on the ground again.

I did soon find out that "life is real, life is earnest," but in that April entry I continued

> I went to a demonstration [for the aluminumware Banks was selling] with Banks last night. I like to hear him talk business. I can see that he is a good businessman. I am *so* proud of him, and more and more I know that I have a splendid husband and an unusually good and strong and true one.

> Last Sunday we had our first guests, brother Con and his friend. From what he told me I'm very worried about Mama.

Unfortunately, that worry was not without cause. For the last year my mother had been fighting a losing war with cancer. She lived in Ohio, in Doylestown with my younger sister, Ruth, who was married and had several small children. With Mama ill, Ruth was over-burdened. And so, after a week or so I was called home to help her. But by May 18, as my diary says, I was able to leave again for "Home and Banks."

For a surprise I didn't tell him, but arrived there (by train) that evening and wrote

> I'm so excited! Banks is having a Party [Wear-ever]. He'll be *so* surprised, and if he's as happy as I am that I'm here, won't it be the happiest moment ever!

> Oh, it was awful going away from my perfectly good month-old husband. The week at Doylestown was interminable and now this last hour until he comes in!

Then, the next day, May 19:

> Oh, boy! Wasn't he surprised when he came in and stumbled over my grip in the dark and then he gave one look — Life here is all pure, beautiful, wonder of living. Every moment of this blessed carefree time so transcends even my wildest imaginings of happiness that I'm simply in the world but not of it. I'm living in Utopia, a little Paradise of our own.

> Banks came in tonight about 10. He had sold $100 worth since 4 o'clock. He wanted to go for a walk in the park. I dressed and went along and we got all the exercise and child-like glee out of the situation — our perfect companionship, the lovely balmy evening, the park so beautiful, shadowy, rain scented, the song of the croakers in the lake.

A few days later, June 4, another entry:

> I watch him as he starts down the street for the day's work, carrying his two heavy sample cases, and a tight feeling comes in my throat and chokes me till I turn away in tears. Why tears? Just a feeble response to the sense of bigness — such a sense that I've got to measure up, such a feeling of rejoicing. And then too always the thought, how could I live without him, if something took him from me. But I shut that thought out.

But then, June 8, the happy scene had faded. I had been called back again to Doylestown because my mother was worse. I wrote in my diary

Back here again and my bright little dream faded out, only it isn't. It just seems so, but I know it isn't really by this life-sized ache in my throat and the size of my lonesomeness — it will be so long before I can go back.

It hurts so about Mama. She is weaker and more hopeless. We all feel as if somehow there just *must* be a way to help her, to make her better for a few years at least —

On July 7 I wrote that Banks had come to Doylestown for a week's visit and that my mother, accompanied by my father, had gone to Baltimore for an operation at Johns Hopkins. We hoped it would help her, even though we almost knew there was no hope. Banks and I then went back to Zanesville.

It was such wonderful fun to be going again to home and daily companionship. I was happier than I've ever been before, with few exceptions. But in just a day came the telegram saying Mama was back home, the cancer in her lungs was inoperable and so all hope of recovery was gone. She was growing worse. Oh — it was hard to leave Banks to come back here to conditions like this.

That last evening Banks tried to make so pleasant for me. He succeeded. We had a lovely buggy-ride down the valley of the Muskingum. It was a perfect ride even though we went over a dangerously decrepit old bridge and the harness broke as we went down an unbelievably steep hill.

I've been here [in Doylestown] half a week now and Mama is a little more comfortable than when she first got back from Baltimore. It was unbearable then. I'm afraid she's strong enough to suffer a long time yet. If it must be that, how much better if it could end suddenly. Why should she have to suffer so and from an unavoidable disease? I can't understand.

I got a box of candy from Banks tonight. Miriam [about four years old] said when I gave her a piece, "Banks is a pretty good fellow, isn't he?" She's right!

On July 24 as Mama slept and I was watching at her bedside, I wrote a fragment about my feelings that somehow has been preserved:

She talked to me yesterday afternoon when I was alone with her. She said she now had more strength "to do His will." She hoped that there would be mercy for her for she had always tried to live a sincere life. But she said, and I remember her very words still, "The Old Tempter stands at my side and tries to tell me, 'Yes, that's a good thing to say. They'll like to hear you say that.'"

She used a good many more of the old church phrases about the Evil One trying to get her down at the last minute, etc. She also warned me not to let "Science" lead me astray.

It made me angry at that old religious thinking and at the system that makes such as she, one of the most faithful of its followers, be bothered at such a time by purely theoretical fears. She hasn't sinned! She deserves to feel fully confident for she's never done wrong. But it's this habitual way of thinking that is to blame.

On August 5 the sad story goes on, and I write

Still at Doylestown. Mama stays much the same. When she wakes up she smiles so wanly. It makes my heart ache so very badly. I can't really imagine how it must be to have only death to which to look forward.

On August 11, another sorrowful note, when apparently even Mama had misinterpreted my "exterior" as heartless, when it was only calm because I knew I couldn't control a breakdown if once I let it start. I remember that as I sat resting, by her bedside, dozing off sometimes, I kept handy a book to turn to. And so, that was the reason that that night I got called hard-hearted.

... I'm *not* hard-hearted. I can't see why those who ought to know me best have accused me of that. I wouldn't mind Mama's saying it now if it had not been said before. It just breaks my heart. And Mama is so weak and sick and miserable. That breaks my heart too, and I haven't seen my precious husband for almost two weeks. That almost breaks it too. If I ever get away from here I'll have quite a job of mending to do.

When at last that agonizing and hopeless time had passed and I was finally back in Zanesville, I wrote on September 4, 1920,

More than ever it is attractive to look into the future, for the recent past is so sad. The relief of being here again and of seeing the end of the painful time of Mama's illness is unspeakable. The funeral was August 23. That whole time was just awful. I was shocked, numbed with sorrow and pity for my poor mother. Only now from a little distance of time and space can I look back with any realization.

So long I had known her only in suffering and in an abnormal condition that when the end did come I could hardly any longer realize that it was *my mother* who used to be with us always to cheer and help and give her unfailing sympathy. But now, how can I ever go back with her not there? She always appreciated my homecomings more than anyone else. She'd be watching for me from the porch if she knew I was coming.

But she must be glad in heaven now for she has nothing about which to feel otherwise. And she can know now how much we cared for and needed her.

In contrast to that from me — and showing Banks' approach to the same situation — I find recorded in a diary entry that fall, on November 16, 1920, the following, which I quote from Banks' letter to my younger sister Sylvia, who still was greatly saddened by our mother's death.

The greatest and most beautiful thing is that your mother lived. Nothing can change that. *Think of that* and *not of the fact that she couldn't live always.*

Why must we (all of us) pass up the beauty of a whole life for the bitterness of one hour? You love her most, you revere her most for the dear days when she did not suffer. There is infinite sweetness in those memories. I would not have you lose one bit of the feeling you have — it is sacred.

But I wish you could smile through your tears and feel uplifted and inspired by the very thought of that beautiful and saintly life you know so well. You may search all the records of every religious faith in vain to find as much truth, devotion, and love as you find in that one short period that shall ever be so vivid in your mind — your mother's life.

Won't you raise up a monument in your own life, in the glorious womanhood that shall be yours, will you not build a splendid statue that shall not only honor this dear memory of yours, but shall reflect its golden sunlight as long as memories lighten our souls and sweet reminiscence inspires our hearts.

Although out of chronological order here, the same attitude is reflected five years later in a letter that Banks wrote, in February 1927, to this same sister of mine after his own mother died of a stroke, suddenly and without suffering. He wrote

I find myself groping for a God to thank (that she did not suffer), groping too through science and philosophy — to find a Heaven for her to go to. She cannot go out of my thoughts. I must find a place for her to go to.

After that sad and hopeless summer, a ray of cheering light broke through the gloom. We had applied for scholarships at the University of Chicago, and I had asked my old friend and professor, Strasy, still working on his doctorate at Chicago, to sponsor them. His response came quickly, and a copy of my letter to Banks transmitting the news still remains. I wrote

> I'm excited! I got a scholarship! Now if you get one, or even if you don't, won't we be fixed? Seven hours of service per week, 12 weeks or 82 hours of service per quarter for $50. That's a rate of about 60¢ per hour. Do you think that's bad? It will probably give us a key to the botany building as well as advantages with the professors.
>
> Don't you think Strasy's a friend worth having? I sent him the request on Monday and tonight I get this response. I feel like starting for Chicago right away. Oh, we're going to have the greatest time this winter. We'll study our heads off during the week and play our heads off on Sunday. We'll enjoy all the pleasures of poverty too, because we'll want to save a little nest egg for another year. We'll have enough money to get everything we really need.

I also find a fragment, apparently written the same time, in which I tried to sum up our probable expenses:

Probable Expenses		Probable Savings
Carfare	$120	$60
Rent	360	0
Board	380	70
Tuition	90	0
Lab fees	54	0
Chemistry deposit	10	0
Clothes	25	0
Books	45	25
Trips (field)	100	0
	1184	155

Amusements probably out of the $155 we will save. I believe we can get along nicely on $1200.

That note was written on a Monday evening. By the following Saturday I apparently had a note from Banks with comparable news in it. Another letter fragment dated Saturday night, probably at the end of the same week, says

> I was even more excited to hear of your scholarship than I was to hear of mine. I'm so glad! Now the U. of C. won't be any more expensive than any other would have been. And you don't even have to work for it. And you can be there the first day for sure, so you won't have to risk forfeiting it as I may have to do with mine because I may have to continue on here with Mama. But if I can't go October 1 I'll be so glad to know that you can begin alone and not have to be held back by me.

Later, I continue, explaining that

> Before I was married I wanted to get an education to make myself a member of society able to render a service to it. Had I remained unmarried, I would have tried to do so in a direct impersonal way. As it is I want to do so still, but in a personal, if indirect way — through my family. I really think you understand all this, but I must repeat it for emphasis.

> Oh, I think it's going to be the greatest fun. Deep down, I've always wanted to go to school to the limit and then sometime to make something out of my education. I want to get to the stage when I can think independently and constructively. But I've always felt the need and longing for companionship, for sympathetic understanding. During the course of my college life I've lost lots and lots of time just in blind and hungry longing for this I've lacked.

> But now we're to go together. That's the splendid, the best and greatest part! Now I'm to get that schooling under ideal circumstances!

3

Graduate School and Botany

In the fall of 1920, Banks gave up his canvassing job and we went back to my old university (Chicago) with enough money to last at least a year if we were careful. Banks knew how I dreamed of sometime doing graduate work; and so, although I would willingly have tried to get a job of some kind, he insisted that I, too, attend the university. Unable to resist the chance to study beside him, I agreed to let the future care for itself while we allowed ourselves this one glorious year we had within our grasp. My diary after we arrived at the University records that

At last we're here after having anticipated coming for so long. We got a light housekeeping room today and are trying to get settled. It's cold and wet outside and the heat hasn't been turned on yet, but I know it's going to be a different place to me than the Chicago of two years ago. Being *at home* will put an entirely different color on everything from the one it had when I was only staying here. [I could not forget how unhappy I had been during much of that year.]

As a background for the forestry Banks meant to study later we decided that he should begin his work in the Department of Botany, where I was already well acquainted and in which I now was going on into graduate work. It was not exactly a choice of work for him, but rather a matter of convenience and familiarity. We thought, too, that basic courses in botany would serve the same end in forestry as in botany when later he would enter that field. But at this beginning stage, my familiarity and almost affectionate standing with the professors in the botany department was a factor. It earned me an assistantship and also a little research office which, just as I had dreamed, gave us a convenient shared location at the university.

And in the department, as I expected, Banks was an immediate success, although not so much because of me and my good standing with the professors under whom I had worked before. At the beginning I suppose there may have been a bit of that to account for their ready acceptance of him. It was not because of the excellence of his drawings showing plant development either, for although I don't think I ever told him so, it was obvious he'd never get very far on his drawing skill. No, it was because of his record as a marksman.

Several of his professors were members of the University Rifle Club. Even in my earlier undergraduate days, their enthusiasm for shooting and marksmanship had been so great that my roommate and I had gone to the rifle range a few times to try it out. But the experience had led nowhere for me. In time, I had managed to hit the target, though never the bull's-eye. Now the professors learned that my new husband had won the President's Match and that was all it took to ensure his standing with them. However lacking in esthetic value his botanical sketches may have been, at least they were meticulously correct — and discussions of them with the professor could well be limited in favor of that professor's interest in marksmanship.

During that first year at the university, I wrote in my diary on December 11, 1920,

> Banks went out to Ft. Sheridan today for his first day of shooting and didn't get back until an hour or two after I expected him. — And I began

to think of all the things that might have happened to him — and of the dull, agonizing life I'd have if any of them were true. He's the whole of my life now, all the joy, color and interest.

And then, after a discussion of my paper on potato diseases that was giving me trouble:

It's fun to watch Banks get deeper and deeper into the life here. He'll soon be a full-fledged botanist. He doesn't realize yet how much of a one he is, but I do.

Still later, several entries mention Banks' work at the rifle range. For instance, on January 21, 1921, I wrote

Banks is studying tonight. He took the afternoon off for shooting and must work now. He and [one of his professors] Dr. Land (a Rifle Club member) are getting to be regular cronies.

Then, an added note on a different subject:

I made an apple pudding tonight and Banks said it's about the best thing I ever made. Poor old neglected man with his clothes unmended and his socks undarned, yet just tonight he wanted me to promise not to iron his pocket handkerchiefs or shirts except the cuffs, to save time. But that promise I wouldn't make.

And while on the subject of clothes, I should add a few words about my own, that first summer at the university, showing how unimportant they were in our scheme of things.

I have only two dresses — ginghams. Last week I spilled glass cleaner over one and it "ate" the front of it full of holes, and the dress is beyond repair. [I had used all the extra cloth to make a dress for my little sister back home.] This week I spilled $AgNO_3$ over the other one and now it's full of black stains. I tried to cut them out and put in patches but that doesn't look well either. I'll have to take time off next Saturday and make myself something to wear.

And, as I remember, that is exactly what I did. I went over to 65th Street from our room on 57th and bought enough gingham for a dress; and then, by working hard and fast, I had a dress for myself on Monday. Luckily, the idea that one would not want to wear the same thing each day had not arrived yet — at least, not for me.

I was also learning something quite unrelated to academic life, since this year in a Chicago rooming house began, as the next few lines remind me:

> We're having an awful time with the bed bugs and cockroaches. Out in the kitchen the roaches have almost full — though not undisputed — possession.

After that, however, I turn to other topics including further references to Banks' exploits at the rifle range.

> I caught myself as he left about to ask him please to come home early tonight. Then I made up my mind not to do that or I'd get into the habit and he'd surely hate it. I'd like to be a good wife....

> Banks shot 167 tonight, standing. I think whenever a success of any kind comes to one of us the other is even gladder than if it were his own. For instance, Banks got 100 in his chemistry test today and the best grade in his rock quiz in geology. I was tickled to pieces. I told the two men in my class about his grades — and they wondered "how would it feel to be that way?"

When we first went to the university, my actual scholastic standing was higher than Banks'. He had lost two years of college work while in the Marine Corps, and so he still had a couple of years of under-graduate work ahead of him, while I had finished mine and was in graduate school. And so I was able to help him sometimes, at first; but soon his stronger mental impetus took him beyond me in all but actual academic standing. Then our respective characteristics came to the front, as of old, in the questions and differences of viewpoints that the new situation presented.

By the spring of that first year, 1921, although I did not notice it then, the first signs of a change in Banks' attitude toward botany were reflected in my diary. For instance, in June I noted

> Banks worked all night last night with his osmotic pressure studies [on plants in situ, out on the sand dunes, an all-night job] and he slept this afternoon while I ironed. This evening just before dark, we took quite a walk up through parts of the city "where the wealthy nobles dwell." When we came home we started a discussion of some of the botany courses here. Banks is always saying that too much of the Ecology and Morphology courses are only theoretical, "nice to know" perhaps, but of no practical value to justify anyone in his own position taking them. I

keep arguing against specialization now. I feel that we still need generalization and that the other can come later. It seems to me we now have specialized enough by limiting ourselves to botany without trying to specialize in that.

We talk of our ideals. For a long time I've had a very effective set — to keep me going on, but when I try to state them definitely I don't succeed very well. I don't want to be *little*. I don't want us to be too small for ourselves, but I can't seem to tell Banks what I mean by that. For instance, I think the university man generally is less likely to be *little* than the agricultural college man because he has a broader background. I wonder if I'm too hazy to make sense, but I make sense to myself.

I'm dreadfully tired of Chicago and eager for a change of scene, but if there is any way possible we don't want to leave before Banks has another year at least. I'm eager to see him try graduate work. And research. I'm sure he'll do it very well. He has *ability*, though he hardly knows it yet himself.

At the end of the first year, Banks was given an evening job overseeing at the Rifle Club. With my continued assistantship in the Department of Botany and the remnant of our savings, our second year at the university became financially possible. After that, increases in our salaries permitted us to continue until in 1923 I finally had my Ph.D. and Banks, only a year behind me, had his master's and was headed toward a doctorate.

Those years brought mental growth and many changes. Always, Banks and I worked side by side, often in the same classes, meeting the same people and problems, having similar experiences and the same influences. We worked, studied, and played together and rejoiced in the fact that we could do so, realizing all the time that circumstances and habit were helping us to cement ever more strongly the union through which we felt lay our best preparation for the future.

Our third year at the university, beginning in the fall of 1922, was made possible, as the previous year, by the savings we were able to make during the summer and my continuing assistantship. I believe this was the season when I went back to Ohio alone for a short visit home after the summer term ended, and Banks wrote me there that he got a job as "pilot" with the university. When I returned, he explained that it actually was a "pile it here and pile it there" job, as he spaded up designated spots on the university grounds.

By this time, we felt quite proud of ourselves for somehow having managed to achieve the financial ends I bragged about in a diary entry:

Unusual as it may have been, through all these years the same Fate, smiling and kindly, has never left us. We have spent these years at the university, lived in the heart of a great city, each carrying full college work. And now instead of confronting a huge college debt, we have nearly as much to our credit as when we entered. So has Fate made possible for us the practical side of living.

As to the thrust of our college work, however, the record for Banks was not so smooth. In a diary entry of August 28, 1922, I recognized that as a field of life work, botany could not satisfy him. By then, I had practically forgotten that his introduction to botany had been only provisional in the first place. As I note in that entry,

Gradually it has been borne in on me that botany isn't going to afford Banks the real measure of development he needs nor is it the field into which he ever will be able to throw all his energy with no question at all as to whether it is worthwhile. Very frequently something comes up that shows how hard he has to work to make himself believe that this field is just the one for him. Somehow the men in it and the problems on which they are working do not seem quite the kind that he, and consequently I, demand. We say, "Those problems may do for some people, but not for us."

Banks' work *must* be something that in its very nature seems to him worth all that he can give it. And to be that it must be of the greatest and most far-reaching use to the world that it possibly can be.

As for myself, university life had for so long been an aspiration only that now that I had the chance, I nearly swallowed whole all that went with it. Even though at times in botany, especially the first year or so, the stiff impracticality of the extreme "pure science" ideal had left a fish-bone feeling in my throat, I had swallowed it all anyway, thinking that it must be good for me.

But Banks was not so docile a student as I. Research and science might be spelled with capitals for some people, but with his propensity for looking behind the mirror, not so for him. Now as valiantly as I had once argued for an orthodox and accepted religion, I now argued for cold, formal research, for knowledge for knowledge's sake.

But he would counter, "No, Louie, knowledge for *man's* sake." One whole section in the botany department met with his special objection, although it was the most popular one of all. About it he said, in effect, "I can't see what it's all about. I don't doubt that a lot of facts are presented, but to what do they lead? What help is it to know them? I don't see why one should major there, even if the course *is* so attractive."

I answered, explaining that the work was not only pleasant and attractive, but that it must have real value or the university would not pay for two full-time professors to handle it. Besides, for him it would be a background for forestry, at least in a general way; and also, should one not be interested in everything, even if it doesn't fit one's own narrow margin of immediate interest?

"Well, I don't see it that way," he would reply. "The university will offer any course for which students will enroll, but that does not mean necessarily that the courses are worthwhile."

Then to my general and oft-trotted-out argument that all knowledge is valuable, he was just as negative. "What's a science for, anyway? It's because scientists have lost perspective, that they can cry, 'Science for Science's sake'." And then he'd reiterate that science began because man needed to know the facts of nature in order to live better. But as soon as knowledge began to stack up big, it got heavy and cold and formalized and spelled with capitals. And men began to fall down and worship, "Oh, Great and Glittering Golden Calf..."

In his argument that research and research problems should be evaluated according to their value to humankind, Banks insisted that one problem was indeed more important than another. The gospel on this question which I had picked up from Strasy was that one could not make that value judgment before the research was done, because it was impossible to tell the value of a research topic beforehand. For instance, early research on the optimum diet for rats may have had no value at the time it began. But when rats became test animals for investigation on humans, knowledge about their dietary needs became very important.

Banks, however, was not convinced. He was impatient with the remoteness of many botanical research topics from any conceivable human value. To him it did not make any difference whether the first cell division of the embryo in an obscure plant group cuts off diagonally or horizontally (to make up an hypothetical case). It didn't matter (to make up another out of my rusty old botanical memory) if the sporophyte of an obscure liverwort has a flat or a round foot or no foot at all. He quite disregarded the significance of such minute observations for the evolutionary thesis which the professor of the course had seen in his own firsthand observation of the details and which that professor had found fitted into the great evolutionary process which he glimpsed in the background. And then Banks would hurl his biggest bolt, not only at me but sometimes at other students in the laboratory poring painstakingly over their microscopes, and say, "All knowledge is *not* valuable! Lots of it is not worth the knowing. A man can have no better excuse for giving his time to an ill-chosen research topic than he has to waste it in any other way. The cloak of 'research' or 'science' may cover it but cannot justify it."

In all this, I perforce must leave out all of the patient and un-revolutionary study and research that Banks and I carried out during those years at the university. After all, I picked out these episodes to show that Banks' mind, in a way, was open and unsettled like a prepared seed bed; new ideas could come in and find space for growth. It was particularly true by the end of our second year at the university. It was not until the beginning of the third year, the fall of 1922, that a diary entry of mine in October hints at new directions of interest. In it, I mention my bacteriology course of the previous summer and the important advances I had learned about that were being made in that field. These advances had impressed Banks, too, as seeming to bear directly on human welfare, as did new findings in medical fields which he learned of from medical students in his classes.

I mention in this same entry it seemed as if a blind man could see the great scope and bearing of the work the people in these branches were doing. Their keen purpose and enthusiasm, I thought, contrasted pretty strongly with

> the easy-going self-satisfaction of our good old Botany crowd here.... Those are some of the reasons why we almost decided to try to enter the Medical School next spring. But if we should do that it would mean that it would be five years before Banks could hope to get an M.D.

> Of course, we can't wait five more years for our home and family, and so a few years would have to be counted out for that. And there is where the question stood when we came back here [to Chicago] two weeks ago, after the summer break.

> Funny, when we got here the looks of things seemed to change. When it came right down to it, Banks said he had a sort of feeling of dread instead of elation when he thought of entering five years of Medical School. He doesn't want to be a practicing M.D. anyway. He wants to do investigation work. He wants his work to be worth something—or at least on a question that is worth something—something that matters to human beings.

> And so the debate went on for several days until he had to specify the courses he will take this term. He finally decided still to walk on middle ground, get an M.S. in botany and at the same time work up related

sciences — physics, chemistry, physiological chemistry, etc. and thereby sooner or later fit himself informally but directly for the sort of work into which, as time goes on, his major interest leads him. As he says, "I'm not in training only these present years while I'm in college, but I still will be for years thereafter." And so I know it will work out. We'll try to help, but not force, circumstances.

And now this week has come Dr. Crocker's unbelievable offer! A year at Yonkers [the new Boyce Thompson Institute for Plant Research] for both of us at $1500 apiece! The best thing we could dream about! We are the most fortunate people in the world!

But when is my home coming? I can't wait much longer. It calls to me from every baby I see on the street.

I was then 31 years old. Fortunately for my peace of mind, no statistics had yet come out to show the hazards of childbearing in older women.

On December 1, 1922, on a different topic, another little reference to Banks tells something about a characteristic of his I was beginning to recognize.

I'm so proud of him. No one else would work at one physics problem all day. I would give it up after the first fifteen minutes and try another one. But not Banks! And eventually he gets it. And I know, whether he knows or not, that the mental stress to which he puts himself at times like that, and the habit of sticking to a thing until the end — is a trait and a habit that makes him the strong man he is and is going to be.

On February 26, 1923, I find a reference I am glad was inserted because it refers to one of Banks' special characteristics, his great love of music. While I, too, enjoy music, I apparently lack the tone sensitivity which in him was very acute. Perhaps that is the reason I had forgotten until reminded by this entry that he once had a violin. But here I say, "Banks is so interested in his violin. I'm sure it was just the kind of interest for him to get."

Even though I have forgotten the violin, where it came from or where it went, I will always remember his lifelong absorption in music for relaxation, and his accordion, mouth organ, and ocarina, each of which he played by ear beautifully and sensitively. So, at least, it seemed to me, but I don't know why it never occurred to either of us that he should take music lessons. We agreed early in our life together that I should supply the color, since he was colorblind to red and green and could not appreciate as much, while he would supply the sounds, to which I was much less sensitive than he.

Later, on May 8, 1923, another diary note touches incidentally on a mental characteristic of Banks that I put into these words:

> It is easy for me to note the improvement in my very mental caliber which being with Banks is bringing. His mind is keen, mine is lazy. If someone comes with a new idea I have a tendency to say Yes, I see, etc. when I don't see and when by agreeing I eliminate the need for thinking about it until I really do understand.

> But Banks isn't that way. I have watched him getting a new idea many times. He thinks about it, asks a question, raises an objection, and eventually he knows all about the topic. It has become an integral part of his knowledge.

I might have added, too, that he had also sensed its bearing and implications long before they occurred to me, even though my thought processes are quick while his generally were relatively slow.

Another incidental observation I can add now but probably had not then recognized, is that as a result of my tendency to agree with the person with the new idea and Banks' to look it over critically before accepting it, the effect on that person would likely be to regard us differently. He would tend to be pleased that I agreed and irritated by Banks' more skeptical reaction. A standing joke between us came to be that when a person first met us both, he probably thought, "She's all right but isn't he horrible?" and never see beneath the exteriors.

But my good sense was showing, I'm sure, when I added in that same entry

> I am consciously trying to copy his methods. I believe I have just as good an ability to grasp a new idea as he has only I have the lazy habit of not using fully the brains I have. That's just one way of mine I'm trying to change.

> I'm growing, too, I know, by constantly being forced to defend a position I take, against him. We have many discussions in these hours we spend reading Bergson and other philosophical stuff. I wish so much that I could record these stages through which we pass.

As Banks' rebellious line of thought about the botanical questions increasingly took possession of him, his continuing in the field came more and more into question. We both knew that the general training we were getting in scientific method was very good. Banks, with no inherent aptitude for drawing, for instance, might turn in a rather casual sketch of cell division in a sprouting embryo, and then elicit the order from his professor to go back to his microscope and look again. And sure enough, he would have missed some of the detail. Later, perhaps long after information about cell division in that embryo was entirely forgotten, the lesson was remembered that in scientific method you don't take the unimportance of details for granted, and that to be painstakingly accurate in every observation is just as important as making certain in the first place that the problem is an important one.

More and more, Banks' interest turned to the chemical, the organic, the physiological aspects of botany, rather than to the more obvious and conventional side. And, of course, in those areas, too, the strictest standards of research were demanded. As a result, the use of meticulous methods, regardless of content and regardless of how important or unimportant that content may have seemed to him, was confirmed as the enduring lesson of his botanical research.

About this time, another seed was planted and began to germinate, however unnoticed it may have been to either of us then. This came from an article we read in the *American Magazine*. It was an account of a remarkable kind of photography reported from England, spirit photography, in which a recognizable image of a departed loved one appeared beside the picture of the sitter. If any of the facts given were true, something inexplicable was going on. Banks remarked that if anything like that photographic claim could be proved, if by any objective means whatever real proof of spirit life could be obtained, then he would believe in a spiritual world because then he would *know*, for him the only kind of believing possible.

I agreed, but could not help adding that if such a thing as spirit photography could ever be established, then indeed all of my old orthodox ideas of the spiritual world would be knocked to forty pieces. That kind of spiritual world would be so much more earthy than anything religion and the churches taught, that the two kinds of worlds could scarcely have much relationship.

But after this, nothing more along this line came for months, and Banks' drudgery in botany continued. Ever since the fall before we had been looking forward to our new jobs as plant physiologists at the just-established Boyce Thompson Institute for Plant Research at Yonkers, New York. These positions as I said had been offered to us by Dr. Crocker, who had been one of our professors at the university and who would be the director of the new institute. The offer to us for $1500 each seemed magnificent. We were to begin on October 1, 1923. We accordingly moved to Yonkers that fall, as did also my former professor, Dr.

Sophia Eckerson, or Ecky, under whom I had written my Ph.D. thesis in her specialty, plant microchemistry. She now would be on the research staff at the institute.

When I look back at my diary entries during the entire period of our stay at the university, I see only one thing that points to something new coming onto Banks' horizon, i.e., spirit photography. I see in this lack of other mention of the new interest, what now appears to be a blind spot on my part as to the indications that even then were beginning to foreshadow the direction of Banks' life involvement. But diaries are only sporadic and incomplete records of events, or at least mine were, governed as they were by impulse and snatches of available time. And after all, I knew of no formal channel into which this interest of his could be directed.

At any rate, I'm sure I was more aware of the direction Banks' attention was taking than is shown by the fact that I never mentioned in any of my diary entries during this third year at Chicago (1922–23) a lecture we attended one night by Sir Arthur Conan Doyle, then on a United States tour. We had known of him mainly as the creator of Sherlock Holmes. But in this lecture he spoke very earnestly of his belief that deceased persons can communicate with the living, and that the fact could be taken as proving survival after death.

We were very much impressed by Sir Arthur's utter sincerity. Whether or not his belief was justified, his certainty that his dead son had communicated with him had given him a deep and all-pervading optimism about the meaning of life.

We had gone to the lecture with several of our botany student friends. They, however, were not touched by the lecture as we were. Instead, they were almost hilarious in their ridicule of Sir Arthur's credulity. We tried to talk with them about the substance of his message, but they were uninterested. One or two of them were almost openly digusted with us for even considering the matter. They disregarded the fact that the reason we did so was that something more was suggested than we could explain, and that it was, we thought, on a supremely important topic. Banks urged that it was not the part of openminded scientists, even embryonic ones like all of us, to deny an unexplored idea or claim before giving it some study. To do so, he said, just because it was on a revolutionary instead of an orthodox topic was unworthy of the true spirit of science. Conan Doyle's lecture thus did not affect Banks the way it did his botanical friends, but he did wonder how good was the evidence on which the man had based his conviction and whether that evidence was strong enough to be counted as more than the fulfillment of wishful thinking. Banks' own critical way of thinking, augmented now by the training in the need for strict and careful observations, colored his judgment and kept him from a quick decision for or against. But one aspect of Conan Doyle's lecture was entirely convincing. That was his joy in the knowledge he thought he had of the survival of the spirit after death. This certainly strengthened Banks' belief that the world needed to know whether or not that conviction was justified, needed to know whether or not the question could be answered decisively by the method of scientific investigation.

As a result of this lecture, Banks looked in the university library to find publications of the Society for Psychical Research in London. He realized then that research on the question of survival of the spirit had long been studied in a scholarly way by a group of eminent persons in England, where that society had been formed in 1882; and he learned, too, that a similar society had been formed soon afterwards in New York, the American Society for Psychical Research.

Our attention was arrested, and we attended such public seances as we could find in the city around us. But in them we found no evidence on which to feed our interest and only what seemed to us to be gullibility, suggestion, wishful thinking. We soon gave up the effort as unprofitable and a waste of time.

None of this is even mentioned in my diary. Quite obviously, I had not yet sensed the drift. Now, in retrospect, I can see that it was already showing, as evidenced by Banks' interest in a story he heard in a plant morphology course. But perhaps I should say in my own defense that I did not know then how deeply that story intrigued him or how often he would refer to it in years ahead, or that it would be the one item he seemed to remember from that course, far from botany though it was.

The story was told to Banks by the professor in that course, Dr. Charles Chamberlain. It was an episode from the professor's boyhood on an Ohio farm and which he said had always been a puzzle to him.

The professor's story was that a neighbor woman came to his home one morning very upset because of a dream she had had about her brother, who lived some seven or eight miles away. The dream was so real, she said, that she had to go and check on it. Would someone drive her over to the scene of it? The professor offered to do it. On the drive there, the dream (which I now would classify as a realistic clairvoyant one) was told him in detail. The woman said she had "seen" her brother return from a trip, unhitch and stable the team, then climb the ladder to the haymow, take a pistol, and shoot himself. She saw just where he lay and she said that the revolver had fallen in a certain place which she described.

The sequel was that the dream was true in all details. As the professor emphasized, "It was true, but how could she have known it?"

Banks' reaction to the story, as he told me afterward, was amazement that after an experience like that anyone could have spent his life in botany, as that professor did, and never have tried to find an explanation of this strange occurrence. Although at the time of the telling, Banks probably simply marvelled with the professor that such a dream could be, I know he was never able to shrug it off as just a coincidence, and the seriousness with which he took it impressed me even then.

But even though our own venture into the city to find evidence on the topic of Banks' interest had been disappointing, he was not discouraged, for he knew from his library reading of SPR publications how difficult it was to find any wheat among the chaff in such demonstrations, and that the Society only did so after careful screening of the mediums through whom the evidence came. Our failure, therefore, did not necessarily mean that such evidence did not exist anywhere. It had to be patiently winnowed out by the most careful methods. Obviously, the place to look for guidance was the American Society for Psychical Research in New York City. Accordingly, on June 6, 1923, although ignorant even of the name of the president of the Society, Banks wrote simply to the president of the ASPR. He stated first his credentials:

> My situation in brief is this: Six years ago I was intending to become a divinity student. I lost faith and went into Science. My training has been largely physiological and plant chemistry with an attempt at a broad scientific background. I have been moderately successful, belonging to two honorary fraternities, one paper going to press (Botanical Gazette), the M.S. degree and a Ph.D. in about a year. My wife is a Ph.D. and holds a minor position at the University of Chicago. We will both be on the staff of the Boyce Thompson Institute (in Yonkers).

> Having read Myers' *Human Personality* and some other books of the kind, I have been deeply impressed with the importance of the subject to the human race. If I can in any way further this research I'm sure it will be the best work I could do. I am fully prepared to devote my life, or rather that part of it which is left after a livelihood is earned, to psychic investigation.

> I am writing you now at a time when I may make some choice of my future (as we use the word choice) to ask if there is any opportunity known to you for me to enter this field of research and leave the other behind? Do you know of a fellowship or position that would enable me to get some of the special training I would need to go on with investigational work?

Can you give me the names of a number of reliable mediums in Chicago?

On the same date that Banks wrote to the president of the ASPR, he also wrote to Professor William McDougall in Cambridge, Massachusetts, the head of the psychology department of Harvard University. In this letter he said

> I have become deeply interested in the work of the SPR and wish to know if there is any fellowship or position open in the next two years that you know of which would enable a student to maintain himself and carry on investigational work on psychic phenomena?

> I am not however merely looking for a position. I am comparatively sure of my future in my field of training, Plant Chemistry. But the tremendous importance of the problems of Psychic Research to the individual and to the whole social order has deeply impressed me. This field is so much more vital that I would not hesitate at a complete change, if means of livelihood were forthcoming. This I do not expect. It is possible though that there is a fellowship which would enable me to get the necessary special training.

The strength of Banks' interest in psychical research is emphasized again in the third letter he wrote on the same date. This was to Dr. Joseph Jastrow, Department of Psychology, University of Wisconsin.

> I have become very interested in the field of Psychic Science and intend ultimately to leave that which at present engages me, bio-chemistry, to devote my life to the study of psychic phenomena.

> Having seen your name in connection with the ASPR, I venture to ask if you know of any means by which a student can enter this field of psychic investigation to give it all his time and at the same time earn a livelihood? At least, I would like a year of "adjacent" psychology if it is possible that there is a fellowship available for this kind of work in some institution.

> Any suggestion you can make on the subject will be greatly appreciated.

In due time all three men replied. The president of the ASPR, Mr. Frederick Edwards, was encouraging in that he stressed the need for young men with Banks' interest, but he had no job to offer. Instead, he urged Banks to continue to study and read in psychical research while remaining in his present field of training.

A handwritten reply from McDougall reported that the Hodgson Fellowship, the only one in the field, was already filled by Gardner Murphy and although "there is money at Stanford University for psychical research, it does not seem to go very definitely into that line."

Dr. Jastrow advised against giving up

> ... your present pursuit in favor of the career you propose. I am of the opinion that psychical research, so-called, is largely concerned with the elucidation of error, though partly with the explanation of obscure phenomena. Positions are few and often the critical attitude is the very obstacle.

He then advised writing to Professor Coover at Stanford University and Professor Troland at Harvard.

Banks' reply to Professor Jastrow (July, 1923), or at least a copy of the one probably sent, has been preserved. It runs as follows:

> I thank you most kindly for your advice on the subject of Psychical Research. I may say that my natural tendency is not to release hold upon my present position until amply assured of certain essentials in the new. This assurance will I suspect be long in coming. I shall this day however write Profs. Coover and Troland, more to satisfy myself that I shall have left no stone unturned than in the anticipation of any opportunity eventually to enter the field of Psychical Research.

> I may say in dismissing the matter also that I am not at all prepared for this work except in that a biological and chemical training may have given me a point of view and method of attack and that therefore the opportunity I should now like to have, may well await the greater preparation and maturity that a few more years may give.

Although of course I knew about these letters and the less than encouraging replies I, too, had hoped that through them an opportunity would come to Banks for more direct involvement in this problem that so interested him. By then I, too, doubted that botany was the field for him. But I knew, and he did too, that in it he was getting good training in scientific thinking and method, even though he had no deep interest in the facts of botany. More and more he was turning to chemistry, organic and physiological, lying as they do at the basis of life itself.

In this uncertain time, however, it was not Banks' old-time interest in forestry that was reviving. Instead, he began to think of changing from plant to animal tissue, and a turn toward medicine began to come into focus. I encouraged it, for I knew it had been my influence that had drawn him into botany in the first place and I didn't want him to feel constrained to stay there if something else interested him more deeply.

In the meantime, we were finding that our initial excitement and pleasure at the prospect of working at the Boyce Thompson Institute was subsiding into disappointment. Although the place was still in the stage of bricks and mortar and our first assignments were of the nature of sweeping out the carpenters' shavings and of arranging books on bookshelves, menial tasks such as these were not the source of the discontent that we, and Ecky too, soon began to feel. I'm sure that all three of us could easily have been enlisted in enthusiastically helping to build, in actually attending at the birth of the new institute. But instead, the management and we, the workers, soon became two different social classes. We who had been expecting to be researchers were definitely made to feel that we were on a lower level. The nature of the difficulty is suggested in a little note that Ecky later wrote on the traits of department heads. Her words were

> How do men get into positions of authority? How do heads of departments, directors, etc. get chosen? Not by their scientific ability, not by their ability to plan or direct research, not even by their ability to organize. No, by their political ability; by a certain ruthlessness and desire to use other peoples' brains and ideas as if they were their own.

In the uninspiring, even unscientific, atmosphere that we soon felt, our resulting unhappiness meant that our stay at the Institute terminated at the end of the year for which we had been hired. We could leave then because we had an alternative to which I shall come directly. But Ecky was not so fortunate. She had resigned her position at the University of Chicago and did not have a better opening to turn to, and so she had to continue on at the institute, although she felt her second-class status as much as we did ours. However, her hope was that by the following year research possibilities would be greater and that then she could establish her own department of plant microchemistry. But this was a hope that never was fulfilled, although she stayed on for several more years.

That year before leaving Yonkers, we found one circumstance of living near New York City that had some lasting value for Banks. He was able to make personal acquaintances at the American Society for Psychical Research (ASPR). Under the Society's auspices he attended a seance in the city with one of the Society's members, and that was a valuable experience.

Because of the cost of getting to New York City (every penny counted), I did not go with him. But this seance again proved disappointing as an opportunity to see psychic phenomena at first hand. The circle of sitters at that seance were apparently hallucinated and certainly deluded, he decided, for they saw lions and other animals in the room, of which Banks and his companions could see no trace. But far from discouraging him, the contact with the Society proved more interesting to him than anything at the institute.

Our alternative opportunity came about because during our stay in Yonkers, I had kept in touch with my old botany teacher, Strasy, at Wooster, Ohio. Since he was devoted to the field of botany, he naturally was much interested in the new botanical institute and in our connection with it. He had watched with interest and sympathy as our initial enthusiasm had changed to disillusionment, and so now he offered us an escape. His own situation had changed, and it was now possible, even desirable from his viewpoint as well as ours, for him to make us this offer.

His change from Wooster was to a new position as the head of the Department of Botany at West Virginia University at Morgantown. Needing to build up a staff there, and aware of our unhappy situation at the institute, Strasy offered Banks the position of teaching plant physiology in his department. It was, of course, an alternative we eagerly accepted. And so the fall of 1924 saw us in Morgantown and Banks an instructor in botany.

Incidentally, a characteristic of Banks' which should be mentioned here is illustrated by his reaction to the University of Chicago correspondence course in writing that I was able to take that winter. From the beginning of that venture of mine, which he enthusiastically endorsed, to the high level of encouragement he gave me continually, I felt supported throughout. But this kind of husbandly response was not a universal one, as I kept hearing from friends of mine, other wives, who in comparable ways tried to satisfy their urges while their husbands were busy and they were not. The general consensus seemed to be that the husband wanted his wife to stay at home, be quiet, and have the house and a meal ready for him when he got there. Banks, however, was not only supportive of my course but always appreciative, although helpfully critical of my writing attempts. He even suggested that I try for publication of some of them.

This attitude of his, it seems to me, was a mark of his own inner strength and self-assurance. He did not fear competition, as I think may have been the explanation of the husbands who seemed to want to keep their wives in the kitchen where they would offer no challenge to the husband's superiority.

Banks' year of teaching plant physiology at the University of West Virginia was pleasant and successful. His sympathy and interest were aroused in an extra-curricular way by several of his students. The reason was, I think, that they and their situations reminded him strongly of features of his own early background. These, too, were mountain boys, sons of the hills, and they were just managing to get a peep at the outside world, if only the little metropolis of Morgantown. Some of them had left wife and children at home and now were here at the university, subsisting as best they could on little stints of night work. I remember one case, especially, because Banks brought the young man home for lunch one day. He had told me beforehand that this student had been falling asleep in class. Banks had talked to him about it, and learned that the young man's wife, with their several children, was managing somehow back home in the cove they lived in, high in the mountains, while her husband had a night job in Morgantown. He fell asleep in Banks' class one day after working all night and having had no breakfast. Sleeping in class in cases like that was to Banks entirely excusable. And so, he was, in a way, in close contact with his own early life.

That summer of 1925, we went back again to the University of Chicago, and Banks finished the requirements for, and was awarded, the Ph.D. degree. But at the same time — and the main thing for him — his interest in psychic research was continuing to grow. My own admiration for him was too. That fall, November 25, 1925, I wrote in my diary

> He is a splendid man. In his complete human-ness, his active mentality, his keen analytic ability, his stimulating interests and ideas and his aspirations and "goodness," I think he's nearly perfect.

This may be as good a place as any to remark on Banks' affiliations in honorary societies that were made that year, largely at Strasy's urging. In January, Banks became a member of the American Association for the Advancement of Science, and at about the same time of the Botanical Society of America; in March, Phi Beta Kappa, University of West Virginia chapter; and shortly after, the honorary chemistry fraternity, Phi Lambda Upsilon. He never again was a member of so many organizations, for his attention was never centered on them. But Strasy knew the way a young man climbing up the latter of scientific advancement should go.

However, during this second year at Morgantown, the counter-attraction for Banks continued to grow until finally it triumphed over botany completely.

4

Change in Direction

During the years at the University of West Virginia, Banks' attention had to be centered first of all on his classes in plant physiology, although his older and deeper interest remained in psychic phenomena. His attention was caught by a series of articles on the topic that had been running in the *Scientific American* written by the editor, J. Malcolm Bird. The series had begun in December, 1922. A prize of $5000 had been offered by the magazine "to be awarded for a conclusive psychic manifestation." To implement the contest, a committee of eminent persons had been set up to judge the contestants, with the editor, Bird, as secretary.

After a few unsuccessful contestants had been reported, a Boston medium known as Margery, who had gained local notoriety, entered the contest and soon overshadowed the others. The report was that she produced manifestations of her dead brother, Walter, and it was claimed that he spoke through her. Although in England and else-where claims of direct communication from deceased persons through mediums had often been taken at face value in historical times, as it also was by Sir Arthur Conan Doyle, few such claims of any substance had been made in the United States. This one, however, was exceptional since the medium was the wife of a prominent Boston surgeon, Dr. L.R.G. Crandon, and therefore her involvement did not appear to be the result of any of the ordinary commercial motives so frequently at-tributed to mediumistic claimants.

Reading of this case in the magazine, Banks was interested at once, especially because of the report of direct communication from a deceased person. He wrote a letter of inquiry to the editor, Bird, on April 4, 1925, and, as it developed, this was the beginning of Banks' first actual adventure in the field of psychical research. It was in more ways than one a learning experience in which the main lesson turned out not to concern psychic phenomena per se so much as the need to judge human nature especially critically in a debatable field like psychical research. In spite of his own generally very critical tendencies which I had come to know to be his hallmark, in this instance Banks' in-experience and eagerness betrayed him when judging the curious per-sonality of Malcolm Bird.

A response to Banks' letter came from Bird at once, and a rapid ex-change between the two ensued, even including later that spring a per-sonal visit by Bird to us at Morgantown. The general message Bird brought to Banks in these exchanges was that Margery produced bona fide evidence of supernormal effects but that the committee judging her was prejudiced, especially Dr. William McDougall, the Harvard psychologist, who had even said publicly that Margery was fraudulent, and also Dr. Walter Franklin Prince, the research officer at the ASPR in New York. Bird said that as a consequence, the members of the ASPR were divided, although the majority of them believed in Margery. Prince, however, was so convinced that she was a fraud that he had split off from the American society and had formed a new one of his own in Boston, the Boston SPR. Bird's report of the controversy sounded as if these two men, McDougall and Prince, were blocking the way to a scientific investigation of the possibility of spirit survival.

In one of these letters from Bird, this one on May 27, 1925, a hint came which, had we been less eager, might have been a warning about the character of this man who seemed to be opening such interesting vistas to us. But we didn't notice it then. In this letter, Bird asked Banks to undertake "a little detective work" for him by writing to Prince in Boston to ask for the pamphlet that Prince had written, and then to send it on to Bird. "If you find this request at all repugnant, pray do not hesitate to say so."

Banks accordingly wrote to Prince and asked for the pamphlet. He must have mentioned Bird in some connection, for Prince's reply on June 1, 1925 was to send the pamphlet but to say in an accompanying letter, "I regard Mr. Bird as a very unsafe person to place any reliance on."

But Prince's warning did not fall on receptive ears. Bird's influence on us at the time was the stronger. He seemed to stand for a straightforward, unprejudiced attitude, no matter how unconventional the facts, and that was what Banks so intensely wanted. If in truth a psychic world existed, he wanted to know it.

In the summer of 1925, we returned to the University of Chicago for Banks to finish his graduate work and obtain his doctoral degree. In the fall we were back at the University of West Virginia for Banks' second year of teaching. There his interest in the Margery case led to another letter to Bird (on September 20, 1925) in which he asked, "Is the Margery mediumship still continuing? When may we expect something further?" "That split in the ASPR," Banks also remarked showing his trust in Bird, "is going to do things to America." (As Bird had represented the situation, with McDougall and Prince out of the Society, then the Margery investigations could go on unimpeded.) Banks then continued, "I would give a lot to be able to sit in on such a seance," and he asked if it would be possible to do so if he went to Boston the next summer.

Bird replied on September 28, 1925, saying, "The Margery mediumship is moving along.... You can get a sitting...." On January 11, 1926, Banks wrote to Bird that he has "pretty well decided to resign his teaching job and go to Chicago or Columbia and get training in Philosophy or Psychology." (I remember how uncertain we were during this period about these two disciplines, as to which would be the better background for psychical research.)

In February of that winter, my old teacher and colleague of the unhappy Thompson Institute days, Ecky, came to see us at Morgantown. After our disastrous year at Boyce Thompson Institute, our sympathies and friendship with her were much stronger than in most associations of teacher and pupil.

Ecky, of course, knew of Banks' interest in psychic matters, but

I'm sure she considered it an aberration he would outgrow. She was openly hopeful that I would continue in microchemistry. It was ironic that, as it developed, her visit to us had the opposite effect from the one she wanted. I hope she never knew how directly it did so. Reminiscing in my diary later, December 26, 1926, I say about that visit

> While Ecky was here and Banks and I were both rather absorbed in thinking her thoughts about plant physiology and Thompson Institute with her, we made a discovery, or rather Banks did. It was a re-discovery, actually, a reminder to him that he was not basically interested, even when he tried to be, in botanical questions. They still did not seem to him vital enough to warrant the absorption and devotion of a lifetime.

Suddenly, the night of Ecky's visit, after we had retired and were waiting for sleep, Banks said, "Louie, if I'd chuck it all and go off to school somewhere to study philosophy would you go along?"

"Sure thing," I replied unhesitatingly, and in another minute the step was taken, at least figuratively; the pact was made, the bridge crossed, all but the details of practical plans and procedures. We did not tell Ecky in the morning, or ever let her know that our decision was precipitated by the reminder her visit had given that botany was not sufficiently interesting to Banks to warrant his complete devotion.

That spring of 1926, in spite of Strasy's protests, Banks resigned his position in the botany department. We sold our furniture; the "family" members that had accumulated dispersed to their various homes (Banks' young high-school-age brother, two younger sisters of mine, and the high school boy friend of the older sister had been staying with us); and we went to Boston, veritable babes in the wood, although quite ignorant of that fact.

We had a little money from Banks' salary, from the sale of the furniture, and from savings. It was sufficient, we hoped, to last until we could find some source of income in Boston. All our expectations were focused on Margery and the sitting at her seance the evening after we arrived, admission to which with Bird's help we had been granted.

At the home of Margery Crandon that evening, we found ourselves before long in the seance room with quite a few other visitors, some of whom were accustomed "sitters." They were loud and gay and very much at home, so that they created quite an hilarious atmosphere. It was not at all the semi-reverent one we had expected to find at the unveiling of a contact with a departed relative.

Without details, I should say here briefly that the room was darkened and much went on, including "Walter's voice" and testimony from "the other side." When all was over and Banks and I were alone outside, and I, still confused and uncertain, Banks burst out with something like, "Oh, Louie, Louie, what fools we've been!! That was the most fantastic fraud I ever could imagine!" And then he proceeded to take the whole event apart for me almost literally piece by piece.

He ran over the list of the various exploits of the evening, which I too had noted and which had puzzled and confused me. But, one by one, he told me of the tricks he thought had actually been played on the observers under cover of darkness. One of these tricks involved a chemical balance with two pans. One of these, unweighted, had gone down while the other, heavily weighted, had gone up, just the reverse of what normally they should have done. Later, at the end of the seance while the crowd was exclaiming about the marvels that Walter had produced, Banks, to whom such balances were familiar from his chemistry classes, had gone up to that one and attempted to move the little rider at the top to see how easily it might slide from side to side just by gravity. But he found it stationary and saw that it had a little screw which he could turn with a thumb nail in order to move it across to the opposite side, where it then could be fastened. He had noticed its position before and again after the seance had begun, and now he knew it had been changed from the heavier side to the other. No wonder the lighter pan went down!

As Banks stood by the balance, the medium's husband and chief manager of the seance came up and said to him curtly, "Leave that balance alone before you get it out of order." Banks knew then that we would never get another invitation to a Margery seance.

Subsequently, Banks wrote an account of the evening's experience which was published in the *Journal of Abnormal and Social Psychology*. It thus went down in history along with several exposés by others.

But what did all this mean, especially about Bird, who apparently had believed in Margery, but also about McDougall and Prince, who had said that she was fraudulent? Now we knew that the latter two were right and Bird was wrong. But how could he have remained ignorant? He had been in many Margery seances and was to an extent a friend of her family. He was too intelligent, we felt sure, not to have had doubts, at least, if not outright proof that she faked her results. Later, the suspicion was raised that he had become a confederate of hers, but this was never proved.

The subsequent history of this man, Bird, has left him as somewhat enigmatic and his connection with the ASPR never clarified his character, but the situation for Banks was clear. His feeling was expressed in a letter he wrote to a former colleague back at the University of West Virginia, one of the few people there who had been interested in our adventure into psychical research. In his letter to this man, Banks said about the Margery episode, "We found abundant evidence of very elaborate fraud. It was sufficient to condemn it completely," and he added that consequently he had to "retrench, after Bird had led us to accept Margery's genuineness." He remarked on the difference in his attitude now from what it had been a few months before.

And so I must observe that Bird had inadvertently been a teacher for Banks, and he taught his lesson well, that in psychical research one dare not take individuals at face value. It was a lesson that Banks never had to have repeated.

But what were we to do now? Here we were in Boston, bridges burned, and the hopeful quest that had brought us here nullified so soon after our arrival. The obvious thing would have been to telegraph back to Strasy in Morgantown and ask if the position in plant physiology was still open. As a matter of fact, however, to the best of my memory, that line of procedure was one we never even thought of. It only occurs to me now, so many years later, when I think over the situation.

No, I'm sure that even this major disappointment gave Banks no idea, even a momentary one, of turning back. The glimpse he had had from his reading of the history of psychical research of the possibility of the existence of objective evidence for a spiritual element in human nature was too important to forego, no matter what the difficulties. The false lead that Bird had given was only that, a false lead. And Bird had told us that the two men, McDougall and Prince, had said that Margery was fraudulent. Now we knew how right they were.

And so, the next day, we set out to make contact with each of the two men. I remember quite specifically the trip we made, or rather that Banks made, to meet McDougall.

We had found temporary lodging in a rooming house near Harvard Square. I remember how, walking from it as we approached the McDougall address the next day, Banks began to get nervous for fear it would seem strange for a young man *and his wife* to appear on their doorstep. I took the hint and parked myself on a bench nearby and Banks went on alone. I must interject here that this was not chauvinism on Banks' part, but that neither was it then the day of women's rights. He knew that few or, more likely, no American man would have taken his wife along on such an occasion, and that no Englishman like McDougall would have done so.

And so I waited in the park. Before long, Banks returned. As it had happened, his call had not come at a suitable time. Today he would have phoned for an appointment, but this was 1926 and phones were not the commonplace they are today. And so to have made a phone call, even had the McDougalls had a phone, would not have occurred to an unsophisticated young couple from West Virginia. The McDougalls were departing on a trip around the world; their taxi with their luggage was waiting as Banks arrived. He certainly was not an opportune caller.

But when McDougall learned about the disastrous Margery seance of the night before, his attention was arrested. I think he must have been impressed by the fact that Banks had been sharp enough to pick up the signs of fraud when so many observers had missed them. He also must have noted, even in that hurried meeting, Banks' deep interest in the question of the total nature of man, which was a major interest of his own. But the time was too short for more than a few words. And as Banks learned, the McDougalls were not coming back to Cambridge. McDougall was leaving his Harvard position to develop a psychology department at a new university in the south, Duke University, in North Carolina.

However, in the back of Banks' mind all along, and in addition to anything he might do in psychical research, was the intention to attend lectures at Harvard, both in philosophy and psychology. He did not need them for credit, since he already had his Ph.D., but he needed them for his education. My own role was less clear, but I hoped that I could get some kind of job and help to pay for our living.

Before settling all that, however, after the contact with McDougall, we called on Prince at his Boston Society for Psychical Research home and office on Beacon Street. There, I think I was part of the picture from the start. Prince at once recognized a kindred soul in Banks and in me, too, I guess, because I was soon to him "The Doctoress," and I was in the midst of things both in psychic matters and in his family situation. Prince was a widower, and his family included only his adopted daughter, Theodosia, with whom he lived in his "haunted" house. The house was thought to be haunted because Theodosia had reported hearing peculiar knocks which she took to be signs indicating the presence of spirits. Banks and I slept in the house one night and heard the knocks, but Banks' investigation resolved their mystery. A leaky skylight high above, and a second skylight a storey below, were the unsuspected culprits. A drop of water from the first one, striking the second, gave the resounding "ting" that Theodosia had interpreted as ghostly.

Prince, like McDougall, was at once interested in our Margery experience and also in our disillusionment with Bird. He, too, was glad to welcome a young potential psychical researcher like Banks. Before long he had a commission for us. A well-known, honest, and respectable medium, a Mrs. Soule, he told us, lived in a nearby Boston suburb, and he needed an investigator to undertake a series of sittings with her under approved conditions. In these, the chance or opportunity for her to get information from ordinary channels concerning topics upon which she might give information for individual "sitters" would be entirely cut off, and the information she gave allegedly from the spirit world would be taken down by a stenographer, just as she uttered it. Later, the sitter would be presented with copies of several sitters' records, including his own, all unsigned, to see if he could recognize his own.

We said we would take the opportunity gladly, if Prince thought that I could perform well enough as stenographer. I had had a little typing in college, though never enough practice to do it well. And though I'd had no shorthand, I could write rapidly — and I'd learn shorthand. I immediately enrolled at a Boston business school, worked hard both on shorthand and typing and managed to function sufficiently well in my job as notetaker.

Prince and Banks at once worked out all the details of an approved method for research on a medium like Mrs. Soule. Needless to say, with two men like Prince and the young Banks Rhine on the job, the medium could never by any chance find out the identity of any of the hand-picked stream of sitters who then in turn occupied the room which was set aside for them. The procedure was that, first, the medium would be given time to go into trance in her room, guarded carefully by Banks (than whom, I daresay, few masters of ceremony could have been more vigilant). Meanwhile, the sitter, toward whom the medium's impressions would be directed, sat in his room out of sight and sound of the medium.

I heard, but never saw for myself, any of this. I sat in a room just around the corner from the medium, where I could hear but not see. I was brought into my place there only after the medium was in trance, so she and I never saw each other. But I faithfully recorded all she said, hoping by the end of each incident she reported, that the Uncle John or Aunt Sadie she described, the fancy box of jewelry on the dresser, or whatever, would eventually be claimed by the sitter of that period, the identity of whom the medium never learned.

But why go on? The experiment, so carefully and meticulously planned, and which continued each week that summer, yielded us $12 per week — but *no sitter* (even myself as one) claimed any of the aunts or uncles or jewel boxes. As I recorded in my diary,

We have only been disappointed. The lantern in that quarter [of psychic phenomena] is glimmering more and more feebly. It will go out if we don't get legitimate oil for it soon.

At least, I know I was beginning to feel that way, but I doubt that Banks was. His lantern was better provided with oil than mine.

At Christmastime, for a little personal touch, I added

We went to Beacon Hill to see the candles and hear the carols. It was too cold and wet to stay, but we were there to glimpse a city valiantly trying to maintain its tradition.

Banks got me a beautiful picture of a bunch of nasturtiums for Christmas. It brightens up our little bare wall so bravely, we squeeze each other every time we look at it. That wasn't all he got me, the dear old kid — even the lavendar vase I had admired and bedroom slippers and note paper.

I wanted to get the Copeland Reader for him but I didn't get money enough [as I remember, it cost $10] until too late and the co-op was closed, so all he got was a promise. [We eventually got the book and enjoyed it, though never had as much time for it as it deserved.]

During that summer of work with Mrs. Soule, unprofitable although educational as it turned out to be, we managed to make living arrangements that were a bit more possible than was the first rooming house, where the regular rent made inroads on our slender cash resources. We found another rooming house farther up and off Massachusetts Avenue, at which we were able to earn the rent. An elderly spinster there rented rooms to "respectable" girls. (She seemed on the verge of an apoplectic stroke once when she suspected that one of her girls had entertained a man in her room.) She needed a man to tend the furnace and a woman to clean the halls and bathrooms. Banks got the former job and I the latter. For these, we earned the back downstairs bedroom and cooking privileges. Providently, the room had its own outside door, so that the landlady couldn't monitor our visitors as she did those of the roomers.

The room was a bilious pea-green color, but the landlady was glad to have Banks paint it any color we wanted (at our expense, of course), so he painted it white. We felt very comfortably located and remained there all that summer of 1926 and the following season, 1927, until we left Cambridge.

During our period in Cambridge, beginning in the summer of 1926 while we were carrying on our unprofitable but educational work with Mrs. Soule, we, and especially Banks, read much of the history of psychical research. In addition, he read some psychology and philosophy, going into each much beyond our introductory college studies in those areas. In the fall, he took courses at Harvard in both of those disciplines. But as I note in a diary entry that December,

It was soon apparent that the strong active stimulus to further thinking Banks craved was not going to come from those courses. Our ideas of Philosophy—academic—have changed. It is not alluring as it is handed out by the unscientific to the unscientific. It leaves us as cold as a preacher's sermon because, like the latter, it has no solid ground to stand on.

But in the meantime through his continually urging me to write, Banks is beginning to recognize his own trend and talent in that direction, and he has written several short stories and a poem or two. Next term since he knows now that there is nothing at Harvard he wants badly enough to pay tuition for, he is going to take his time for practice in writing. I too am giving it more time and feel some development. Banks however is the one who has the faith. I see the obstacles, he sees the possibilities. But I have promised not to be a wet blanket, but instead to await developments in the next few months and see which way we grow. If we are at all successful, we plan to spend the summer back home in Ohio both for the pleasure of being there again and for the material we will accumulate.

Those plans, however, did not work out. Instead, they illustrated again the lines from Robert Burns about the best laid plans of mice and men. These also went "agley," for Banks' writing attempts, like mine, never got very far toward earning us any income, although they netted each of us some rejection slips. But Banks expressed his attitude toward life very clearly, I think, in a poem he wrote and called "World-Worship."

> O wondrous Mechanism we call World,
> I bow to you
> In deepest awe, yet gratitude no less,
> So much I owe.
> Though guised to many eyes as cruel Fate,
> Grim Destiny,
> And seeming to grind out the lives of men
> Remorselessly,
> You are the light of suns, the beat of hearts!
> The one assurance 'gainst all Chaos, you!
> The means and promise of our future Good.
> You, Great Machine, are Beauty, Life, and Love!
>
> Within you, O Great System, plays my mind,
> Attuned to you.
> Works through and with you, from you get its life,

And yet is free.
For in the little world of imagery,
In my mind's-eye,
I flit about and try the various ways
Ere I make choice.
Though made within your system, yet my will
Is spent upon you, changing you in turn.
Thus, free I am through you to work with you;
More liberty than this would be our bane.

What Causes caused your Causes to create
Defies our ken.
How you made Life and how emerged the Mind,
Baffles us still.
Through forces inconceivable to man
Governed by Rule and System each variety,
He studies to bring forth
Most wonderful creations,
Laughs at the thought of toil and loves the use
Of Culture which, with Nature's Law,
Gives beauty and delight to humankind
In rarest tint and fragrance.
His Reason gives more harmony to sense!
His Logic makes a landscape for the eye!

But I am one who loves a wooded glade
More than the garden's formal row;
To me the daring buds that brave the frosts,
The timid stalks of longer days,
The elfish bloom that peeks around old stumps,
Or coyly sits upon a lofty ledge —
These wild uncultured things
Have beauty, personality,
Unreasoning Nature all alone can give.
I do not need the Purchased Things,
For I find both philosophy and bloom
In nature and in Life.
I would not lose the tang and zest of things
By taking Metaphysics ready-made!

Yet these great souls are set to noble tasks.
I may not need, but still may love them both;
Their work means much to those who still must find
Their Thought in books, their Beauty in a vase.

Then, too, I now find a prose fragment Banks wrote dated January 23, 1927, called "Summary of the Situation, Past, Present, and Prospective Future," which shows that by then the "oil" in his "lantern" was also running a little low. In this short, single-page effort, he says

I came up here to study Psychology, Philosophy, and to see if there is anything to Psychical Research. Perhaps a real explanation of the enthusiasm we manifested was that we were escaping thereby from the narrow limitations of the field to which we had affixed our interest. Naturally in our eagerness we held the subjects toward which we were directing ourselves with more hope than understanding and yet there were certain well defined principles which claimed our deeper interest.

We hoped to find the solution for these somewhere in the general region of the three subjects mentioned. Our experiences of the half year with Psychical Research have disappointed us, leaving faint hope of genuineness.

Our experience with Philosophy has led us to expect little from its method that can be relied upon, much as it may comfort the soul (some souls). At any rate, it cannot answer the problems that we are interested in.

Psychology remains, a subject of very great interest, a science whose method may be dependable and which may contribute to the solution of our problems, at least if anything may. But somehow we have changed. Having once cut loose from things we find it easier to change, and to change quickly, being constantly on the alert for leads and indications. We are finding out more about ourselves than we have ever been able to do before. I think, too, that we are tiring of chasing the Psychic rainbow or the Philosophic pot of gold.

We hope now to get down to real work and to have the time to do some real studying of the work we seem to like to do, and to try to put into good readable form some of the experiences which we have had.

And so we continued on in our rooming house and at the Boston SPR. At one point, Banks added a bit to our tight little budget by teaching carpentry, of all things, in a little nearby kindergarten, though just how good a teacher of it he was I do not know, but neither do I have much idea of how much carpentry preschool youngsters could absorb. At least I know that he liked the kids and enjoyed his little exposure to them.

We were still living at the same rooming house when one day in the summer of 1927 opportunity again came knocking at our door. This time it was in the form of a very engaging middle-aged man who said we had been recommended by Prince as possibly open to a proposition he had to make. Naturally, by this time we were ready to listen to any proposition that might point in the direction we knew by then that we wanted to go, the kind that Prince would be likely to recommend for us.

5

Explorations in a New Field

The caller at our door was Mr. John F. Thomas, a now retired official of the public school system of Detroit, Michigan. He gave us a very interesting account of his situation, of the help he needed, and of the way in which we very well might fit in and fill that need. We were much interested because the situation he described carried a definite promise of something psychically significant.

He told us of his long and happy marriage, his sons now grown and away from home, and of his wife's sudden death the previous year,

April 1926, while undergoing minor surgery. Then, on the advice of a friend who had earlier had some striking results with the medium, Mrs. Soule, he, too, had had a series of sittings with her. She had transmitted "veridical" information, a word he used for facts she gave which were true, many of them such that no one but his wife and he would have known. With this encouragement, he had to go on and try to get more veridical information from other sensitives as well.

One alternative to the "spirit" interpretation of his messages, as Thomas knew, was that Mrs. Soule had learned his identity and in some way had secured this information from normal sources and presumably in trance, simply played it back to him, dramatized it, as it were. In view of all the empty sittings we had had with Mrs. Soule that summer, which had begun, we learned, only shortly after his, we were particularly interested and intrigued to hear about this meaningful experience Thomas seemed to have had with her. Could the difference between his results and ours have stemmed from the fact that in Thomas' situation both he, the sitter, and Mrs. Thomas, the "communicator," probably were much more highly motivated than our experimental sitters and communicators? This was only one of the intriguing questions that the Thomas records raised.

We knew very well, as did Thomas, too, that mediums, fraudulent ones, or even honest ones sometimes, piece out the information they may give a sitter with material they have secured by normal means. Mrs. Soule was reported not to do that, consciously, at least; but still, the possibility could not be ruled out that she had used accomplices or had even demonstrated telepathic ability, however unestablished and scientifically unrecognized such an ability might be.

Thomas told us that he was now on his way to England, where he hoped to get incognito sittings with some of the famous mediums there whose honesty and reliability had been well tested by the London SPR. If, as he hoped he would, he still got messages ostensibly from his wife, he would feel convinced of her survival. In that event, he would want help, presumably of the kind we could give. Would we be interested? The alacrity with which Banks accepted need hardly be mentioned, nor the eagerness with which we awaited word from Thomas upon his return.

In the meantime, it was necessary for us to turn to the more mundane problem of earning some money. The quickest way for Banks was to go back again to canvassing, selling Wear-Ever cooking utensils. He then got territory for it near our homes in northern Ohio. With this in prospect, he bought a secondhand "Tin Lizzie," our first car, and in it we travelled home from Massachusetts, and after a few days there, to Cuyahoga Falls, Ohio, the scene of the summer job. (There, one day, when rounding a bend in the road, a rear wheel flew off the Ford and we ended up ingloriously but safely in the ditch.)

Again that summer, Banks was at least reasonably successful, while, as my diary says, we lived in a three-room flat (what luxury!). The important event there, however, was this wire from Thomas, dated September 2, 1927:

Would you think of spending the first semester at Duke University working with Professor McDougall on my material? I would stand the expense.

Banks' reply shows his general outlook and state of mind:

Dear Mr. Thomas:

I have come up from the deep waters of salesmanship for air and to write long-due letters. One must completely submerge oneself in this type of work, and then must occasionally come up for renewed "inspiration" too. At last tho, I have reached a paying rate. I hope to do still better and may yet get into shape for Columbia, at least by the second term.

Your letter reassures me very much. I am not able to rest calmly on the question of your findings, it seems. I am vacillating between a tremendous elation and a gloomy despair with regard to the whole field. Of course, I strike a balance and use some judgment but I cannot rest as it is. I think I shall have to study the whole case now for my *own* peace of mind and will certainly welcome the opportunity to do it.

I wish it were possible for us to see you for a day on your return west, in order to go over some of your results. Would it be possible for you to stop off at Cleveland on your return? We could spend a Sunday without any loss of time but would consider it a good investment to take any other day of the week for that matter.

I am interested in the response you get from McDougall. I would be glad to spend a part of the year at the new University if circumstances allow it. I respect his psychology and philosophy very much even if, in Psychic Research, he seems to me a little too tolerant and patient. I should be curious to see how a man like John Dewey reacts to your evidence for the supernormal.

Let us know if we can have the opportunity of a day with you....

Thank you again for letting us share in your discoveries. I can't understand what good fortune brought you to us or what merit in us held you. At any rate we are entirely at your service.

Sincerely,
Louie and J.B. Rhine

Soon after, Thomas did come to see us, and he brought the stenographic record of the sessions with the English mediums whose responses had so elated him. Nearly all of these sensitives to whom he had gone, one after another, incognito to the best of his belief, gave meaningful evidence which was ostensibly from his departed wife, as had been that from Mrs. Soule. At first impression, it seemed to us as it had to Thomas almost as if his wife had been with him as he went from one sensitive to another. On the face of it, the evidence of communication from her seemed very strong. To Thomas, it was strong enough to be all but convincing. He knew too much, however, about the pitfalls in such communications not to be on guard. He wanted the opinion of outsiders either to support his own feeling about the material or to show him the alternative.

As we read over a few of his records and listened to his corroborations of some of the points, we too were very much impressed. To us the situation could scarcely have been more intriguing. And Banks' interest and eagerness to study the material in detail could hardly have been greater.

Together the two men agreed that seemingly the only alternatives to direct communication from Mrs. Thomas to the mediums would be either that somehow the mediums had spies in his household, or that they had drawn the facts that Thomas certified were true from his own mind (by telepathy?) and unconsciously played them back as if from the discarnate personality. These were possibilities, however remote they seemed to Thomas, and he wanted to eliminate them. He needed to have a competent psychologist study the material and pass on it. He thought the best one would be Dr. William McDougall, because of his interest in psychical research, having been president of the London and the American SPR's both. As early as 1926, in his "Psychical Research as a University Study," McDougall had written

If mind in any manner ... transcends the physical world and its laws, surely it may somehow and somewhere be possible to obtain direct evidence of the fact by the methods of science, by observation of phenomena, and by reasoning from them. Psychical research proposes, then, to go out and seek ... phenomena pointing directly to the transcendence of mind, and, if possible, to provoke them experimentally [reproduced in *William McDougall, Explorer of the Mind*, by Raymond Van Over and Laura Oteri].

McDougall, however, as we knew, was no longer in Cambridge, but by then in North Carolina. Thomas had thought of sending the material to him by mail, but he was afraid the huge parcel it would make would be neglected while the professor was busy with his new job. Thomas therefore thought it should be sent by messenger, by one who would see that it was not neglected. Would Banks serve in that capacity? Thomas had $2000 in hand for a six-month errand of that kind.

To us, this promised to be the Real Thing at last and we accepted the offer at once. It was nearing the end of the summer. We would drive south to North Carolina and take Thomas' material to McDougall in person.

The drive south in itself turned out to be a notable one for us in a quite unexpected way, which calls for a chapter of its own. But before starting out on our new adventure, I had to make an explanation of it to the folks at home. My own reaction to the way that explanation was received is recorded in a long, still-preserved letter I wrote back to my sister, Esther, after we were in North Carolina. Obviously, in that explanatory session at home our venture had been written off by my family as one into Spiritualism, for I begin

> The only thing I minded in all the talk about Spiritualism was that all of you were so ready to think that we would be *taken in* so much easier than you. I had supposed you would think we have as good sense as you and that it must be that we have some facts you have not had a chance to know about. I thought you would trust our judgment farther.

> It's not a *religion*. But it is a scientific fact that it's not possible to prove that spirit communication has *never* occurred. I don't believe in Spiritualism, as an *ism*, any more than you do, or than I ever did.

> We went to three or four spiritualistic churches, had about a dozen readings purely to *find out* at first hand. We came away almost entirely disgusted.

> Now, the other side. We have studied science and scientific method for years, and we know something about the way to judge if a piece of botanical or physical or chemical research is sound. We're accustomed to going to *sources*. We don't *believe* just because a textbook says so, that

plants take CO_2 from the air and make sugars and starches out of it. We believe it after we go to the source and find out how carefully the researchers carried out their experiments. Then we have an intelligent basis for deciding if the textbook version is to be believed. If you ask me, I believe our training in scientific judgment is the biggest thing we got out of our graduate experience.

Now, by the same rules, if I find out that under certain conditions actual spirit photographs can be taken, and if the ground for it is sound, then I can believe it the same as I believe the theory of gravitation.

(I didn't yet know, much as I thought I did, just how difficult it is to be able to distinguish a pseudo fact from a true one. This letter obviously marks a still early learning stage for us.)

Thus, building still on spirit photography as evidence, I argue that "spirits" must exist if they can indeed be photographed and that they do exist, I remind her, "is just what good church people have always believed," as well as that there is a "soul" which doesn't die at death and which, at least on rare occasions, can return. I continued

Also, there is some evidence that under certain conditions actual communication with the living by the dead can occur.

I am not fully convinced of this yet — won't be I suppose until I have undeniable evidence of it firsthand, but I don't see why it couldn't happen. Papa says it's against all his ideas of spiritual things. So is it against mine. But that doesn't prove anything except that our preconceived ideas may have been wrong.

Now you don't have to fly clear off the handle about this and if you do you may be sure it's only because you are not in a position to really have the facts. You or Dad didn't mind if I found sufficient proof to allow me to believe the electron theory of matter, or the Mendelian law of heredity. If the same cold judgment of fact leads me to believe there is a possibility of definitely *proving* there is a life beyond, instead of piously believing it all my life, or infidel-like disbelieving it, I should think you'd grant that it is at least a worthy task and one in which you'd have to be interested.

Suppose it's true that Mama could and wanted to communicate with us — wouldn't you want to hear? Wouldn't you care to get the idea of *death* out of your mind entirely if you could realize for a certainty that it's only a passing over, that it is not an end or even a great change, but only a temporary physical separation during which the departed one could actually be *nearer* you than ever in physical life?

So that's that, I'm not an *ite* or an *ism* or an *ist* and if I ever believe fully in any of this, it won't be a religion, as a Russelite or as a Mennonite or as a socialist — or even as a botanist. I will only go where the facts lead and to begin with we are as skeptical as the skepticalest!

And now my hour for study is gone and only a couple of pages of illegible writing to show for it, which will probably make Ern sneer, you rave, Dad sorry, Dick laugh, Con explode, Ruth look serious, Turp chuckle, and anyone else who may hear of it think we're doggone fools — and that's what a college education comes to and she only got married and wasted it all! And ain't it a cheerful world anyway.

... I'm awfully eager to see the babies. I almost got a little one today. I found a little red-haired mite about 1½ years old who had strayed from a nursery school. She held out her arms to me and said, "Mama." I picked her up and took her back. But I'd have kept her I guess if I'd have thought I could get away with it.

Quite undaunted by the questions about our venture which were raised at my home (Banks had not even tried to explain our wild-eyed doings at his), our plans for the journey and new adventure proceeded.

First, we had to locate the town of Durham. North Carolina, we knew, was just below the Mason-Dixon line. The capital was Raleigh, after Sir Walter. That much we had learned in grade school. But other than that, the state was unknown territory, though Banks had been in South Carolina while in the Marine Corps. But we had never known of anyone going to North Carolina until Banks' meeting in Cambridge with McDougall. We learned then that a tobacco magnate named Duke had left a lot of money for the establishment of a university in the town of Durham. The university was to be named after him: Duke University. McDougall, as we knew, was to head the Department of Psychology there.

For us, going to North Carolina was an adventure, both geographically and psychologically. It was even an adventure to drive that far in an automobile. (Automobiles only later became "cars." Even the pronunciation of the new term "garage," which we knew was French, was debatable.)

At the end of the summer, we started out from my parents' old home in Ohio to drive to North Carolina. We took along a passenger, my young sister, Miriam, who after our mother's death had been living rather irregularly with an older sister or with our father, whose own living arrangements were rather unstable. We all thought it would be better for Miriam to be with us.

We decided to go to North Carolina via New York City because Banks wanted to meet Dr. Gardner Murphy, who as McDougall had told Banks earlier was interested in psychical research and lived there. But somewhere in rural mid-Pennsylvania the Ford made an ominous sound and ground to a stop. Garages and mechanics in that day were still scarce and not easy to locate, but in due course Banks managed to find one, a mechanic who said something was wrong with the engine. The repair, he said, would take several days and he estimated the cost. It was more than the money we had. Besides, it was the weekend and the repair could not be made until after that. Because of this interruption of our plans, Banks sent a telegram to Thomas telling him about our dilemma, which included the fact that we had no money for the repair. Also, he wrote a letter to McDougall, warning him in a way that we were coming. At least, I find a copy of such a letter, written on September 11, "en route to New York City." It runs thus:

> I am on the way to Duke University to listen to your lectures on Abnormal and General Psychology, and to confer with you, if you have time on the very interesting psychic material obtained by Supt. John F. Thomas of Detroit. As you know, he is intending to publish some of this and wants to have a critical study made on the case from the psychologist's viewpoint. We are both especially interested in having your general reaction to his results. I am coming partly as his agent.
>
> But I am also trying to get a training in psychology with some philosophy and consider that a semester spent with you at Duke would be very valuable. I was much disappointed in missing you at Harvard last year.
>
> Are you lecturing in Abnormal this first half? When will the work begin? And are you willing to discuss Mr. Thomas' data with me, if your busy life allows?

Thomas responded to our telegram by wiring us $200, and so we would be able to continue on our journey south when the car was repaired sometime the next week. We decided then to leave the car at the garage and in the intervening days go on to New York City by bus.

Perhaps I should omit here as irrelevant, but can't quite, some mention of the night we spent in a YWCA-recommended rooming house in Newark, Miriam sleeping on a cot in our room. We were awakened sometime in the night by her restlessness. The reason for it, we found, was that she was being attacked by an army of bedbugs. Our bed, too, we realized then, was not free from them, but Banks was able to disarm them sufficiently that after a fashion we could finish out the night all three in one bed. I never think back to that trip to New York without visions of that night returning to me.

The next day took us into the city (our first subway ride). But Banks was not able to meet Murphy, as he had hoped. His wife, Lois, said he was out of the city. It was another instance when the use of the telephone, had it been commonplace then, would have saved an unproductive effort. After it, however, when the car was again in traveling condition, we continued on the trip south. It was one that became memorable because of another wayside episode after we reached the country south of Richmond.

Lodging there in a tourist home that night, we read a newspaper report that interested us. It happened to be the night of a Tunney-Dempsey prize fight, and a "mind-reading" horse in the area had predicted, against the odds, that Tunney would win, as he then did. Of course, Banks decided to find out about that horse, and so after we finished our journey into North Carolina, he wrote a letter of inquiry back to the horse's owner, Mrs. Claudia Fonda, in Virginia and explained that he was a psychology student and interested in studying the horse. The reply from the owner was that she would

> like to have you see Lady. She is not a trick or cue horse. It is really a case of thought transference from my mind to her. And often from the minds of others. She spells words without training.
>
> I do not understand her in many ways. I am enclosing a card, with hours.

"LADY"   Mind Reading
Horse
can be seen
Mondays, Wednesdays, & Saturdays
3:00 to 4:30 p.m.

Will answer questions, add, subtract,
multiply, tell time, etc.

Mrs. C.P. Fonda
Stop 10 on the Petersburg Line

That fall, as soon as we could, we arranged to go back to "Stop 10 on the Petersburg Line" and see the horse. She turned out to be a young filly, her mistress, Mrs. Fonda, something of an amateur animal trainer. I remember the dog she was training to play the piano. At that stage, it would sit up on the piano bench and strike the keys; I never heard whether it eventually learned to play a tune.

But the horse, Lady, was the animal that interested us because of the possible telepathy. For the advertised public demonstrations Mrs. Fonda used a large tent in her backyard. Inside it was Lady with a low table in front of her, on which alphabet blocks were arranged in an orderly row, and also blocks with the digits 0–9. Mrs. Fonda stood beside the horse and observers like ourselves in front of the table where we could see what went on.

The procedure that had been worked out for the customers, who wanted answers to personal questions such as they might ask a medium, was that they would ask their questions aloud, and Mrs. Fonda would say, "Work, Lady, work." Then the horse would begin slowly to touch the blocks with her nose, one after another. The sequence of them was supposed to spell the answer. Surprisingly, it often did, as slowly Lady would pick out the appropriate block and so give an answer. Of course, false movements were made but correct ones too, at least, in that the sequence of letters made intelligible replies. According to report, these answers sometimes gave appropriate information which the questioner did not know. The problem for us was to find the source of the information the horse gave. Presumably it came from Mrs. Fonda, although she insisted she often did not know the answer herself and was as surprised as anyone when the questioner said that what the horse spelled was appropriate.

The explanation that seemed best to fit the facts, Banks thought, was that, in the really test cases Mrs. Fonda did have the answer, whether consciously or not, and that Lady got it somehow from her intuitively or by telepathy, if such an ability existed. Of course, the counterexplanation was that Mrs. Fonda gave Lady sensory guidance, however subtle it might be. But one aspect that became quite impressive as we noticed it repeatedly was a peculiar state of mind, if one could call it that, into which Lady at times appeared to lapse and during which the majority of her correct responses occurred.

In these periods she would settle down, practically motionless, eyes half-closed, and in general would appear as if about to go to sleep. Then, swinging her nose slowly over the blocks, she would pick out (touch) successive letters and give an answer to the question that had been asked. To us, it did look as if the horse was somehow reading Mrs. Fonda's mind. Banks eventually was able to take Mrs. Fonda's place beside the horse, finally even with her out of the tent; and he did get intelligent answers fitting his unexpressed thought. It did appear to be an instance of mind-reading.

Later, our visits were repeated, and McDougall once came with us. He, too, observed conditions, and between him and Banks they succeeded in eliminating (as well as the situation permitted) any cues that could be visible to Lady. They selected target letters silently and randomly, shielded their eye movements from Lady's sight, leaned against tent pillars to prevent body movements, etc. But still Lady succeeded to a significant degree.

All the time, however, not only Lady but her owner, too, had to be cajoled. Mrs. Fonda really did not understand just what was going on, or what these college professors wanted. Only by considerable persuasion, for instance, did Banks succeed in getting her actually to leave the tent and allow him to experiment with Lady without her presence. After all, Lady was her animal, in a way, her creation; and she expected to take her "on the circuit" — show circuit — and make a profitable venture out of the performance. These professors were not helping in the training process — hindering, rather — and interrupting the money-making afternoons when the paying public could see the horse.

In spite of all these practical necessities and difficulties, the general result of this work with Lady was that we felt we had probably seen an actual demonstration of mind reading, of telepathy by animal from man. Although the modus operandi of such a phenomenon could not be decided under the conditions, the hope was that more information about it might be worked out later, perhaps next year after Mrs. Fonda had taken Lady on the circuit.

The following year we were able to see Lady again but, alas, the phenomenon we had witnessed before was not repeated. Mrs. Fonda's now more or less obvious cues to Lady quite evidently prompted the responses she made. Besides, Lady no longer fell into the passive state in which she had made her hits the year before. If we had witnessed telepathy then, now the habits of the summer circuit probably acquired by both Lady and Mrs. Fonda almost obviously guided the responses, as Mrs. Fonda, however consciously or unconsciously, signaled the horse.

The difference between the situation earlier and now, difficult to describe but convincing to observe, was clear to us. As we reflected on it years later, after longer study of the elusive and fragile ESP ability, it did not seem surprising that if present originally it should have vanished when the horse was subjected daily, probably often almost hourly, to the command, "Work, Lady, work," with the accompanying movements of Mrs. Fonda, both of whip and of body.

I doubt if Mrs. Fonda ever understood why Banks' interest in Lady ceased after those demonstrations. To him, however, it would have been a greater surprise if Lady's sensitivity had survived the commercial exploitation, than that she should have demonstrated it in the first place.

The remainder of our trip to Durham, that first summer, was uneventful. When we neared the town our most distinctive impression was one of smell more than of vision, although rows of small houses looking as if they were on stilts were conspicuous as we approached the town. The stilts were only a few feet high, made of stacks of rocks or cement on which the wooden frames of the houses rested. We had seen similar structures occasionally in the country through which we had passed, and always wondered how the inhabitants managed to keep warm in the winter. We had not yet realized how mild the winters were compared to those of Ohio, where the mercury went below freezing for long periods instead of only briefly a few times a year. Apparently those few periods when it did so in North Carolina could be endured without attempts to counteract them. Like the man who couldn't mend his leaky roof because it was always raining when it leaked, we thought that probably these people could not board up the space beneath their houses because it was too cold to do so when it was cold enough to make it desirable.

But the smell of tobacco was even more universal than the shacks when we approached the town. Although awareness of this ubiquitous odor soon faded, not because it ceased to exist but because our sense of smell got tired, we were reminded that this was a tobacco town.

The little shacks on stilts soon gave way to better and more permanently built houses as we entered the city. We soon realized that the shacks were the homes of the tobacco workers, those who made the Chesterfield cigarettes advertised so widely in northern areas like the one we had come from. On a pleasure drive back home in Ohio, one day, accompanied by a rather innocent old relative, I asked if anyone had noticed the name of the town through which we were passing, and he looked out the window and replied, "Chesterfield!" with complete certainty. He had seen it on a sign.

Not the day of our arrival in Durham, but soon after, in driving past the cigarette factory at closing time and seeing the workers pour out, I realized that they were black, and so pathetically poor that the garments many of them wore were far more nondescript, tattered, and worn than even those of the tramps back home, the homeless wanderers that sometimes came to our farmhouse door and begged a handout and permission to sleep in the haymow in our barn.

But in Durham and up toward the area where the new university was being built, the outlook was less bleak. Here were paved streets and substantial houses with well-kept lawns. One area just back of the university campus, however, was less well kept, the houses obviously older, and here were the "rooms to rent" signs. In one of these houses we found living quarters convenient to the campus and to the school that Miriam would attend. The house had two storeys, but even so it was on stilts. We rented the first floor and the landlady and her ailing husband lived on the floor above. Heat, when needed, would be from a fireplace in the living room, and if we had not known that the space under the floor was a part of the unenclosed outdoors, we could have learned it by looking down a knothole in the flooring and seeing the ground beneath. Another thing, too, we could learn by looking through the knothole was the condition of the weather. When it rained, the rivulets of water flowing on that ground could tell us so.

Also, we soon could tell something about the culinary operations upstairs, if not from the smell of turnip greens (which we soon learned to like as true Southerners did but which at first seemed unspeakable), then by the refuse from them and other kitchen discards which our landlady conveniently dumped out her upstairs back window. I asked her for a dustpan at my first sweeping of our apartment, and she said she had had one once but had lost it. "Just sweep the dirt out the door."

All of this may sound worse than it actually was. We knew it would be a temporary place and it was low priced and convenient. We could carry on our necessarily simple domestic life there, get Miriam off to school, and then walk across the campus to McDougall's office and classroom.

This campus was to be for women; another, for men, was still in the blueprint stage a mile or so away, the pine forest where it would be, still standing. The idea of a separate campus for each sex was already exciting comment and raising questions from disapproving faculty newcomers, but they had not been there to prevail at the planning. Like the furrow marks which could still be traced in many then pine-forested areas in the region the separation of the sexes by campus dated back to earlier times, just as it obviously did in the North. Later, the strict distinction was to break down; and although the women's and men's dormitories remained each on its own campus, mixed classes soon were being held. McDougall, from the Oxford-Harvard tradition as he was, told us he was quite unprepared when he found females as well as males facing him at his first lectures at Duke.

Our welcome by the McDougalls was cordial. They too felt somewhat stranded in the still almost pioneer stage of the new university environment. Only a few new faculty members had arrived, and McDougall had as yet found only one person for his new department. That one was a Dr. Hirsch; and although his psychological credentials were good, he, like most members of his profession, was uninterested in psychical research. When we arrived, therefore, Banks was the first person with whom McDougall could discuss his strong interest in psychic matters unpopular as the topic was among psychologists. This became a common bond between them.

McDougall's interest in psychical research, even if personal, was, above all, a professional one. His psychological concept of personality needed what psychical research promised. In his view, human beings are animated by purposes and motives which govern their activities. These put living creatures, and especially man, into a different category from the purely mechanistic one of the behaviorists, whose school of psychology was then beginning to come into popularity. But McDougall was resisting behaviorism in spite of the fact that, in doing so, he was swimming upstream professionally. He and Banks thus were considerably alike in following their own interests, however unpopular they might be.

McDougall was at once interested in the Thomas material, and before long it was an unfailing topic of discussion between him and Banks. At the same time, Mrs. McDougall and I were soon good friends. Even though I sensed in her a bit of uneasiness about her husband's interest in the unconventional subject of psychical research, I think it reassured her somewhat to find that I, at least, seemed to be a fairly sensible person. I think it reduced the fear I sensed she had, that a too fanatic psychical researcher, which Banks might have been, would tend to be a bad or diverting influence when her husband had a psychology department to build.

Both Banks and I were allowed to audit McDougall's abnormal psychology class and his seminars. We thereby had immediate contact with the other psychology students and also with the new faculty member, Hirsch, who had arrived before we did — just in time for the opening of the fall semester. He was our first guest.

As it happens, my first diary entry records something of the kind of interaction of Banks and Hirsch as they became acquainted. It shows the attitudes that developed because of their different backgrounds, if not personalities — Hirsch from conventional psychology and psychiatry and Banks from biology and chemistry.

The diary entry is dated February 27, 1928. (Our first semester at Duke University had been too busy, with all the orientation involved, to leave time for diary writing.)

> We had a discussion in Psychology Seminar today on Jung's idea of racial inheritance of dreams. Dr. H. got quite excited over it. But of course Banks didn't and voiced his objection [that it was only a conjecture, not a

reliable scientific fact]. His introduction to scientific method has made it impossible for him to be a good philosopher. In fact, it almost makes it impossible for him to be a good psychologist, even though I guess it was his philosophic tendency in the first place that took him out of the conventional scientific field.

Anyway today Dr. McDougall, who I think harbored a little rancor for the "box" J.B. had gotten him into on "insight in the lower forms of intelligence," sided with H. against J.B. and rather harder I thought than the circumstances warranted. The discussion ended without anything very profitable being arrived at anywhere, but I'm certain H. thinks because Dr. McDougall expressed himself on his side that it's settled that certain dreams are "a racial characteristic," a definitely heritable element.

Then my own attitude in this argument comes out strongly in a diary entry, though I probably didn't express it at the seminar:

What a pot of mush! No wonder scientists get so impatient with philosophers and psychologists. No wonder Behaviorism!

Understanding, as I did, Banks' definite and wholehearted devotion to strict scientific method, which he was not finding in psychology much more than he had found it in philosophy, I wrote

I wonder if we'll ever fit in any place. This matter of Science versus Philosophy is for us a real issue. No wonder I tell J.B. he must not be a philosopher. I couldn't bear the stigma. We got rid of "botanist." I don't want to take on something just as bad.

And then comes a different topic:

The question is up, shall Banks accept a research assistantship here next year and scramble for the necessary additional funds in order to go on with the telepathic animal research, or not?

The period for which Thomas had hired us was ending. But McDougall as well as Banks was interested in Lady, and he encouraged further research in that direction. For this, the research assistantship, with, however, an inadequate stipend, was available from the university via the psychology department.

The diary entry continues

The present answer is no. I do not think that Banks should take anything less than a faculty position even if we could manage to live on the assistantship stipend. I tried to explain that my attitude on that was founded on a more subtle and far-reaching reason than mere ambition. My idea is that our usefulness in the future would be limited by the consequent lack of position. In order to avoid that, we must make the apparently mundane and mercenary concession to position right now. I remember how Dad always continued retailing when he wanted to be wholesaling because he never made up his mind that he'd do nothing but a wholesale business. I'm all for wholesaling for us.

Then comes a change of topic to our errand for Thomas:

> Banks just wrote up the "Gum Case." [About which, and the Thomas project in general, more later]. It is fine—he made an exceedingly interesting little item out of it. I am very enthusiastic about Mr. T's work. I think it is going to make a great contribution. I'm glad we got a chance to work on it. We're lucky people. I think Mr. Thomas is a splendid man. He has all my sympathy as well as gratitude. It looks like Detroit for us next year.

That entry in February, however, was not prophetic in regard to our next year's locale. But very soon the scene shifted drastically, as I explain in an entry made on April 1, 1928.

> A nice spring evening. We just came home from the banks of the Eno River [a few miles from Durham] where we found a hillside covered with hepaticas and another with trailing arbutus in full bloom. We formally took possession of this country for ours, since just yesterday a letter came from Mr. Thomas which helped us to decide to accept Dr. McDougall's offer of $2500 for half-time of research and half of teaching for next year. He had made the offer two weeks ago but we did not accept at once but waited to get Mr. Thomas' opinion. He now has about decided to come down here himself and work for a Ph.D. and so we'll all be together if that works out.

> Banks' attempt to get the English people to cooperate on absent sittings through Sir Oliver Lodge has fallen through. He would be very much disappointed about it except for the fact that a Mrs. Keene, an American medium, has accepted his offer. Her letter just came last night and Banks said, after reading it, "I'll have to drive more carefully now. I feel as if my life is worth more now."

> I surely hand it to Banks. It has been his fearlessness and vigor that have

gotten us into these interesting things. I have tried not to hold him back entirely but I haven't given him much impetus to go on. I have not had the faith. My best judgment did not tell me that in so few years he could have university connections and be in psychical research too.

The half-time for research is going to mean that Banks can go on with the telepathy work and continue with Dr. McDougall's rats and with Mr. Thomas' work on the side. It ought to be the ideal arrangement.

The mention of Mrs. Keene, even though no later work with her resulted, is a thread that introduces an episode that occurred at this period and which even now, all these long years after, still perplexes me. We were living then at the same place I described above, when we received a pamphlet from one Sally Keene, and the title of it was "Evidence of Things Not Seen." Although I have long forgotten its message, I have not forgotten that title, for after we read the pamphlet we placed it with a few other books and pamphlets we had accumulated since our arrival, on the mantle over the fireplace, supported upright by bookends.

One day when we returned to the apartment after the morning class, we found this pamphlet lying near the doorsill from our living room to the hall which led outside and to the staircase to the apartment above. It was lying face up, "Evidence of Things Not Seen." We stopped in puzzlement, just avoiding stepping on it. How had it gotten there? If it had been there when we left that morning and after Miriam had gone off to school, we would almost necessarily have seen or stepped on it. Surely it could not have been there then. Besides, we were both quite certain we had placed it on the mantle with the other books, and when we looked at them, all still standing as we had left them, a little space still marked the place where the pamphlet had been. But we knew we had not removed it after placing it there, and certainly not that morning, when we had started off to class without taking time to read anything.

Of course, our apartment was open to the old landlady upstairs, and no doubt she sometimes inspected our rooms in our absence. But although she could read, it was almost inconceivable that she would read something like this or pick it off the mantle and leave only its empty space to show where it had been — and then drop it on the floor as she left. And surely no one else had been there. The only one who knew us was Hirsch, and he would neither enter our apartment in our absence nor read such a bulletin if he did.

So, "Who dun it?" We never knew whether it had some normal explanation which we overlooked, or whether it was indeed evidence of things not seen. The answer to this superficially trifling but unsolved incident was only a harbinger of the countless equally inexplicable puzzles with which the following years confronted us.

Although my diary does not mention it, I had a job, too, that year in Durham. The new university had a new botany department as well as a new psychology department. The new botany department had been started a year or two earlier, and the man heading it was a former acquaintance of ours from the graduate school at the University of Chicago, Dr. Hugo Blomquist. When we got to Durham, although he had no faculty position to offer me, he needed an assistant in his department and offered that job to me. I took it and enjoyed it that winter and hoped to continue the second year.

However, again the plans of mice and men — and of a woman, this time — went agley. The reason was that I began to realize that as a married woman I could not continue always to be just an adjunct to the professional life of my budding young scientist husband; and because the result of this realization affected him as well as me, I must inject an account of it here. I must do it also because it shows a facet of his character without which the representation of that character here would be incomplete.

At top, left: Ella Elizabeth Long Weckesser (L.E.R.'s mother), in 1915; right: Louisa Ella Weckesser (L.E.R.), ca. 1917. Above: L.E.R. and siblings, standing from the left, Miriam, Elden, Sylvia, Ethan, Constant (Connie), Ernest, Ruth, Esther, Louisa, and their father, seated, Christian Weckesser, summer 1932.

At top: L.E.R.'s girlhood home in Marshallville, Ohio, ca. 1900. Above: Louie Weckesser, right, at summer school, Wooster College, 1914, with sisters Ruth, second from left, and Esther, third from left; L.E.R. lived in the tent for financial reasons.

At top: J.B.R.'s father, Samuel Ellis Rhine, ca. 1930's. Above: J.B.R.'s father and mother, Elizabeth Ellen Vaughan Rhine, ca. 1912 by their house in Marshallville, Ohio.

At top: J.B.R. with his sister Myra on her wedding day, May 26, 1917, just before joining the Marines. Above: from right, J.B.R. in Marine uniform, L.E.R., L.E.R.'s sister Esther, L.E.R.'s sister-in-law Sadie (wife of Ernest Weckesser), in Ohio, ca. 1919.

The recently married Rhines, posing again in their April wedding clothes, summer 1920.

At top, left: L.E.R. and J.B.R. at her commencement (Ph.D. degree), University of Chicago, 1923; right: the two at the University rifle range, ca. 1922. Above: L.E.R. on J.B.R.'s shoulder, his younger brother Paul Rhine, and Paul's child, ca. 1923.

At top: family portrait in North Carolina, summer 1934; from left, Betsy (about 1½), L.E.R., J.B.R., Sally (about 4), Robbie (about 5), Miriam Weckesser (L.E.R.'s sister). Above: the Rhine children, ca. 1935–36, Robbie, Rosie (in front), Betsy, Sally.

William McDougall (left) and J.B.R. at Duke, ca. 1937–38.

L.E.R. and J.B.R. in the backyard of their 908 Club Boulevard house in
Durham, in 1950.

J.B.R. with students at Duke, ca. 1950.

At top: L.E.R., J.B.R., Farilla David, and Gaither Pratt at a Duke Parapsychology Laboratory coffee hour, 1956. Above: J.B.R., L.E.R. and "Dear Me" after picking blackberries at their new farm near Hillsborough, N.C., ca. 1953.

At top: Arthur Koestler (left) and J.B.R. at the Duke Lab, ca. 1960. Above: the Rhines on the Duke campus, ca. 1960.

At top: L.E.R. at Duke Lab, ca, 1960. Above: J.B.R., ca. late 1970's.

Louisa E. Rhine, Co-Editor of the *Journal of Parapsychology*, ca. early 1970's.

At top: the Rhine children, March 13, 1982, in Wilkesboro, N.C.; from left, Rosemary Rhine, Elizabeth Ellen Rhine, Robert Elden Rhine, Sara Louise Rhine Feather. Above: J.B.R. and daughter Sally, ca. 1979.

Joseph Banks Rhine and Louisa Ella Weckesser Rhine, life companions, in 1976.

6

Early Years
at Duke University

As every biology student knows, Nature in the course of evolution made many experiments as to the method of reproduction of species. We all know what it is on the human level, and that — whether or not it is the best of all possible ones for the species in general — at least it's the one we are stuck with.

And it was the one that I, in particular, was stuck with, whether or not it was the one I thought I preferred when, in 1927, after seven years of marriage, we still were childless. By then I had become very tired of explaining to the good old mamas we met that, no, the fact that we were still childless was not because we didn't want a family but because Nature had not sent us any. I knew very well that on every trip back home that Banks and I had made, I had been looked over, especially by all the older female relatives, both his and mine, for any family signs that might be showing. I was sure that it was a slip-up in the reproductive system of humans that had permitted to occur such an anomaly as I presented in my prolific family line. The reproductive system would certainly have to evolve on beyond the possibility of blunders like I seemed to have been, I thought, if it were ever to achieve perfection.

At that time, however, I was much more interested in continuing to try to help Banks professionally than to drop out and have a baby. I was the eldest of my parents' flock of nine children, the youngest being 24 years my junior. Babies therefore had been rather a commonplace in my girlhood. Although I had been normally attached to each of my siblings as they came along, my goals in life had gone beyond them.

More and more, however, I had become aware of Banks' attraction to children. He always cast an appreciative eye on any smiling cherub in a baby carriage that we might pass on the street or in a grocery store. Not to sell myself too short, however, I did too, but that, I thought, was only natural. The fact, however, that Banks noticed babies so obviously told me something, so that even back in Morgantown our continued childlessness had led me to a gynecologist, and as a result of his findings I had had a corrective operation. Now it was several years later and the operation had not fulfilled its purpose.

Of course, we recognized all along, or at least I did, that childlessness had advantages. We had been able, for instance, to go back to the University of Chicago in the summers and to make trips for Thomas. Even our headlong venture away from the security of the job at Morgantown, to the uncertainties of Boston, we would no doubt have considered impossible if we had had a family.

But Banks' interest in children, even though I don't remember his ever actually putting it in words, was impressed on me especially strongly one time during our first year in Durham. After our experience with the horse, Lady, his interest in unusual abilities in animals was high, and by the spring of 1928 we went on a trip to see a dog that was reputed to be telepathic. I don't remember much about the dog by now, though I believe the verdict on it was that the owner unconsciously gave it cues by which it performed its feats.

The item on that trip that I do remember clearly was a small photograph of the dog owner's little daughter, a sweet little two-year-old smiling out at the world quite charmingly. Her name, the proud father said, was Sally. Banks fell in love with her, and so obviously that the father gave him the picture. It graced his dresser top for years.

In view of all this, I knew again I'd be a flop of a wife if I didn't somehow manage to produce a real Sally for him. Also, if I were to do so it should be soon, for it was very clear, I wasn't getting any younger. Now I was 36! And Banks had this opportunity at Duke University, "half-time for teaching." Life ahead looked reasonably stable at last, and I knew it was time for a family if we were ever to have one.

Another medical examination. No hope, the doctor said. All right. We'd accept the verdict. We'd adopt a baby sometime. But by then it was near the end of the school year and a trip for Thomas to Oneida County, New York, was coming up. On our way there, we stopped in Ohio for a short visit home. We found the younger children there half-ill with three-day measles, the rubella, since known for its bad effect on pregnant women. But that effect was quite unrecognized then, and we were equally unaware that the very test that had labelled me sterile had itself removed the cause of the sterility. And so we were unaware that at last and against all expectations, I was in an early stage of pregnancy.

On our way to our destination in northern New York state we took a roundabout detour in response to an invitation from the McDougalls to visit them at Joy Farm, their much-loved summer retreat in New Hampshire, which was, as I recorded,

> a mountain farmhouse of the more romantic type. The setting is perfect— miles away from anywhere in a clearing in the forest, overhung by mountains.... Banks and Kenneth have gone to climb the mountain. It's almost a day's undertaking. Banks will enjoy it. I didn't go along because I thought my rate of speed would only be a dampener on them. They started off about 8 this morning and will probably be gone all day. But tomorrow we are starting off for New York State where we'll do some work for Mr. Thomas.

The next morning, incidentally (as I thought then), I had an unaccountable rash on my body. I hoped it was not too noticeable. It soon disappeared, however, and I forgot it. We never guessed until many years afterwards that it was rubella, nor did we have any hint then that it was preparing a tragedy for Banks and me.

Quite unaware of what lay ahead, we went back to North Carolina, Banks first of all to prepare lectures for the classes he would teach that winter, and I, as I thought, to another year of assisting in the botany department. But before that semester started, I knew that my future was different, as I noted in my diary on September 28 that fall of 1928.

Another year started, and a new one indeed for me. I'm all unadjusted yet, in spite of frantic strivings to realize the different destiny before me now. It seems impossible to realize, even impossible to believe that the future, the next few months, will be so different. If I could realize it, it would make this period smoother and I'd be less discontented. It's only by fleeting glimpses — little short hours or minutes against the great All-the-Time that I seem to get the significance of the situation. When I do I'm glad, glad, glad, and awed that such a thing [as my pregnancy] can be.

The rest of the time I don't feel quite like myself, a little tired, a little — or more than a little — cross, disappointed because my tangible "bird in the hand," the botany teaching, had to get away from me. It's so easy to remember that with that I'd be up at the University now, meeting students, talking and thinking about intellectual things, and getting rid of my mental staleness.

It's easy to imagine all that, and the very idea is most attractive. But instead, now I have to realize that I had to give it up — for a hope, a dream, a sentence — which as yet has not, and never before in my life has had — any meaning. And even if the doctor said it, it's possible he was wrong. There may be nothing to it — and here I'll be with nothing — a modern "Niobe" for sure.

I still recall how I often sat looking dejectedly out the window, mornings after Banks went off to the university and remembering how last year I used to go across the campus with him, out into the world of stir and activity, while now I had only the little light housekeeping job to occupy me. But yet, as I continued that same morning of September, 1928,

Still I do know that *something* is happening to me. I'm certainly abnormal physically from some cause or other. The doctor says it's the cause we want. Why don't I believe it? Banks does, the dear. Oh, I wouldn't have him disappointed for worlds. His disappointment would be the biggest part of my own, because one can't really be disappointed about something the very fiber of one's being still disbelieves.

And then I went on to describe the material aspects of our living, that after the summer of "chasing all over creation," and living now in a fairly comfortable apartment on the second floor (we had moved to a better neighborhood), I remarked that we were nicely set up materially. I got a new rug, a kitchen cabinet that Banks is as proud of as I am. Miriam is established and contented at the Junior High, and Elden [my young brother who was with us that year] is getting his first experience at facing an unsympathetic world. [Canvassing, to help pay his college expenses while living with us.] In a week or so Mr. Thomas comes with the interesting vista he represents. Everything is starting off nicely—all but myself. I'm going under a cloud—but oh, I hope it is a happy one. I must try to realize that it is, to imagine it, to believe it.

It wasn't a happy one. It was a cloud, a dark one indeed that I went under, and it covered Banks too. The rubella had done its work. The baby was born prematurely and died at birth.

The final reality of it came to both of us then. And the curious consequence of it was that now our attitudes toward parenthood, Banks and mine, reversed. Now I had to have a baby, right now. Nine or ten months from now would be too long. Now I could not face those empty-armed months ahead. Now, at once, it seemed, I *had to have a baby*, but Banks was unconvinced. He too wanted a family, as I knew very well. But he could wait the months, the year or two until our hopes might be fulfilled.

If this were my own story only, and not mainly Banks', I would have to quote the diary pages, February 8, 15 and 28, 1929, that record my disappointment and how more and more I began to think that we must adopt a baby, even though the doctor said we could have our own quite soon. But my feelings, feelings which must have been very real to Banks, are summed up in the diary a month after the little tragedy:

But what's the use of thinking of it? It's all over now. Today we drove over to the cemetery and Banks showed me the little grave. That's all that's left, and here I am with nothing to do. How can I get interested in cold, intellectual things, or in trivial evanescent time fillers? I thought I was going to touch a reality—it escaped me and nothing is left but emptiness.

It's worthwhile to help Banks a lot. I have an intellectual interest in the History of Science that he is studying [the subject of the course he was giving] as well as a personal and emotional one in helping him—but it's not vital enough to be a main issue. I could do it so gladly and interestedly on the side, but I can't get absorbed in it enough to forget the other.

It's not necessary here to recount the difficulties of the decision we finally made to adopt a baby boy, the one we found that was needing and waiting for a home, at the local Children's Refuge, although Banks really thought such a step should not be rushed into so fast. But he realized my need and so helped to do it. I'm glad to say that I'm certain he never regretted it and that he furthered my project to adopt the little Robbie, in every possible way he could, and he continued to be supportive during the infancy stage and afterwards always. His first test around the house came, when only a year later, another baby, the Sally he wanted, was born. Then during my hospitalization, a two-week period in those days, and after I was home again, he helped with Robbie every available minute. His devotion to the children was complete, as was theirs to him, then and always.

For one thing, Banks was an imaginative story-teller, which I was not. Consequently, it became a habit as the little ones reached the listening stage that he would tell the bedtime stories preliminary to sleep. I tried to do it upon occasion but usually without notable success. Long after, Sally told me that when her father told her a bedtime story she always quieted down and *tried* to go to sleep because she knew he wanted her to and would be disappointed if he knew she often was still awake and only "pretending" when he tiptoed away to keep from waking her.

I said, "But when I tried to put you to sleep you rarely did so. I too wanted you to sleep and would be disappointed if you didn't. Didn't you know that?"

"Yes, I did, but I didn't care. I felt sorry for Daddy."

Apparently the same feeling was shared later by the other little girls, Elizabeth (soon, Betsy) and Rosemary (soon, Rosie), who came along in succeeding years. To all of them, Daddy was the story-teller. The one advantage of it to me was that thereby I was free to finish up the kitchen work the quicker. I was always grateful *not* to be expected to manufacture childhood fantasies, which it was clear Nature did not mean me to do.

One aspect of Banks' home life that should be mentioned for completeness was his attitude toward medical men, and especially their role in the problems that arise as children are growing up. My tendency when an illness threatened was to "call the doctor." But Banks was different, and only extremity would drive him to it or lead to his acquiescence when I wanted to do it. Not that he ever would have forbidden it, but I seldom would have done it without his approval as well as simple assent.

The background to Banks' attitude concerning medical advice went back to his boyhood and his father's nearly fatal experience. It seemed that earlier his father had only rescued himself in time and, as he was convinced, saved his own life, by ceasing to follow the prescribed line of medication the doctor had given him for severe and chronic digestive trouble, when he discarded the prescription and instituted a stringent "natural food" diet for himself. It was a diet advocated by Mr. T.B. Terry, a man who contributed to the farm paper that he and my father both read. Incidentally, Terry's writings affected my own father too. But mine took them less seriously while Banks' father continued experimenting with his diet for the rest of his life. Consequently, his children early absorbed their father's distrust of medical practitioners and his belief in diet as the one and only defense against almost all physical illnesses.

Banks' attitude in this affected me the most during Sally's infancy, when instead of turning to the pediatrician as all the young mothers of my acquaintance did, Banks disapproved. He said the doctor only knew routine practices and his opinion was unnecessary. I, being a more easily influenced person than he, acquiesced, even though the baby was very unadjusted and cried most of the time for the first six weeks of her life and in spite of the fact that she was gaining in weight, that was supposed to be the index of infant well-being.

Until then I could not bring myself to go counter to Banks' advice, but when at last I did so and a supplementary feeding was prescribed, the trouble disappeared at once. The baby had been gaining a little weight, but now she gained much faster and her life and also those of all of us were eased thereby. It was one time when my judgment was better than Banks', but such were few. Most of the time, as I soon learned, his was the better.

One reservation about that, however, must be made. Banks' way was always the best—for him. But it was not always so for me, although I do not know if he ever recognized that, or if so, very fully. Probably his strong-mindedness and my—shall I say—more easily influenced tendency made it possible for us to live together successfully, as we did, although added to it of course was our deep devotion to each other.

During this period of my absorption with family beginnings, Banks' life on the campus was divided, as he had arranged with McDougall, between teaching and research. His attitude and reaction to this arrangement was expressed in a letter he wrote to my sister Sylvia on January 28, 1929. In it he says

Dr. McDougall has just secured for me an Assistant Professorship at $1000 increase. This will enable us to begin to expand our family—and paint the Ford. Besides, this gives me an entry into Duke staff that will I hope launch me on my real work in life. I am going to give an "Outline of the History of Science," and a "Constructive Survey of Modern Science" which will consist in a condensed resume of all I know and can learn before the lecture. The courses will be given in the Department of Philosophy, but I will still be a part of the Psychology Department too. You can bet, kiddo, that I am happy over it. The work will be lighter than I could expect elsewhere, one course of 3 hours — and my research with Dr. McDougall (we are working on his problem of inheritance of acquired or learned responsiveness to light — Lamarckianism). I will have time this spring for much of my own reading and preparation. Oh! I am the lucky feller, Oh!

Planning the teaching part, Banks then made a list of courses that he might give. The much abbreviated course list illustrates very well the direction of his interest.

COURSES SUGGESTED FOR 1929–30
to be given by myself

1. *An Outline of Science*: This will have to be a general course dealing in the main with the principles of rigid scientific method.

2. *A Constructive Review of Modern Science*: An orientation course designed to aid the student to gather together his fragmentary knowledge of the natural world into a synthetic working view.

3. *The Relation of Body and Mind in the Light of the Sciences*: Following upon a review of the significance and the philosophical modes of treatment of this old problem, the facts bearing upon it will be considered from the following sciences: Physics, General Physiology, Comparative Zoology, Genetics, Endocrinology, Embryology, Neurology, General Psychology, Physiological, Experimental, Comparative and Abnormal Psychology, with some use of "Parapsychology" at the close. The aim is primarily to formulate the various approaches of these sciences toward this rather central problem, affording a chart of present status. A general summary of the physical and psychical data will be evolved incidentally around this theme.

4. *The Nature of Human Personality*: The substance of the course will be a consideration of the bases for the different theories — heredity, environment, ductless glands. Finally, the question of the survival of the personality will be viewed in terms of the evidence presented by psychic research in its behalf.

Eventually—say in a year or two, if I am here, I should like to offer a seminar course for general free discussion on one of these subjects:

1. Religion and Ethics in Relation to Science and Its Methods

2. An Evaluation of the Evidence Presented by Psychic Research

3. Philosophy and Science, a Scientific Approach to Philosophic Problems

The letter of explanation to McDougall accompanying the proposed list is of some interest, showing as it does that Banks was not unaware of the boldness of the idea of giving courses of these kinds:

> While I feel very unfit at present to give any of these courses adequately, I feel that I shall be able to make fair preparation for two of them by next year, and for two more by the year following.

> In view of the possibilities of your leaving, Dr. McDougall, and because of the general character of the subject matter of the courses suggested which would not probably find much support from your successor, I I had better "make my nest" now rather than later, in the field of Philosophy, if I can and if you agree with me in this. While I am not appreciative of Philosophy as defined by many, yet I am devoted to it as defined in my own way—and what subject allows for so much personal latitude in defining it? At any rate I hope to be useful in the courses to which I will give my energies, and I do not mind what names they are called by. Of course, this arrangement would make no difference in the work I do with you, or in any other help I may be able to give, as in Psychology 1. My disinclination to specialize in psychology would soon leave me unsheltered, whereas my own greatest interests coincide with a real need in the Phil. Dept., in a History of Science, and general science and orientation courses. I should be interested in getting your reaction to this, at your convenience.

The half time for research was to be divided between Thomas' material and McDougall's rats. The rats were the animals used in the professor's long-time research project. This was on the unpopular Lamarckian theory of heredity, a theory that ran counter to the conventional one which says the genetic factors are isolated in the germ plasm and cannot be affected by experience on the individual level. The Lamarckian theory had long been quite generally rejected by biologists even without test or experiment.

McDougall, a psychologist, but one not afraid of unpopular questions if he thought they had any merit in them, had while still in England rushed into this one where (biological) angels feared to tread and had undertaken to test it. He had taken this research problem with him to Harvard and now had brought it to Duke University. When Banks, a young biology student interested in psychical research, appeared at Duke, McDougall, noting his biological background, thought that the young man might also be able to help in the Lamarckian research. Banks was at once interested and in agreement with McDougall's argument.

The argument for the Lamarckian theory, as McDougall saw it, was that when evolution occurs, the changes which come about over generations could only do so if at least a trace effect of individual experience was inherited. Even though in the frequently cited example, giraffes always reaching for higher branches might not show a longer neck immediately, that fact did not prove that a slight effect, only measurable over many generations, might not occur. One might say, therefore, that, in this view, although evolution was not in a hurry, it was moving nevertheless.

McDougall's experiment had involved training individual white rats to perform a specific task until they learned to do it without error, and then to continue to breed them and to train their progeny similarly over succeeding generations. The number of errors they made before the task was learned in each generation was recorded. The expectation was that if the learning that was involved was in any degree inherited, then the number of errors would gradually decrease. But if no decrease was shown over a large number of generations, the fact would support the idea that acquired characteristics are not inherited.

While McDougall was at Harvard, the experiment had already run for about a dozen rat generations. And it was encouraging for the Lamarckian hypothesis, since the records showed a slight decrease in the average number of errors made by the current generation as compared to the original one. That original one, to put it simply, had consisted of half of a litter of white rats which had been trained to perform the task and then bred, while the other half had been bred but not trained. This second half of the line thus constituted a control and a continuing one over succeeding generations as the individuals continued to be bred, but never trained.

The specific task to be learned by the animals in this experiment was that each individual rat when placed in a water tank should find the painless one of two exits. One exit would be lighted, the other not. One would be electrified, the other not. The rats, presumably would tend to choose a lighted exit. It, therefore, was electrified and an animal climbing over it to escape the water would get an electric shock, mild enough that it would not be injured but strong enough to be unpleasant. The dark exit was safe and when, by repeated trials, an animal learned which one to choose without error, the two exits would be shifted from side to side until the animals learned to choose the painless one unerringly, regardless of the side. When an individual animal could do that, it was then considered to be trained and would be bred. The average number of errors the individuals of each generation made in leaving the correct exit would be recorded.

Banks' test procedure was to drop the animals into the water and watch them swim to an exit. With the test repeated daily, he would record the number of errors of each individual, each day. When he took over the experiment, several technical points still needed to be improved in order to make the result even more reliable than it had been. One of these was to decide on the strength of the electrical shock to be used and get it standardized. Another was to be able to choose from litters of each generation, comparable individual animals for testing from each stock, the experimental and the control, and in all ways to ensure that the only uncontrolled variable in the test would be the heredity of the two groups.

In time, J.B.'s results, like McDougall's, began to show a slight reduction in the number of errors made by the experimental over the control strain. Banks continued with the experiment for several years, until finally when his own projects became very time-consuming he was able to turn it over to others. But this first year, "running the rats" was one of his daily duties, and something of his attitude to it I find reflected in a letter he wrote about it to my sister, Sylvia. Evidently, she had asked him about his reaction to working with rats, generally considered to be rather repulsive animals. Dated March 11, 1929, his reply was that

Rats can become fascinating—a handful of cottony, fluffy, clean-as-silk little baby ratlets, pink and white symphonies in innocence, with clean little soft paws that cling to your fingers so timidly, and tiny soft everinquiring little pink noses touching your skin so lightly that you know, only thus, how fairies feel.

Of course I have lots of data, curves, tables and *Conclusions*. These are interesting and of some importance, maybe—but not fascinating. Just the baby rats are that, poor little wet fellows trying pitifully to clean themselves off, all over again, each time I put them in the water maze—at last getting so tired they can hardly lift their paws up to get the cleansing lick to scrub with—yet still struggling "nobly" to make their bedraggled coats shine again with their snowy cleanness.

The other half of Banks' research time, was, theoretically, to be given to the Thomas material. But before going into that, I should give a bit of my own personal history reflected in a letter of mine, a copy of which I retained, which gives at some length Banks' and my own outlook on the questions we were facing.

That first year at Duke, I had been given an assistantship in the botany department. The next fall the job was open to me again but I could not take it because of my pregnancy. And finally, now, I had "news" to tell my friends, as I did in this letter. It was a long one and written on December 30, 1928, to Ella, my former roommate at the University of Chicago.

Ella was then a biology teacher in her hometown in Ohio. She responded warmly to my "news" and then went on to ask if I was convinced of the survival of human personality. She asked also what she should read to bring her information on the topic up to date. She also said that she had just read McDougall's *Character and the Conduct of Life* and went on to say, "I just love it! It's so wholesome, sane and inspiring and it seems so very sound in its philosophy."

She knew also that McDougall was now at Duke University and she thought that we must be working under him. "Consequently," she said, "in class I have been talking about you all week — because a lot of us are reading his book. Did my thought reach you to prompt your letter?"

My reply reflects at some length Banks' position then on the survival question, although it is given as my own, since by this time after eight years of marriage, his ideas and mine were no longer separate. I know, of course, that his were still his but his now were mine also. I therefore could answer Ella's question at length and in so doing the stage of his thinking shows plainly through my words.

Was it a coincidence only that I wrote you just when you had been thinking of me? The world is full of strange coincidences. Whether many of them are more than that who can say? I would not be surprised however if many times we get and are influenced by another person's thought. *Something* prompted me to write you when I did. I had thought of doing so for some time because I thought you would be interested in what I had to tell. But several others to whom I did write to tell this — to me — great news, appeared to be so much less so than I had expected that there was a little hurt spot inside me somewhere and I decided that I had expected my affairs to seem too big to others and I had better keep them to myself.

But on an unpremeditated impulse I wrote you and your warm and prompt little note was just the response I wanted but didn't get from the other quarters. So was it a coincidence that I wrote you just then or not?

Dr. and Mrs. McDougall were with us for impromptu dinner last night and I took the liberty of reading him the paragraph from your letter regarding his book. He seemed much pleased as I knew he would be. He is quite naive that way and enjoys praise and appreciation as much as anyone; this particular book has somehow drawn so much of the opposite type of criticism that I think he appreciates commendation all the more.

I'm glad you liked it. I haven't read it myself, sorry, though I know the general character of the contents, partly from trying to defend his general position from local critics. They say he is mid-Victorian, antiquated, etc. largely because of his attitude toward the position of woman, sex relations among the young, etc. and there have certainly been cutting reviews in the American Mercury etc. and much cheap and thoughtless and undeserved ridicule heaped on him. Fortunately, he lives out of the world so much — in his own inner life, I mean, that I don't think he knows the worst of it. I hope he doesn't. He doesn't understand or appreciate the American spirit very well anyway. He is so dignified and reflective himself that the lightmindedness and flippancy and materialistic attitude so common here is quite foreign and distasteful to him.

Among psychologists in this country he's a lone wolf too. They jeer at him for being "religious." He does have an appreciation for the deeper and more intangible *reality* which they are too narrow-minded to grasp. It is that element in him of all American psychologists which attracted Banks and keeps us here. We do not agree with him fully, of course, but we are not disappointed. On the other hand we think it is a great privilege in our development and education to have had this opportunity to have known both him and Mrs. McDougall so intimately.

You ask me if I am fully convinced of the survival of personality. And then I ask myself if I am. I certainly am very nearly convinced; whether absolutely, I don't quite know. I believe I know firsthand more affirmative and convincing evidence on this question than I do on the rotundity of the earth, for example. But it is a question on which one naturally requires more convincing, overwhelming proof than on almost any other topic I know of.

Since we have been studying the material these last years, we have found not only undreamed of evidence, but also unthought of objections. I had not supposed there were so many possible other explanations for "supernormal" occurrences than the spiritistic one. And the study of these and the evidence has certainly made us critical. We realize now that if tests as strict and critical as we apply to psychic evidence were applied to half the commonly accepted facts of science, to all the beliefs of established religion etc. the slate would be wiped pretty clean.

But in spite of all this, Banks and I believe, though not all psychic researchers by any means do, that the survival hypothesis explains and fits more data than any other. (Personally, I realize that I have accepted it as a certainty in my practical thinking. And it does for me in a sane and balanced way, what emotional religion was never able to do. It gives me a kind of peace as well as a tangible working philosophy and goal which I had never been able to get from religion.) It's an utter relief to me to have no more dealing with heaven or hell or sin, as concepts, I mean. And death seems so much different. I know I could face it now with a calmness I never could have known with the imperfect religious faith which was the best I ever was able to get. Leaving Banks and the rest of the world now would just be as bad as leaving him for a temporal separation of indefinite length — bad enough, since when he's gone a week my world is pretty empty, but still it's endurable if we are reunited in the future.

In the nature of things this idea about life after death cannot be proved. Evidence seeming to bear on the future state cannot be evidential. Mr. Thomas' deceased wife may tell him (in a seance) that his daughter is going to have a child seven months beforehand, when he's in England and she in Michigan is scarcely sure herself yet and having told no one besides her husband her suspicion. And she (Mrs. T.) may tell him (Mr. T.) of intimate things he does in solitude, or of things he knows nothing of and scarcely can check out — and all this is evidential. It shows there is an intelligence of some kind in touch with the facts. And if all possibilities of fraud are excluded it would certainly seem to be his wife's personality and intelligence somehow showing through the mist.

But if she tells him along with these things how she felt when she realized she was dead, or how she's living now, we cannot call it evidential. It may be the mind of the medium breaking in with purely human imaginations. And so I don't think we can ever know much of that existence beyond the fact of its reality. That, I think science can establish, if it has not already done so.

I know you cannot have much time for reading and I wish I knew what you could read to get the most out of in the shortest time and with least effort. I'm not sure. Our information has sifted in from such scattered sources, and much of the best of it is not generally in libraries. A lot is rather technical too and rather discouraging if not distasteful reading. Its study really is not put up interestingly.

I have a bulletin here I'm going to send which we feel confidence in, and which I think is rather interesting. The author, Mrs. Keene, we do not know personally though Banks has corresponded with her some. But as you will see she is vouched for by Dr. W.F. Prince who edits her material, and who knows her well only to speak highly of her. And we know him very well — stayed in his home this summer while in Boston — and there is no one more critical or well-trained and experienced in these things without being the least bit credulous than he. And so you may depend on Mrs. Keene's story I am sure. There are two recent books you'd enjoy, but I'm afraid they're not available — *The Bridge* by Nea Walker, Sir Oliver Lodge's secretary, and *Some Evidence of Human Survival* by Rev. Drayton Thomas (of England). If you can get them, however, they are dependable beyond doubt, and *The Bridge* at least, if you can get past a certain cumbersome presentation, is a dramatic story of the highest merit — a true story much stranger than fiction. Dare I take the space to outline it to you?

Mr. and Mrs. White were a devoted English couple whose relations seem to have been of almost poetic beauty. Mr. White died and Mrs. W. in her bereavement wrote to Sir Oliver Lodge for any assurance of survival he could give. She had never met him or his secretary however. The secretary, Nea Walker, was then engaged to hold some sittings for Mrs. White with one of the best English mediums, but not to tell the medium for whom the sitting was intended. All the correspondence is given, so that Miss Walker could have told the medium very little, even if she had told all she knew. In the sittings so held, however, Mr. White purported to communicate and got some evidential material across which is quite surprising under the conditions. A lot of material was accumulated in this way (though not so good as our Mr. Thomas' we think) before Miss Walker and Mrs. White ever met.

Later they met and Miss Walker learned for the first time the degree of correctness of much of the material, which she had relayed to Mrs. White. Needless to say, Mrs. White was more than convinced that her husband was communicating and she wanted the material to be given to the world. Her health was bad and she really wanted to die and go to him, he seemed so real, but she felt an obligation to get this material publishable first. Her husband told her she would come to him only after several years — I forgot how definitely he foretold it — and after she had completed this obligation.

So she and Miss Walker worked on it and it looked as if Mrs. White's health wouldn't last — the latter months she was confined to bed I believe.

And then finally, when Miss Walker had all the essentials for publication, Mrs. White's strength failed and she died. The curious part is that in this story one's sympathy is such that her death is the happy ending. You know they are at last reunited. After a time some messages were received from Mrs. White which contain some evidential material though only moderately striking. But on the whole it is a convincing and touching story, and the material seemingly collected under unassailable conditions.

Sir Oliver Lodge's book, *Survival of Man*, is a pretty good first book to read. Don't be swayed by the popular opinion of Sir Oliver [that he was credulous because he believed that his son, Raymond, killed in World War I, had survived death.] He really is a great man in this, and I think something of a hero. He was not easily--nor only after the death of his son—convinced, but he had been a student of the subject for twenty years before, and had arrived at his conclusion before the war. He goes farther now than we can go, but maybe he has reason to. At least he is no fool, though Conan Doyle approaches that in his naive credulity.

If you cannot get *Survival of Man* and would care to read it, I can send it to you. Also a little book we have of Dr. McDougall's by Sir William Barrett. It is *Psychical Research*, one of the little volumes of "Home University Library of Modern Knowledge," dollar books I think published by Henry Holt and Co., New York. It's a very good beginner's discussion of the field as a whole.

I hope I haven't bored you by all this. An outline of Mr. Thomas' material will come out in the spring I think. I'll send you that of course, though I don't know yet just what it will amount to. Mr. Thomas and we are trying to adjust our difficulties.

Dr. Blomquist [whom Ella too had known at Chicago U.] called me Christmas evening to tell us how he was being married next day and going on a trip. I was so happy over it. He's such a kindly man, but shy, and I think the woman he selected will make him happier than he could have been through all these bachelor years.

We had such a happy little Christmas here. The world seems just right these days. Didn't mean to write such a long letter. Yours are so short, and mine so long, yet you say just as much.

This letter, at the end of 1928 and early in Banks' time at Duke University, shows by reflection his position on the survival question — undecided, because he felt the evidence was not quite conclusive. Even though it was sufficient for Thomas, Sir Oliver Lodge, and others, especially in England, Banks was as wary now of jumping to an attractive affirmative conclusion as he had been in youth when he would not accept an easy answer.

But now, at last, the question was definite. Does the human personality include an element that is not physical and can survive the death of the body? The answer depended, Banks realized afresh, on the possible role of telepathy as a human ability. Is telepathy real, or only another catch-all word, a kind of pacifier for those who are content to dodge the issue?

Also, the Thomas material had to be considered. The aspect of Banks' research dealing with this material was the most engrossing part of his work, as would have been no secret to anyone who knew much about him or why he had come to North Carolina to work under McDougall. It is clearly expressed in a letter he wrote to Thomas on December 4, 1927:

> What a thrilling world is ours (the undersigned, I mean). As a boy I used to mourn the fact that there was no short cut to the Indies to be searched for today, no continents to be discovered, no living Spanish Main. And here I am as much moved to excitement as ever Balboa, Cortez, or Columbus — in the exploration of the Supernormal, to search for hidden Lost Worlds, the conquest of the psychic jungles.
>
> You must allow me this flight of exultation, for we have had three unusual experiences since I last wrote you. First, Mrs. McDougall recited to us her unusual experiences in hauntings that are the most impressive ones of the kind I ever heard or read of. Second, we have witnessed a neat and definite demonstration of telepathy from man to horse. Third, we have read your London material. Joint result is that life is many times more interesting and I am going to be a psychic researcher, as far as possible — the rest of my working days!

Thomas' material, more definitely than any other of the psychic puzzles that had yet come our way, bore on the survival question, which in turn was, broadly, that of the place of the human personality in nature. If the spirit of the human being survives death, then the fact would indicate that the human mind is more than a mechanism like the physical systems, the muscles, the sense organs. In this material that Thomas had received now in the form of records of mediumistic utterances, the obvious although superficial answer seemed to be, yes, the spirit does survive, for in one after another of the records it appeared that Thomas' dead wife had given evidence that she still "lived," was aware of what went on in his life and had been able to send back these communications telling him so.

But the question was, were those communications reliable and did they really come from her? They were based only on mediumistic reports. They were not the result of experiments which could be evaluated statistically and therefore would not depend so largely on personal judgment. The experimental method more and more was becoming the accepted one in science generally.

Early in our undertaking to study this material, Banks tried, none too successfully, to formulate what would constitute persuasive evidence for the spirit hypothesis. He probably hardly realized that the method that had been used on this topic in the past was not an experimental one, and that results of a nonexperimental method cannot be objectively evaluated because individuals can disagree as to the conclusiveness of the evidence.

An adequate resume of the material that Thomas had accumulated can hardly be given in a few paragraphs because it is so voluminous. But to put it as briefly as possible, scattered liberally through the verbatim reports of the words of the many mediums are references to occurrences in the past experiences of the Thomas family, the great majority of which Thomas recognized as true. Also, some of those which he didn't so recognize at first, later inquiry revealed to be true also. Only a quite inconsequential number of items were definitely wrong. All of this, of course, was quite in contrast to the lack of veridicality we had found in the material we ourselves had received from the same medium, Mrs. Soule, in our sittings with her.

At some time after the study of his records began, Thomas wrote a resume of 25 of the best of these individual cases. This report of his, which he wrote in the third person, was published in 1929 by the Boston SPR as a small book under the title, *Case Studies Bearing on Survival*.

In this resume, Thomas reported that he had held 159 seances with Mrs. Soule in Boston and 55 with mediums in London. He had had no idea of making so large a study when he began. But even though he doesn't actually go on and say why he did so, the reason is easy to see. The fact was that in nearly all of the sittings, he was given meaningful material. It was meaningful to him because in spite of all the mediumistic patter, it seemed that his wife, to whom he refers as E.L.T., "came through" and gave testimony which was appropriate and true. In the face of this, no stopping place had occurred, for one interesting session led to another.

As Thomas summarized the situation in this book,

There can be no doubt that these records give a clear and faithful picture of the personality of E.L.T. It makes little difference whether Mr. Thomas is the sitter with Mrs. Soule who knew his name in advance, whether Mr. Thomas or his son J.G.T. was sitting with London mediums who did not even know their names or whether secretaries were conducting experiments along with mediums who did not know for whom the sittings were being held. The same person is being described in each instance and correct traits of mind are given and appropriately emphasized. None of the mediums or secretaries had ever known E.L.T.

In all of this material as given and as I mentioned above, the patter and the actual message are mixed together; but Thomas sorted out these 25 instances and presented each as a unit. Among them is the "Gum Case," mentioned earlier. As he explains, this episode was one that dated back years before to a time when he had been "an addict to the gum-chewing habit and his wife was his severest critic." Her attitude finally led him to discontinue. Then, some twenty years later and after her death, someone offered him a stick of gum. He put it in his pocket. Later he came upon it and unwrapped and chewed it. His daughter-in-law said, "Why Mr. Thomas — you chewing gum?" "Just for fun; someone gave it to me," was his reply. About a month later in a sitting with Mrs. Soule these words, as from E.L.T., were given:

> I have been watching everything that has been going on at home — I want to say something about gum, gum-chewing and someone who has taken to it as a little habit which is not serious, as a kind of joke, for I have seen a piece taken from a vest pocket, unwrapped and put in the mouth with a little smile and someone cried out, "You chewing gum!" — And the answer was, "Just for fun; someone gave it to me," and then there was a general laugh. Gum-chewing is not tolerated in our family, is it? It has been tried before in younger days. Then I took a hand in the matter, but I never expected then to speak of gum after I died, and I feel the joke of it is that I never died.

In many ways that case is typical of most of the others of this 25, which also were detailed, but of only casual content. They were records of items in the daily life of Thomas or some member of his family and were reproduced by the medium with a high degree of accuracy. For instance, another of these episodes concerned a picnic basket which had not been used for the last two years before Mrs. Thomas' death but was stored in the attic of their Detroit home after they built a house on Orchard Lake. As Thomas explains, the basket was made of leather but divided into compartments in which were metal boxes, some for sandwiches, some for utensils. It was a very complete outfit designed for carrying in a car, and Mrs. Thomas always packed the food in it very efficiently.

On Thomas' sitting with Mrs. Soule, April 11, 1927 (and reproducing here only the main points as he gave them), the medium's control said

> Then I see her with something like a little trunk—a little bit of a trunk affair—it isn't a trunk—it's a case of some kind—it's metal—I hear the noise of things dropped in it, and I don't think it's money—it looks like silver—like spoons and forks dropped down. Did you have a picnic trunk, or anything? It seems like that—It's shiny so it looks like metal. I really think it's more—I can see as if it's lined with something inside, not all metal—It's partly a good time. Seems as though everything is arranged by her. She's as good an executive as ever was—She was orderly. This little trunk you can put in the car and take along with you. In the trunk are dishes—I rather think there's food—I can smell coffee—I think there's something else—other drinks.

The record later returns to the picnic theme, as the control continued

> When she comes down to arranging for a picnic or a party, everything is right—nothing forgotten. Somebody says, "Any salt?" "Right here." Everything is right at hand and it's just as orderly and nice as it can be and she enjoys it, to do things.

As Thomas explains, "The completeness of the outfit was one of its unusual features. Coffee was always taken—and cold tea."

Even just these two cases show, aside from the nature of their content, that the messages vary in their form. In the Gum Case the medium purports to reproduce the message from E.L.T. in the first person, "I have been watching everything that has been going on." But in the picnic basket case it was in the third person: "Then I see her." Whether or not such variations had any significance we, of course, had no idea. In the face of the larger meaning, they seemed insignificant and had to be ignored. In the long run, however I think they affected Thomas differently than they did us if they affected us at all, although I think they did have an effect, probably unrecognized then, on us, or on me at least. They raised a doubt about the process, though I hardly recognized it at the time.

Thomas, in his report, then reproduced some comments on the fraud theory made by Banks, perhaps in a letter. They include references to more than the picnic basket case alone. Banks had said

One cannot question the fact that definite knowledge is shown in the statements by the medium. Also, it is knowledge that could not safely be inferred or guessed; the possession of such an object [as the picnic trunk] is not a common or probable occurrence. The question is, could the supposed agent of a medium obtain undiscovered the necessary information given about the trunk? It is conceivable that he could, provided there was such an agent.

But stating it conservatively, this spy would, in order to gain all the information given in his entire sitting, have had to enter Mr. Thomas' town house and make a number of observations, including comparisons with the house as it had been a year before; he would have had to go to Orchard Lake and make similar observations and comparisons, both inside the house and on the outside; he would have had to glean such items as certain friends and relatives of the family and facts about them, what kind of pillow E.L.T. preferred, her outstanding qualities and ways, and a general understanding of the family. Had he successfully bribed the devoted friend of E.L.T., the Swedish woman [who came in to work on Saturdays — to the Thomas family she was genuine beyond question], some of this could have been furnished by her, though not all of it.

Now all this espionage, activity and bribing, if any, as well as the medium's own time and energy must be paid for from the five dollars that Mr. Thomas paid for this sitting. To expect the full sum (i.e., leaving nothing for the medium herself) to recompense the necessarily expert detective-spy for eking out all this detailed information and carefully covering up every track and leaving no trace for suspicion is clearly expecting what is utterly impracticable.

This [the picnic basket case] is in one of the better sittings, it is true, but when the entire series is considered, it shows a mass of knowledge that would require continued surveillance for more than a year and a half; and this for a payment to the eight mediums altogether [in the series under consideration both in Boston and in London] that would be insufficient to hire an expert detective for remuneration of the mediums themselves. Even if we allow them half of the income for themselves, we have left for the total paid for the one hundred eight sittings of that year and a half, at five dollars per sitting, scarcely a month's salary and operating expenses for a second-rate detective.

Banks might have included among the kinds of information the medium had given a number of references made in the course of it to ancestors of Thomas' father, references which went back in time and place beyond Thomas' own recollection or that of any living family member. He knew that long before the family had moved to Detroit and before his own birth, his father's people had lived in Oneida County, New York, and that consequently the only record against which he could now check these names given him would be in old cemeteries in the area in which these ancestors of his might have been buried.

Consequently, in the summer of 1928, after our first year at Duke University, Thomas commissioned us to go to Oneida County, New York, and try to find any old gravestones that might confirm any of this material. Accordingly, that summer we traveled from North Carolina to New York State and visited the old cemetery where Thomas' ancestors were buried. Banks' record of that attempt still remains, although it does not indicate just which of our "discoveries" were "hits"; but some were. And at least the record shows we tried and also that the medium's information must have involved this bit of family history which had all but been forgotten by the Thomas family.

Banks' record reports

> The graves of Richard and Mary Thomas, John and Eleanor Thomas are in Copelucha Cemetery near Remsen. The details on the stones correspond to those on the charts. Other members of the Richard Thomas family are buried there.

Without quoting here the rest of this fragment of our report, one reference helps, in the absence of any dates, to suggest the antiquity of some of these references. This one concerns one Evan P. Thomas, who at one time taught school, according to the memory of one old resident whom we found and interviewed. In his report, Banks characterized her as

> a dear old lady of 71, in Remsen, who said that he [Evan P. Thomas] later took up peddling, gathering rags, etc. and selling tinware and "Yankee notions," spices, etc. She bought dandelion coffee from him during the Civil War, and said "It was good coffee, too."

Even without citing a greater number of cases and facts that Thomas received in these sittings and which he certified as true, the inadequacy of the fraud or espionage theory to explain them seems clear. In the final chapter of his book, Thomas gives his conclusion. He leads up to it by first listing five possible explanations for the material.

These explanations, as Thomas saw them, were: (1) chance, (2) inference, (3) fraud, (4) transcendent properties of the incarnate human mind, in other words, telepathy, and (5) the spiritualistic hypothesis.

The first three can be discarded and need no further mention here, and as he says of the fourth, this material would require

a kind of telepathy that (1) draws from the mind of the sitter when he is at a distance, (2) draws appropriate information from the minds of people who have never been present, (3) draws separate items from the minds of several persons not present and combines the items into a correct whole. There is no experimental evidence for this kind of telepathy.

On the final point, then, Thomas says

My own attitude toward survival is easily inferable throughout the report. To make my position explicit, I am quoting with full agreement a statement made by Dr. Hyslop in the A.S.P.R. *Proceedings* for 1912, as follows:

"Taking the whole history of this problem and the facts recorded in connection with it, I think the evidence of personal identity is sufficient to satisfy any intelligent man who understands the problem. We may have accessory problems to solve like that of impersonation, mistakes and confusion, the influence of the subconscious upon the phenomena, the fragmentary nature of the communications, the ethical relations of the present and the future life, the character of a spiritual world, the intelligibility of the whole process involved in the acquisition of the evidence, but these are purely subsidiary to the main question whether the facts do not require the hypothesis of survival to explain them and we can prosecute our inquiries for the solution of concomitant problems without implying that the whole complex system shall be intelligible before we admit the territory that has been gained. We have perplexities enough still to be removed, but they are not a part of the question of survival. They are only difficulties connected with the process that limits our information, but does not impeach that which we have. We shall make no progress if we do not assume that the main contention is won, at least as a working hypothesis, and then proceed to make similar conquests in the remaining fields of investigation."

Banks, however, could not come to the same conclusion to which Thomas came. He too would have dismissed the first three of the possible explanations, but he was not so certain as Thomas that the fourth could be dismissed, and consequently that No. 5, the spiritualistic hypothesis, could be accepted. Even though Banks felt strongly the weight of the evidence that suggested that fifth explanation, it still was not quite convincing to him. He felt that the answer was either survival *or* telepathy, but this impasse to which the material drove him was not one he could decide; "the transcendent properties of the incarnate human mind," as Thomas put it, could not be ruled out as firmly as Nos. 1, or 2, or 3. At that time Banks had already started a research project on telepathy but it was far from a conclusive stage. Until it was, until telepathy could definitely and conclusively be ruled out as a possibility, he was not at all ready to draw any final conclusion about survival.

And so, as the collaboration between the two continued, Thomas' conviction about survival became complete, but Banks with his researcher's carefulness, was still unwilling, or rather unable, to draw that final conclusion. Thomas' patience, however, began to wear thin. I'm sure he could not fully understand the scientific viewpoint. He felt that the survival question was answered in these messages from E.L.T. Thus it was that, in time, the relationship between Banks and Thomas had to cease. What was "persuasive evidence" for one was not quite that for the other.

By this time, however, Banks like every faculty member would have been expected to have a research topic of his own. The old slogan, "Publish or perish," had real meaning. Advances in salary were obviously influenced by the notice reflected on the university by such publicity. In Banks' case, however, the motivation for his research did not derive from such a cause, but from one deep in or basic to his world outlook.

7

Parapsychology:
A New Science

Survival or telepathy—which was it? Again and again, the question was raised. The basic issue, of course, was survival, the one that more than any other had motivated the pioneers of psychical research and the one which had brought Banks and myself to Duke University. The early psychical researchers had noted human experiences like the apparitions of the dead, which suggested to them the answer to this question.

If such reports were true and their implication reliable, then the dead not only survive, but upon occasion return and communicate with the living. In order for such communication to occur, however, a thought in the mind of the deceased person would have to be transferred to that of the living one without any physical clue. That (hypothetical) process had come to be called telepathy. In the Thomas material the reasoning was that telepathy would have to occur in order to account for all the information the mediums had given, supposedly from Thomas' deceased wife. No simple "reading" of another person's mind would be adequate. It would have to be much broader, much more extensive and complex than that.

McDougall was also very much concerned about the question of telepathy. He had asked in his article, "Psychical Research as a University Study,"

> Does telepathy occur? Do we, as minds, communicate with one another in any manner and degree otherwise than through the sense organs and the bodily organs of expression and the physical media which science recognizes?

By this time for Banks, the first question of all was, does telepathy occur even among living persons? Fortunately, that was a question which was open to direct experimental investigation, as survival itself was not. Even though telepathy had long been a word in common usage and some scattered experiments purporting to confirm its occurrence had been made in the past, the question was far from being reliably answered because the experiments had not been repeated and confirmed sufficiently. It was of first importance then to determine in a conclusive way whether telepathy was an actual mental ability, and if so, when and under what conditions it occurred, as well as how broad was its range and how wide its coverage.

During 1928 and 1929 after the experience with the horse Lady, Banks made a considerable effort to find other animal subjects that might give evidence of telepathy. When this failed, he began a search for good human subjects. In the summer of 1930 he was very encouraged to get a grant of $400 from the University for the purpose of pursuing psychic research. As he wrote Thomas on June 22, 1930, it was "probably the first (grant) on record" given by a university for this subject.

One of the objectives originally proposed for this grant was to make an exhaustive survey of psychical research, "a thorough digest of all important evidence for survival" as Banks wrote Thomas. He added

It would of course, as we know, be a brief for survival because the evidence does unmistakably point that way.... I would avoid taking a stand—simply edit and weigh. Few people living know all the evidence

Soon after, he also wrote to McDougall, who was spending the summer in England, making the same proposal. Banks said he would try to develop a technique for evaluating the material and so help readers "to see the problem squarely, disassociated from religious beliefs and occult practices." The replies from both men must have been encouraging, because he did go ahead with a study of the Thomas material, though I find no record that he ever made this broad survey.

But he did begin a research project, which as he later reported (*Extra-Sensory Perception*) was undertaken because of the need to resolve the conflict in the system of beliefs caused by the phenomena of psychical research. These phenomena, he said, seem to escape well established laws as to man's place in nature, and the solution was not merely an academic one, but one which could lead to a better philosophy for living. The question raised, according to Banks, was, whether there is a human function of extra-sensory perception.

In reports of telepathy it appeared that a person became aware of the thought of another without any outward sign. It was as if he could guess it correctly. The question was whether that could be done to a greater extent than could be accounted for by the laws of probability. Tests to determine whether such significant guessing could occur were in order, and in the summer of 1930, Banks began to give them. As he reported (*Extra-Sensory Perception*),

I began by giving "guessing contests" to some groups of children in summer recreation camps. The tests consisted simply in having each child guess the numeral, zero to nine, which was stamped on a card that I held concealed from him in my hand and looked at.

He made about a thousand such trials, but no one individual stood out sufficiently to seem to warrant further investigation.

However, in the fall of 1930 with the help of his colleague in the psychology department, Dr. K.E. Zener, he tried having students in their classes guess the numerals on cards enclosed in sealed envelopes. Once again, the objective was to see if any student could guess the symbols at a rate high enough to suggest telepathic ability. He also would measure the scores of the group as a whole. Various target materials were tried, such as numerals or letters of the alphabet. Eventually, he asked Zener, who had worked on the psychology of perception, to design a special set of symbols, images that would be easily distinguished and easily remembered. The result was a pack of 25 cards on which were stamped five of each of the five symbols, ○ + ≋ ▢ ☆. This in time became the standard ESP deck. At first, these were called Zener cards, but later at Zener's request, simply ESP cards.

During that first semester in the fall of 1930, Banks gave "guessing tests" to 63 students in over 10,000 trials. The results were slightly higher than chance alone would produce, although not high enough to be conclusive. However, it appeared that if continued long enough even at that low rate of hitting, the tests might eventually be significant of something more than chance.

In order to understand how much significance to assign to these results, Banks early realized the need to evaluate them statistically. At that time this was a much less commonplace procedure than today. As he explained in *Extra-Sensory Perception*, he used the mathematics of probability to evaluate the results. He explained that by adhering to the use of five simple card symbols, he had been able to keep the probability of success at 1/5 for each. The basis of judgment was the numerical evaluation of the difference between the experimental results and that to be expected if chance factors alone were operating. This difference, in order to be considered meaningful or "significant" had to be large enough to yield a value (in statistical terms, a critical ratio or CR of 2.5), which would indicate the likelihood of about 1 in 100 if chance alone were operating. Such an experimental result would then still need confirmation by other workers to establish that the point in question was a reliable finding. Lower CR's, a 2.00 for instance, could be considered as suggestive, but not significant: encouraging, but needing more work and a higher CR before it would be considered reliable.

As already suggested, Banks' classes offered a ready-made opportunity for such tests. In the history of science which he then was officially teaching, he had introduced the puzzle of telepathy, and I have little doubt that he made it a live issue to the students, since it was for him such an interesting unknown.

Some of the most striking of the early reports of telepathy from other parts of the world had come from France, where subjects under hypnosis had apparently shown knowledge of the thoughts of other persons at a distance and of which, of course, those subjects had no sensory information. Banks wanted to replicate this work and fortunately, Dr. Helge Lundholm, one of the new men in the psychology department, was an expert hypnotist. Banks soon interested him in the question of whether, under hypnosis, any of the students could give evidence of telepathy. Hypnosis then was still a novelty and the general attitude toward it was tinged with suspicion. So it was necessary for Banks to proceed with caution if he should use it on his students; and, of course, he would first have to learn to use it himself. He and Lundholm were soon collaborating and managing to do so quietly enough to arouse no adverse reactions from the university administration. They meant to select only students who were willing and eager volunteers; as it turned out, most of them wanted the experience of being hypnotized, whether or not they succeeded in the telepathy tests.

Before long it was apparent that inducing an hypnotic trance in each subject before testing was quite time-consuming. Some individuals fell into the state more quickly than others, and in some it could not be induced at all. Also, soon Lundholm could no longer give time to the telepathy research, although by then Banks had learned the technique himself.

In his learning to use hypnosis, incidentally, Banks and I both thought it would be interesting to try the technique on me, but either I was a no-good subject or our relationship was too close. We tried again when I was pregnant and the use of hypnosis in childbirth was being advocated. Again, the effort failed. We thought it might be necessary to try again and again before I could fall into a real hypnotic state, and we planned to try at least every week. But it was then about the seventh month of my pregnancy and nature thwarted the plan. The baby did not wait until I learned my part; she was born safely, but prematurely, before the next hypnotic session.

Banks' hypnotization efforts with his students were more successful than with me, and continued in the 1930 summer session. The work that summer included 12,000 telepathy trials with about 75 hypnotized subjects. Again, the results on the average were slightly higher than chance alone should have given, and so were encouraging, although far from decisive. By then it appeared that results without hypnosis were just as good as those with hypnosis, so it was abandoned.

All the telepathy tests in Banks' classes were only suggestive as a whole; out of that group one subject, a college sophomore, did emerge as an unusually high scorer. As Banks himself reported in *New Frontiers of the Mind*, almost by accident they discovered Adam Linzmayer, whose scores averaged about three correct out of five, especially when in a light hypnosis. One day, Linzmayer called correctly nine ESP cards in succession with Banks holding the cards out of his vision. Elated, Banks tested him again and the score was repeated. It was then the end of the school year and Linzmayer was about to leave for vacation, but Banks induced him to stay a little longer for further tests. By the time he left he had guessed 1,500 cards with 405 correct, where only 300 would be expected by chance.

I was almost as excited about Linzmayer's high scores as Banks was, for knowing his deep interest, I realized how much this encouragement meant to him. My satisfaction was not from any idea that he would get any scientific notice from the study; I was pretty pessimistic about that. Banks, however, was less so than I; he thought the world might change in a few decades, at least enough to admit these topics as worthy of serious investigation. But I thought it would take a hundred years. We had a big argument about this, in fact. In it he commented on my tendency to be a "wet blanket," which I realized that I did tend to be. (I'm not certain yet, however, which of us was right about the length of time it will take for the results of parapsychological investigations to receive full scientific recognition.)

As I told my diary then, I didn't care so much how the world took it. Two other considerations were paramount for me; one was that Banks should have a chance to pursue his most fundamental interest; the other was that in our lifetimes we should go a little way on the road toward satisfying our own intellectual curiosity. He and I both wanted to know what kind of a world this is we live in, even if no one else was interested. And so I began to get a pretty deep inward satisfaction when Banks began repeatedly to bring home reports of high scoring in telepathy tests from this one student, Adam Linzmayer.

Quite incidentally, I recall that since this question about telepathy was a real one to me, too, I thought that if it is an actuality, then two persons as close as Banks and I should offer fertile ground for its occurrence. Yet we had never noticed a spontaneous instance of it. I could "telepath" him to bring a forgotten grocery item home for lunch — no grocery item. And he could "telepath" me that unexpectedly he was bringing a guest along for dinner, and it would be the very time when all I had prepared was leftovers. And so, if telepathy was real, we apparently were not providing proper conditions for it. In an attempt to do better on such a test, I tried a different approach.

Banks liked pancakes with syrup for breakfast, but I only prepared them occasionally. When this bright idea about testing telepathy occurred to me, I recalled that we had not had pancakes recently, so why not "telepath" him to ask for them? To make the test bona fide, I wrote my intention on a flyleaf of my diary, and said that I was going to have in mind all evening that he should ask for pancakes for breakfast, and as he was falling asleep — which he always did more quickly than I — I would "send" the thought most forcefully, and also I would reinforce it if I awoke in the night, "Ask for pancakes for breakfast." The sequel is recorded in the diary too. "Banks apparently never thought of pancakes." And this, of course, did nothing for my wavering belief in the reality of telepathy.

The telepathy tests with the students continued to yield encouraging results, however, despite my own lack of personal evidence. Banks continued to get good results from Adam Linzmayer, and before long there were a few lab assistants to help him with the testing. Two of them, promising young psychology graduate students, initially had been subjects in the telepathy tests in Banks' and Zener's psychology classes. They were Gaither Pratt, who had transferred to the psychology department from the divinity school, and Charles Stuart, who had transferred from philosophy and mathematics. In fact, Stuart had become interested in the idea of telepathy because of successful results on tests he had made on himself.

One of the intriguing questions to Banks about these positive results after a while was just what was really being tested in experiments in which a card bearing a symbol was used as the target of the subject's guesses? Were these necessarily telepathy tests? As he says in *Extra-Sensory Perception,*

> These experiments illustrate the dangers of following experimentally one hypothesis without full recognition of other possible hypotheses — perhaps the greatest danger point in all human thought. The early experiments grew out of the need to test for what appeared to be non-sensory transference of thought from mind to mind. This was early given the name "telepathy" by Frederick Myers ... and experiments were framed so as to exclude sensory and rational cognition, but not any possible parapsychic cognition.

As he explained, all such tests, including his own earlier ones, failed to exclude clairvoyance, for invariably the experimenter in selecting a target symbol to send used a symbol-bearing card, a physical object on which to concentrate as the target for the subject to guess. Therefore, the source of the hits might not be the experimenter's thought, but rather the symbol on the actual card. If so, the test would exemplify clairvoyance rather than telepathy. The distinction between the two conditions was described at that time simply as that in the telepathic condition the experimenter knew the symbol on the target card, while in the clairvoyant condition he did not. The earlier work, Banks' own and that conducted elsewhere, had not distinguished between these two types of ESP. Even if general ESP (GESP) had been shown, Banks now realized that it was not necessarily telepathic. The information secured might have come from the card and not from the experimenter's mind. In the testing carried on subsequently by various student assistants, the distinction necessary between clairvoyant and telepathic conditions was recognized and maintained. Results of about the same level of significance were then found in each condition.

The average level of scoring in class experiments of either type, however, continued to be only slightly better than that expected from chance alone, so that attention came to be centered increasingly on the occasional individual, like Linzmayer, whose scores were markedly higher than the average. Before long, eight such good subjects were found, and the research continued with them predominantly. Within the next few years, two of these subjects stood out especially, Linzmayer and then Hubert Pearce. Their individual scores when totalled were statistically very significant.

In 1934 Banks published his first report of this research in the monograph, *Extra-Sensory Perception*, already referred to, and he could say in this report that extra-sensory perception had been established both as clairvoyance and as telepathy; results had been significantly high under both conditions and at about the same level of scoring. Also, similar fluctuations appeared under both conditions. For instance, the effect of drugs like the depressant sodium amytal and the stimulant caffeine was the same in tests under both clairvoyant and telepathic conditions. Results were also obtained under both conditions with varying distances between the subject and the target. In fact, the distance as such seemed to be immaterial.

All of these similarities, Banks thought, suggested that a common process might underlie both telepathy and clairvoyance, and that the difference was only in the kind of target. Yet on account of the obvious physical difference between thoughts and things, it was difficult to conceive of any common method or process by which such perception could occur. Since the distance between subject and target did not seem to affect the ease of reception in either type, obviously a wave theory, as in sight or hearing, did not apply. Besides that, no sense organ seemed to be involved. But the evidence did suggest that the process was at least subject to a measure of voluntary control. As Banks said in the 1934 monograph, it "integrates naturally with the other cognitive and with the affective processes of the percipient's [subject's] mind."

And so these hundreds of experiments did not solve the dilemma of survival versus telepathy as they might have done if no evidence for telepathy had been found. Instead, if anything, they accentuated the problem by showing that information which might be received need not necessarily have its source in another person's mind but could be in an inanimate object, and so be clairvoyant rather than telepathic. This made even more complicated the interpretation of mediumistic material, such as Mr. Thomas', and added more difficulties to the survival hypothesis.

But this research raised a further question. As Banks asked in an article in the *Journal of Parapsychology*,

If distance in space is not a limiting condition in ESP tests, what about remoteness in time? In this space-time world wherein any measurable objective event is necessarily both spatial and temporal at once, if anything could escape space it could be expected to be free from time as well. If an ESP subject can in some way transcend spatial barriers might he not be able likewise to transcend temporal limits? [1937, vol. 1, p. 183, "The Effect of Distance in ESP Tests."]

Certainly the temporal as well as the spatial dimension would have to be studied before any research on the question of survival could begin. Research on the effect of time in ESP tests was then undertaken, as is reported in the following chapter.

But now these experimental results that seemed to suggest telepathy raised the same old question in my mind. I continued to wonder why, if telepathy is a real ability, we saw no sign of it in our private lives. Repeatedly, I raised the question with Banks, which no doubt he too was asking himself.

His answer was that the conditions must be right. He knew that many of the tests that he and his colleagues, Lundholm and Zener, made with students did yield evidence of ESP, but he also knew that many of the subjects scored only at the expected chance level. Subjects like Linzmayer whose results were higher when averaged in with these others raised the average a little above that to be expected by chance alone. Apparently, then, the conditions were just not right for many of the students too.

Of course, a sensory ability such as vision that seems to operate every time one opens his eyes also does so only when the conditions are right. But in sight, the main and most obvious condition necessary is light, which is present so generally that one scarcely thinks of it. And in addition, individuals differ in their visual ability because of anatomical and physiological differences. In the ESP situation, on the other hand, no one yet knew what all of the necessary conditions were. The challenge, accordingly, was to study the ability under a wide variety of conditions and find out.

Apparently, for the class tests with only slightly positive results, the conditions necessary for telepathy to occur were, in the main, just barely sufficient or proper. For the special subjects, it appeared as if, either their ability was naturally greater than that of the average subject, or else they were less inhibited by adverse conditions. At any rate, it seemed clear telepathy was easily affected by external conditions.

And so, when I continued to wonder why we never saw any evidence of telepathy in our daily lives at home, Banks could say that apparently the conditions were not right, or that it did occur and we just did not notice it. Obviously, if the world could exist until the twentieth century and still not generally have recognized ESP, it must be a very subtle process; it must be so subtle that the very application of careful scientific ways of "making sure" tended to obscure it. Not that it had never been suspected; it had been. But more and more, that suspicion had been "educated out of" the culture, so probably any evidence of it had come to be suspect, "old wives'" tales, imagination, superstition. If ESP occurred in families like ours, it was not in a very clear-cut or obvious way.

These talks made me more sensitive to home situations, however, and after several "coincidences" that I wondered about and then forgot, I decided to keep a record of any future ones that might occur. It would not be that I was expecting to say they were evidence of telepathy, but at least I would have something to consider. The following are a few from the list I eventually accumulated over the next four years.

Early 1936, Nation Avenue, Durham, N.C. — Betsy (about 3 years old) had been ill in the night and was not sleeping well. I had been up with her but had gone back to bed. She was in her room beyond the little connecting hall. I dreamed that some terrifying black shape was coming down the road. It was night and I dreamed that I had to put the milk bottles on the porch. I was afraid I couldn't get them out in time, but I did and rushed back in and slammed the door just as the "thing" — I couldn't tell if it was human or animal, came upon the porch. In my dream I was cowering in terror just inside the front door when a cry from Betsy awoke me. I got up and went over to her, noticing that I was really damp with perspiration from the fright I had just had. I said, "What's the matter, Betsy? Why did you cry?" "What 'kared me, Mother?" she asked me. She was evidently badly scared, but had no idea why. Only a short time had elapsed since she had been awake before, so I don't suppose she had been soundly asleep yet when I had my dream. Was my mental state somehow communicated to her?

1936 — I had driven in and out of (unpaved and muddy) Vineyard Street at dark a lot of times without ever thinking anything about the difficulty one might have there if it were necessary to pass another vehicle.

Then driving out one evening, and just as I turned onto Vineyard I suddenly thought, "I'm going to meet someone on this narrow stretch ahead and what will I do?" It was just light enough still to see the length and no other car was on the road. But I felt perfectly certain I'd have to pass someone. When I got halfway and still no car, a curious feeling came —

"I'm going to pass someone, but how can I when there is no one?" I was trying to feel relieved in spite of my certainty when I began the ascent of the little rise near the end of Vineyard and the junction with Chapel Hill Road. Just then, a huge covered van approached on Chapel Hill Road and I thought, "I know it's going to turn in." But my common sense said, "No. Nothing like that would be coming down this small sidestreet." But I knew it would and it did. It turned in just as I was nearly at the end of Vineyard and I all but went into the slippery ditch to miss it, as I turned onto the highway.

I started to tell the experience, which really was rather vivid, to Banks that night and as I began, before he knew more of the story than that it had to do with the difficulty of passing on Vineyard, he said, "Just wait. Let me tell you something first. I drove out there about half an hour ahead of you tonight and as I did so I was suddenly and for the first time worried as I thought, 'What would Louie do if she had to pass a car here?' But I thought surely she'd have sense enough to back up and not try to pass." (I couldn't have backed — it was too dark and too much on the slippery hill to have made that possible.)

January 17, 1938, Club Boulevard, Durham, North Carolina — After supper this evening the children listened quietly to some records for awhile, then went up to bed. We discussed which story I should read and I urged Betsy to hurry up and get into her pajamas. No other subjects, and no toy of any kind had been mentioned specifically all day for I was very busy having my book club and did not talk much to the little ones. While Betsy was undressing I opened my small dresser drawer looking for a safety pin and noticed the little whistle Robbie bought Betsy for Christmas. It was under some ties in the drawer. I covered it up again thinking, "Oh, there's Betsy's whistle. But I won't mention it to her. I don't want it being blown in the house." Betsy was standing about a yard and a half behind me undressing. She said just after my thought, "Mother, where is my whistle that Robbie bought me?"

Yesterday morning when I went to town she asked me to buy her a whistle for she had lost the one Robbie gave her. I told her she hadn't lost it, that I had put it away. To my knowledge it had not been mentioned since.

Yesterday forenoon I suddenly thought, "I wonder why Banks doesn't bring Don Adams home to lunch sometime?" I had never thought of it before, because though Naomi (Don's wife) had been teaching all year, somehow, not being in the habit of thinking of him as free at lunch time,

I had not thought of it that this year he would be. At noon when Banks came he said, "I almost brought Don along home today."

May 16, 1939 — This morning Betsy saw a picture in the *New York Times* which she asked about. I explained it was of a theatre.

"What's a theatre?" (I explained.) "Why can't I ever go to a moving picture show?"

Just then I glanced at a piece of bread to eat with the cup of coffee I was drinking. But I thought, "No, I won't take it. I'm getting too fat," though I said nothing. Just then Betsy looked up as if I had spoken aloud and said, "Mama, you're fatter now than you've ever been before." "Why, Betsy, what makes you say that? I'm real mad at you." "Well, you never do take me," she said, reverting to the conversation about the movie as if she was unconscious of her interspersed remark about me.

July 22, 1939 — This evening we were driving through the country which is lush and green. When going by a corn field I thought, "One can almost smell that corn it looks so green and fresh." Betsy beside me said, "Mama, I can smell that corn." Could I smell the corn? No, I didn't really, though maybe if I had been on the side of the car where the field was I could have. Betsy was, but I doubt if she knows anything about the smell of corn. However, if she does, it was a coincidence that she mentioned it just as I thought of it. It's curious that just this one child of the four has these "coincidences" with me. I am on the alert for them with all or with anybody I'm sure, but it's mainly Betsy — and Banks a few times — with whom I have them.

September 23, 1939 — Betsy crawled into bed beside me this morning and as we lay there I thought of her music and wondered to myself how soon Mrs. Wilson (the music teacher) would call me to say which days she wants Betsy to stop after school for her music lesson. I also thought that I'd better get Betsy to practice over her last lesson or two (she's had about a month of vacation while Mrs. Wilson was away). But nothing was said about any of it and after a short pause I said, "Now I must get up and go over to get Jan and Joy." The twins were to play here this forenoon. But Betsy said, disregarding my spoken remark but seemingly answering my unspoken thought of a moment or two earlier, "Well, Mama, you'll have to tell me which days she wants me to stop or I won't know when to do it." I thought it was interesting that while her remark fitted my thought so well, yet she gave hers no ostensible introduction but referred to Mrs. Wilson as "she" just as if we had been talking about her.

June 18, 1940 — It has been quite awhile since Betsy has said anything which seemed to tie up closely with my thought, but several times Rosemary said something which suggested it. Usually, however, it was such that I noticed it only because of the timing. In each case there was too much possibility of it being only the result of similar lines of thought between her and me to make the incident worthy of record. However, the fact that she said what she did so exactly when it was apropos of my thought suggested the possibility that she could be getting it by telepathy and it was worth watching.

And here are two seemingly good cases in two days.

The first was yesterday when we were driving home from a weekend at Harker's Island. I fell to thinking of a bad scare I had had while there, when Sally (about 10) and Mariella Waite, running on ahead of me as I went with them to the beach, were by the time I got there floating on inner tubes on the Sound. I thought they were too far out. Robbie (about 12) started with them but he soon was coming back to the shore. I was there at the beach with the smaller children by that time and I called to him to tell the girls to come in. "Oh, they can't," he said, "they're in the current and they're drifting." He didn't seem to realize any danger in the situation but of course I did, especially when I tried to swim out to them and found how impossible it would be for me to rescue them at that distance being no more of a swimmer than I am. Then I began to shout for help and eventually two fishermen up the beach a ways in a little motor boat went out and picked the two girls up and brought them in. I had had a pretty severe fright although no one else had so much of one, not even Sally or Mariella I guess, though of course it affected Betsy and Rosemary strongly for they knew my reaction. Rosemary and one of the little group of passing fishermen's children had run up the beach to call the fishermen who were visible but almost beyond the range of my shouts as I waded back to land.

All this happened in the forenoon. In the afternoon we started back to Durham. During the first hour or more of the trip the fright of the morning was not in my mind, but after a time I began to think of it again and the mental image of those two little heads and the rubber tubes bobbing off so far in the distance was very vivid. Banks was driving. I was in the back seat with Betsy and Rosie on either side of me but none of us had mentioned the morning's occurrence, when just as that picture returned to my mind, Rosie said, "Robbie was braver than Sally and Mariella wasn't he, Mama, because he came back when he got so far out and they didn't."

Though I knew that she didn't understand the situation, I was surprised to have her pick up the subject of my thought at exactly the same time. I mean that though I had then been thinking of the occurrence for some little time, Rosie got on to the same theme within the same time interval.

The next case occurred tonight when we took Rosie to see some dancers, her first entertainment at Page Auditorium. Rosie sat next to me. During the first number but when it was well along I suddenly got a view of the dancer's face that made me think, "Why that could be a rather masculine type of woman," though at first I had thought it was a man. I hadn't noticed the program very carefully as Betsy insisted on holding it before the performance began. After beginning to wonder about the sex of the performer, I watched carefully to see if I could be sure, but I couldn't decide, and then Rosie whispered, "Mama, is that a boy or a girl?" I wasn't surprised that she should wonder but that she should only do it after I had, and so long after the dancer first appeared seemed to suggest that my doubt was carried over to her mind somehow. I asked Banks at the end of the act whether he or Betsy had wondered, but they hadn't because they had noticed the program and knew it was a man.

November 7, 1940 – I was combing Rosie's hair this morning. It was late for I had not felt good and so had lain down and taken a nap beside her after all the others had gone. When I awoke it was 10:30 so we hurried down stairs with no conversation except about breakfast and how she wanted her hair combed. We hadn't been talking for several minutes and I thought that I could very conveniently take her over to play with Caroleigh since I was going out that direction to a club meeting. The only question was would she want to go. She hadn't of late. I thought for a moment about Caroleigh's parents when Rosie interrupted my thoughts with, "I'm never going to Caroleigh's anymore. She said I wasn't nice to her the last time I was there. But I *was* nice to her."

April 1, 1941 – I was sitting here sewing this afternoon when Betsy came in putting on her things to go out. She danced about a bit and I noticed how shapely and graceful she was and thought to myself how nice she looked and mused a bit about the beauty of all young healthy creatures. And then I thought how tall she was and how rapidly she is growing up. Aloud I said, and that's all that I said, "Betsy next year you'll be in the fourth grade already." She didn't answer directly. She was sitting on the floor putting on her galoshes and she was sing-songing to herself, "Pretty, pretty, I'm going to be pretty when I grow up" – then as if conscious that that didn't sound very modest she said in a matter-of-fact voice, "But I'm ugly now."

June 1, 1941 — Rosie and I were listening to a radio program, neither speaking for some time. I was knitting and getting to the heel of the sock and I thought, "I must get Mrs. McDougall to show me how to make this heel." Then I wondered when she'd have time and fell to thinking of her a little. The radio program (which had been music, not a story which might have engrossed Rosie's mind) came to an end and Rosie said, "Mama, what made Mr. McDougall die?" (in 1938). I'm sure the Mc-Dougalls hadn't been mentioned by any of us for days.

August 25, 1941, Lake Junaluska, N.C. — When we first came up here in June, the woman who rented us this house apparently on second thought changed her mind and wanted to keep us from occupying it. The children knew about the trouble and knew that one of the reasons she gave was that she didn't want children in her house. That seemed to be an incomprehensible idea to them and they discussed it a lot for awhile. However, now, so long after the whole difficulty came up and was settled amicably, it has not been referred to for quite some time.

Yesterday morning I was combing Rosie's hair. We hadn't been talking much about anything beyond the details of the moment. Before that it had been breakfast with no reference to extraneous matters. I ran over in my mind my morning schedule — get vegetables from garden, prepare things for supper, and if possible begin packing up some nonessentials (we're going back to Durham in a week). Then my thought ran over the house in general in a sort of bird's eye glimpse, and I thought of how it looked when we came and that in turn made me think fleetingly of the way it would probably look to the landlady when she came in after we left. Just then Rosie said, "Why doesn't she like children?" Surprised, I said, "What made you think of her all of a sudden?" She said, "Oh, I just thought of how her furniture looks all around here." I didn't notice until afterwards how we both knew with no name mentioned the person to whom Rosie was referring.

September 27, 1941 — There is a question about Rosie's placement in school. With a little coaching, she may be able to get transferred to the second grade. Consequently, I have been giving her a little writing, reading or spelling lesson before she goes to bed.

Tonight she was lolling on my bed while I was in the next room for a minute. While there, I asked myself (mentally only, of course) what I should have her do this evening. I guess she'd better write, I thought. But I haven't been certain what kind of writing is expected, printing or capitals, little letters, or script. Then I thought I might have her spell words as I pronounce them and write them *all three ways*. As I thought that I started for the room where she was waiting for me, but just as I entered I decided, "No, that won't be necessary since I know they don't want her to write script. No use making it hard for her." Then, aloud I said, "I'm going to tell you words to spell, Rosie, and you can write them down in printing letters." She said, "No, I want to do them *all three ways*."

It wasn't until sometime later that I happened to think how unusual it was for her to think of doing her writing *all three ways* just after I had thought of it. As far as I can recall, I never have thought of doing it all three ways anytime before and I know she never had done so nor mentioned it, so the phrase *all three ways* which I had thought the minute before just outside the door of the room she was in, she used so much as a matter of course that at the time I didn't even notice the unusual timing of it.

April 18, 1945 — For some time we've been in need of new drinking glasses, the summer's supply having mostly been broken long since. But transportation being what it is, each time I've been to town I've had my hands too full to load up with glasses. However, a few days ago I found myself in Woolworth's with no load, so I bought some glasses and we used them for supper that evening. When Sally saw the one at her place she cried out excitedly, "Mother! Where did you get that glass? It's just like the one I dreamed about last night. You know the other day I had to give one of the girls who was here to see me a drink out of an old nicked glass and I felt ashamed of it. So last night I dreamed I was giving someone a drink out of a good glass that I was proud of, and it was just exactly like this one." We had not had any just like these before. Sally was so struck by the fact that it was just like the one in her dream that she kept remarking and exclaiming about it for some time. Banks and I thought it was quite unusual for her to be so excited about so trivial a thing.

May 16, 1945 — I was putting up the strings for my bean rows down in the back lot just behind the Tilley's garage. Rosie came down to help me. We were working on different rows, not talking. We had worked for some little time — long enough that I had finished one ball of string and was half through the second.

Vaguely for some time I had been noticing an odor but it was not strong enough that I really thought about it. At last, however, it got to the front of my mind and I thought, "What is this that I smell?" but I didn't say anything. Then I realized it was the Tilley's chicken house. Just as I did, timed like a response, Rosie called over, "Mother, the Tilley's chickens surely smell nice, don't they?" With a wry note on the "nice."

December 6, 1945 — Last night Banks and I were reading in bed, or rather he was still reading but I had turned over to go to sleep, when somehow I found myself thinking of a childhood occurrence so trivial and so long past [and thus so unusual for me to remember] that I considered interrupting Banks' reading to tell him about it. But I've always thought that he's not particularly interested in reminiscences, and he was deeply interested in his book "Looking Eastward," so I didn't speak of it.

I fell to remembering the Christmas cards that Esther (my sister) and I got at school the first winter we went to the little country school "No. 8," at Marshallville, Ohio. The teacher was Irvin Beery and I thought of him a little because as a child I thought he liked me better than Esther and yet the card she got was prettier than mine. I remembered both cards rather vividly, how hers had green pine boughs pictured on the white paper and inside the words of "Hark, the Herald Angels Sing." But mine only had a picture in brown and I don't even remember the song. I commented to myself how trivial things can be important to children. Those cards, however, probably were the only fancy cards we children had ever seen. So no wonder they left an impression. And Irvin Beery gave them to us. This morning, alone here I got to thinking of them again. Banks had gone or I certainly would have told him about the oddity of those childhood, and long-unthought-of memories suddenly confronting me so vividly.

In the morning mail I got a letter from Ruth (my sister back home in Ohio) enclosing an obituary of Irvin Beery. I had seen and talked to him last spring at the cemetery at the time of my father's funeral. He was lots older than I remembered him, of course, but he looked vigorous. And someone whispered that he was looking for another wife. I hadn't heard of or I guess thought of him since.

Did all those "coincidences" — or any of them — extending over some eleven years of family life, represent ESP, either telepathy or clairvoyance or a mixture of both? In view of all now known in the field of parapsychology because of experimental research, certainly some of these incidents raise the question, although none of them *need* be so interpreted.

It was beginning to seem to Banks more and more, however, that the ESP results could not help to settle the survival question, any more than the mediumistic accounts like those in the Thomas material could. Family experiences like these suggested an extra-sensory method of getting information but they did not prove it or give an explanation of the way it could happen. But their occurrence certainly quite clearly indicated the need for our answer.

8

Precognition

As the preceding chapter shows, the original impetus that led to the experimental demonstration of ESP dated back to the widespread interest in the survival question. But, as so often happens in scientific advances, the answering of one question raises many others, and that was what happened here. One of the first of these was, as already mentioned, if ESP does occur, what is the effect on it of distance? Does it, like hearing and vision, decrease with distance?

Already, in some of the reports from the London SPR the suggestion

171

was that "distance is not inhibitory to thought transference." But this impression had not been tested experimentally. In Banks' reports on the early Duke laboratory work in the *Journal of Parapsychology*, he said in effect that although not yet conclusive, "the evidence that distance does not influence telepathy is nevertheless considerable." This restrained statement is followed by a summary of the possible ways in which the distance tests might have been inadequate.

I well remember how Banks submitted these test data to several physicists before he reported in the above article that physicists

> appear to agree that nothing known at present is applicable to the results of the ESP tests. Some of them maintain, however, that the phenomena should not hastily be relegated to the realm of the extra-physical, since physics may expand and since there must be some physical basis for a perception of an object. This apparently reasonable position is doubtless where the problem must be left until further results throw better light on the ESP process. Finding no mechanical explanation (as mechanics is today) need not necessarily exclude a physical explanation by a physics that may yet develop.

How long is it necessary to wait, one might well ask here. Today, some 45 years later, a science of physics that will cover this situation has not yet been reported, and the final sentence of his report is still applicable: "In fact, it would appear that no falling off whatever [of telepathic transmission] occurs directly with spatial separation."

The article on distance and ESP, as the summary states, "was made to preface a series of reports on research on the problem of precognition or previsionary ESP." The problem of precognition or previsionary ESP! Just as the question of whether telepathy occurs was raised by interest in the question of survival, the question concerning distance and ESP was preliminary to and logically related to that of precognition. As Banks commented, "In a space-time world a phenomenon escaping space limitation presumably would be time-free."

But is it? Is ESP free from time limitations just as it has been shown to be free from those of space? As Banks said, "The hypothesis that ESP may be unlimited by temporal conditions thus arises inferentially out of the research already reported." But that hypothesis had not been tested empirically, and in science actual experimental results must take a more final place than logical ones. Logical considerations, however, must guide the framing of the experimental procedure and they also dictate that the relation of ESP to time should be subjected to experimental test.

While at first it seemed that this question might be easy to answer by simply comparing subjects' responses obtained at varying time lapses from the target symbols, again an unforeseen complication arose. This was the result of another line of investigation that Banks was carrying on. Also this research (discussed further in Chapter 12) was on the question of psychokinesis, or PK, a suspected ability of the mind to produce physical effects without the use of physical means. As had been ESP itself, PK was suggested by earlier mediumistic and seance room reports. But now it appeared that the possibility of PK might affect the validity of a precognition test, which depended upon the experimenter's using a perfectly random list of targets, one in no way affected by the experimenter's mind. Now, possible PK by the experimenter in arriving at a random number had to be ruled out in order to test for precognition. In other words, the possibility had to be eliminated that the target list, which the experimenter secured by shuffling a deck of cards, might inadvertently be affected by his PK ability, even though he might have no conscious intention to so affect the cards. Farfetched as this seemed, it was a logical deduction from the PK data.

Again, a detour from the direct path of testing for precognition was necessary to check this out and to determine whether it was a real possibility. Further tests showed that it was; experimenters who knew the target list and who then shuffled the cards in order to try purposefully to match that list could do so to a slight degree. A "psychic shuffle," as it was termed, appeared to be possible and as such it became a real and well-recognized stumbling block in the research, a stumbling block to the easy methodological use of card shuffling as a way of preparing random target lists.

A long series of attempts to find a safer and more dependable random list of ESP targets followed. As Banks said in 1957 (*Parapsychology*), "The experimental study of precognition has gone on for more than twenty years and it is still an active field of inquiry." One new technique after another for arriving at a perfectly randomly arranged deck of target cards was tried. For a while each one seemed satisfactory and then it was discarded for one that seemed safer. Eventually, the basic method used was that of finding a number at which the shuffled 25 card ESP deck should be cut. At one stage a number derived from the official forecast for a given day was considered a safe basis to use in cutting the deck. But before long even the remote possibility that the experimenter could unconsciously influence the weather report (a PK effect) caused it to be jettisoned, and the attempt to find a perfectly random number for the cut went on.

A final method was at last agreed upon by all concerned. It was one that could only be arrived at by an intricate mathematical formula which was considered to be impossible for the unaided human mind to carry out. The final step in it had to be taken by an electrical computing machine.

Even that, however, it came to be suspected, could not be certified to escape the PK effect, for which no theoretical bounds had then (or yet) been found. In the report of this made in 1957, Banks could only say

> Certainly for those who consider that the experimental work was only needed to confirm the rational expectation [that if ESP escaped the restrictions of distance, it should escape those of time as well] the demand for verification had already been met.

Only a very careful experimenter would at this stage feel compelled to carry the argument to its utter theoretical limit. But Banks knew that on a topic as controversial as this, as he says,

> Data of a higher order of significance than are ordinarily required may reasonably be desired for a conclusion that will have such revolutionary consequences as the establishment of precognition.

Testing for precognition continued, however, using that formula, so that by the time a general report was published in the *Journal of Parapsychology*, four years later, the summarized research included the work of eleven different investigators (Banks and assistants) with 49 subjects who in 4,523 runs of 25 cards each obtained a total score of 614 hits above mean chance expectation. This total was so great that it would not be expected by chance in 400,000 such experiments.

With odds so great and because sensory cues were ruled out (since the response column was made before the target list was obtained), Banks felt that precognition was the most likely explanation for the positive results. In his report of this research, however, his approach was considerably more restrained than it had been in reporting his earlier work. In that, he had discussed the results with unrepressed eagerness as research on an interesting and important problem. There he had reported his successful experiments without any inhibition except, as he said, that of "making sure ten times over" that they were reliable. After two years of such "making sure," he had then said, "It seems entirely safe to publish these experiments." He added, however, "It is to be expected, I suppose, that these experiments will meet with a considerable measure of incredulity and perhaps, even hostility." But now that kind of reaction, he thought, would be less strong than it would have been earlier. He thought popular articles like the study of telepathy recently reported by Mr. Upton Sinclair, in which Sinclair's wife was the sensitive, would have something of a preparatory effect. As a result, Banks now said optimistically, "There is today much more natural inquiry ... and less of the older blind intolerant credulity ... for or against."

The article reporting these new results on precognition appeared in the newly founded *Journal of Parapsychology*. In an editorial introducing it, Banks wrote

> The time has come to release the first of a series of articles dealing with a more radical outgrowth of the ESP research, namely, with the question whether ESP is limited by time, whether the process of extra-sensory perception can be directed forward into the future (i.e., can precognize events) — as apparently it can function outward into space....
>
> Although we regard the report of the preliminary studies ... as a very tentative and far from exciting one, the importance of the question makes the venture of publishing seem somewhat bold. Possibly it may be regarded as rashly inviting incredulity upon a field of research only just emerging from the shadow of the gruelling criticism incident to its first impact on a psychological world unprepared with theory for its explanation and acceptance. The situation therefore warrants a word of clarification on the conditions of this step.
>
> The new line of investigation is reported in a somewhat altered spirit — one born perhaps of reaction to the unduly subjective and affective attitudes prevailing among the most outspoken critics. This new spirit is one not so much of impatience as of a desire for less waste of effort in useless argument. [After all of the argument following the publication of the first results, little time had been left for productive research.] It might be thus expressed, "Here is what *we* find." ... [A]nd finally, "The truth must come ultimately from the laboratories, not from public disputation. In brief, less speculation, more experiment."

Banks then added, with again a show of optimism,

> The present barrage of hastily composed critiques running through the journals is not, as far as we can judge, representative of the leadership in psychological thought today. This leadership (happily for all new developments) is a more careful and tolerant one.

For two reasons, as it happened, this optimism was not actually tested then in a thoroughgoing way. One was that since the article appeared in the new *Journal of Parapsychology*, which to psychologists in general was unknown and unread, it was practically ignored by the psychological world. The other reason was that because of the unsettled world situation, with World War II looming just ahead, academic questions like this one quite naturally dropped into near oblivion.

Actually, before the work on precognition was even published, Banks had heard from a number of psychological critics and by 1938 several of their responses appeared in the form of attacks. One of Banks' student assistants, Charles Stuart, undertook to answer them. These criticisms and Stuart's rebuttal of them will be reviewed in Chapter 10.

The philosophical implications of the ESP results were also being discussed during these years by a number of friends and a few *Journal* readers who did not so readily dismiss the reports. As preceding chapters have suggested, Banks' interest and motivation for this research was primarily philosophical. But as a scientist he restrained his tendency toward wider theorizing, as he explains in a letter he wrote in response to a suggestion of this kind:

> Your theory of differential brain development is a very interesting one and it might be possible to throw some descriptive light on it.... I am trying to restrict my theorizing during these working years because I must ploddingly work out as objectively as possible just what the facts are. I will enjoy theorizing about them during the later years of my life. I look forward to that time when I get the facts measured and established. But in the meantime I appreciate the stimulation of men like yourself.

But finding "just what the facts are" proved to be no simple job. It was unlike finding something objective. The human mind, after all, is not that easily measured, and so the time never came when Banks felt that he had "the facts measured and established." But I doubt if it would have come if he had lived to be a hundred.

In a 1945 *Journal* article entitled "Precognition Reconsidered," seven years after the first mention of it, Banks discussed "the incomprehensibility of precognition" and remarked

> If we had to explain a fact before we accepted it, there would be little advancement possible in science.... The very incomprehensibility of precognition is a measure of its scientific importance as a discovery. It must indeed be, like those strange inexplicable sparks of electricity in the eighteenth century, the clue to a great realm of realities silently awaiting the arrival of the explorer.

In 1934 when the monograph, *Extra-Sensory Perception*, was published by the Boston SPR, experimental results at the Parapsychology

Laboratory were accumulating rapidly, but few people except those immediately concerned knew about them. Even the readership of the psychic research societies was limited. Both Banks and McDougall began to feel the need of a wider organ of expression so that the results of experimental research could be more generally known.

The psychological journals seemed to be the natural and normal outlets for material like this, which, after all, was on a topic that should be classified as psychological. But those journals were crowded and all had huge backlogs of reports of regular psychological research. How, then, expect to get news about extrasensory topics into their pages? It could be urged that this research was being carried on at the new and traditionless Duke University and under an English psychologist, Mc-Dougall, who had a reputation for considering "far-out" topics. In fact, according to main-line psychologists, McDougall's research did not even rightly belong in psychology. Instead, if it were worth recognition anywhere, it belonged in biology. It marked him, in the eyes of or-thodox psychologists as well as biologists, as strange, at least. His following in either field was relatively small, even in spite of the fact that he had been picked by the prestigious Harvard University Depart-ment of Psychology as its chairman. If, now, he was reporting evidence for such psychic powers as telepathy and clairvoyance (based on experi-ments carried out by a young and unknown investigator named Rhine), it must have seemed just another ancient superstition come to life. As scientific modern psychologists, few of those who heard of it were im-pressed. Naturally, then, reports like Banks' could not be expected to find a place in psychological journals, probably not even after the few years' wait necessary for experimental work on orthodox topics. (A joke that floated around then in psychological circles was that ESP stood for "Error Some Place.")

An alternative outlet was obviously necessary, and that was to start a new journal, one specifically for experimental psychical research which would differ from the journals already in existence, like those of the London and American SPR's, which published on more general topics in the field. Of course, it could be urged that a separate journal for experimental parapsychological reports would further isolate the work from mainstream psychology. However, it would offer one publication outlet when otherwise none existed, so that the experi-mental results would at least be available.

With this idea of starting a new journal, Banks consulted Mc-Dougall and was strongly encouraged by him. The agreement was also made that McDougall would, in a sense, sponsor such an outlet for ex-perimental work by writing an editorial for the first issue that would ex-plain the reason for the new journal and make its objective clear.

This combination of purpose of Banks and McDougall led to a new publication, the *Journal of Parapsychology*. The first issue, dated March 1937, opened with a nearly nine-page-long editorial by Mc-Dougall. That editorial sketched briefly and succinctly the overriding question on which the subject matter of the new journal would concentrate, "What are the relations of mind to matter?" McDougall first generalized the behavioristic trend of science from the time of Galileo to the end of the nineteenth century as leading to the conclusion that mind is "but a functionless by-product of increasingly complex mechanical systems," a conclusion the existence of which McDougall called "an intolerable situation" and one which he said had led to the compartmental mind so frequently observable — science in one compartment and religion in the other.

McDougall then spoke of the rise of the movement known as psychical research, the objective of which was to seek evidence that mind has independence, an idea which he said seemed to have been overlooked in the science of the day. But the psychical research movement, as he explained, had to be the work of amateurs on the topic because, as a field, it was not organized and financed by the methods that supported research objectives on other, more orthodox topics. However, the question did call for an organized approach, such as might be made in an endowed institute, an institute that would be "more continuous and more broadly based," and yet one in which the research worker could have ready access to specialists along many lines, as in a university. This was necessary, he said, because such a worker needs such contact especially, in order to be "open-minded to all possibilities."

McDougall maintained that research on this topic would be especially difficult and would require, more than most,

> constant severe self-criticism, a disinterested pursuit of truth, and readiness in such a pursuit to face incredulity rooted in massive traditional prejudices, scorn, ridicule, jeers and loss of reputation; it would involve facing the most subtle problems of logic and scientific methods, and grave risks of self-deception in spite of the best intentions.

McDougall saw such objectives as more possible of attainment in a university than in a separate organization. He thought that in a university environment, research could be more disinterested than in a private institution and therefore better suited to this broader objective, "the increased understanding of man, his nature and possibilities."

Besides, as he continued, the function and responsibility of universities is to guide the public, to help it to distinguish between truth and error. Yet, McDougall said, few universities had sponsored such research, so that Duke University in 1930 was playing a pioneer role in allowing a member of its psychology department, J.B. Rhine, to follow "a path which few had trodden, a path of uncertain promise and one beset with risks and dangers." Since this venture had occurred under his own leadership at Duke, these words asserted clearly his awareness, not only of J.B. Rhine's temerity but of his own as well, in thus fostering a research which he recognized so clearly was beset with special "risks and dangers."

He then continued, "Whatever the ultimate outcome of this movement to acclimatize psychical research in the universities, it has prospered undeniably." And this growth, he thought, was largely due to the strict laboratory methods which had been maintained, and which he thought, whatever else their effect might be, would stir up further research in which the procedures would be repeated and varied. The rest of the editorial dealt with the more practical issues that confronted the new publication. He pointed out that the word, parapsychology, would be used to "designate the more strictly experimental part of the whole field implied by psychical research."

As it seemed to him, even then, the amount of material waiting for publication would be sufficient to fill four numbers of the journal per year. If it should fall short, the number of issues per year could be reduced, but he felt that that situation, in view of the need that would exist for repetition, would be unlikely to occur. Such repetition would be necessary, to guard against

> the peculiarly great risks of bona fide error and self-deception, and second to carry conviction of the objectivity of reports and of the validity of conclusions to the naturally and properly skeptical public which this journal seeks to serve.

He added that "all the regular psychological journals seem to have difficulty in finding sufficient space for suitable matter offered to them."

As confirmation of the statement that sufficient material was already on hand to support the projected publication schedule, the first issue led the way with four articles on ESP experiments, each having been conducted by a psychologist in a psychology department in different and recognized universities. These were followed by two articles reviewing significant results reported from foreign journals, one German and one English. The final article was a review of Banks' earlier one, "Some Selected Experiments in Extra-Sensory Perception," which had been published in the *Journal of Abnormal and Social Psychology* in September, 1936.

With the initial issue of the *Journal of Parapsychology* running to eighty pages, not only was the point made that material was available, but also the tone and general length of future issues were set. By the end of the first year, the total paging reached 307, with a fairly diverse and suggestive list of articles included.

As a sequel, in the year 1982, some 45 years later, it can be said that material for publication in the *Journal of Parapsychology* has never been lacking, and that has been the case without a lowering of the original standards set for the significance and reliability of the articles published.

9

Growing Pains at Home and Laboratory

In the preceding pages I have traced the beginning of Banks' research on the question of whether the human personality is more than a complicated mechanism. And going back now, over my records of that story—chiefly my diary, which of course concerns mainly my own part behind the scenes—I find, almost from the beginning, evidence which I think shows his general balance and good judgment, as, for instance, in a diary entry dated June 29, 1929. The episode I recorded there occurred in January of that year, just a few months after we had adopted seven-month-old baby Robbie, a time early in Banks' contact with McDougall and in the beginning of my experience of being the mother of a small child. After the baby joined us, of course, our opportunities to talk uninterruptedly had been scarce. In this entry I wrote

> We went for a drive this evening ... and sat in the car afterward and talked. Banks outlined the ends he hoped to accomplish if he makes the trip to the Boston and Yale meetings [of the American Association for the Advancement of Science] that he is planning next month, while I make a visit home in Ohio.

> I said he would be getting a lot of stimulation and uplift from it all— three weeks or more attending meetings, seeing interesting people, reading in big libraries, while I'd be merely sinking back farther and farther into the mud.

Although I had not recognized its universality yet, I had expressed the problem of most women, I guess, who are faced with the conflict between their professional lives and domesticity. It was a problem much less common in 1929, when even women's suffrage was still almost a novelty, than it is now. The old slogan, "Woman's place is in the home," had not yet been very generally questioned. But Banks' rejoinder to me shows, I think, his good judgment and levelheadedness. He said that my complaint was the equivalent of saying, "How fortunate you are, how unfortunate I am, when in reality it is on account of the baby that you are in this situation, and you wanted the baby." That, I could not deny.

The diary entry continues

> Of course, I know all that and I know that the baby is a compensation to me for my situation. But my critics, myself and Banks mainly, do not always remember that compensation and reason when I get dull and rusty and a mere old idealless household drudge.

> Of course, the discussion went on from there to Banks' problems too, and it helped me to see—even to know for the first time—some of his. They don't show to me without his telling, like mine do to him. His are not as bad as mine nor am I as critical of him. The discussion certainly was very helpful for in the end we each understood the other better.

I should interrupt that entry here to say that from a letter Banks wrote to a friend on January 20, 1929, a copy of which is still available, perhaps I was not the only one who would not have guessed Banks' attitude at this stage. The letter certainly does not hint at any reservations he may have had. He wrote

I heard indirectly that they had hired me on the regular staff here, in the Philosophy Department. This is good news indeed. This is going to be a great place and I should like a chance to grow up with it. Besides, we like the general situation here.... We enjoy the country which is mostly wooded in this region, and find the people easy to live among. Life is a much more serene matter here in this "Friendly City" as they call it, with simple people (many of them black), mild temperatures, "sunny southern skies," than it has ever been before. We are glad to settle for a bit; though it may not be for long—we are such rovers. [Little did he foresee, then, that it would be a lifelong stay!]

Then, after a paragraph about his friend's family, he adds

We have Louie's sister Miriam, 12, and her brother Elden, 18, a freshman, with us. They are fine kids and we really enjoy having them. I am strong for youngsters, not being adult myself.

That Banks had reservations about his situation at Duke, however, became clear to me, as I recorded in the diary entry which I interrupted above. I wrote

Banks' problem is one of main drive. What is it? He thinks he's in danger of becoming "a strawy-minded professor." I suppose he is in some such danger. He has a temperament which needs a cause. He's a crusader. But there is no crusade. That's his problem. It has long been his problem. The implications of psychic research offer the only promise of one either of us can see for him—the only one with which he would be satisfied. But the time for him to be active in that is not now. He thinks his "bearings will rust out with waiting," that his impetus, his "head of steam," his interest will seep away and be dissipated if he is forced to wait and divert his energy—into teaching, for instance. I don't think it will be so, myself. I don't believe he can lose that interest, but I do think he may gain the position from which his efforts can be more availing.

My own problem is how to be intelligent though a mother. Also, why be intelligent? The answer to the latter is that my inward urge, unreasoning as it has always been, is necessary for my self-respect, and that it is necessary too to keep Banks' respect for me.

The *how* is the question. It simmers down to practical details. I get so little stimulation from outside—it means lifting eternally by my own "boot-straps"—but here I go, lifting—

Meanwhile, we were finding our Duke stipend to be inelastic in its support of our little family. Earlier, we had loaned money in small amounts to my sister, Sylvia, who was struggling to get through college as a self-help student. In desperation, I wrote and asked her if she could pay back any small part of the debt. She managed to send some in spite of her own tight budget. On April 24, 1929, I wrote her in a letter she still has, saying

> Thank you for saving our lives. We were about ready to eat boot-straps—only we hadn't any. Our doctor bills are paid now, but we're still behind on the rent. We'll just make out by the end of the term if I don't buy an extra pin, but I must get some clothes for Robbie. So far I haven't even bought an extra pair of socks for him for fear we'd go hungry before next payday. But if we can keep from borrowing, I think we'll be able to spend next summer at the University of Chicago. I'm sure Banks needs it. We both get very stale down here away from everything.

In spite of that initial intention to get back to Chicago for a summer, after the baby came it faded out without discussion. With Robbie and our limited financial resources, it would obviously be an impractical venture and we just forgot about it. Part of the reason we could do so is reflected in another letter from me to Sylvia, this one on May 8, 1929. The pertinent reference is:

> It seems so natural to have the baby now and we enjoy him ever so much. It's more fun to give him his bath than to go to any movie I ever saw.

> Banks comes home on time now, hoping the baby is still awake and the two start playing at once, and then you could tell Banks that the world is on fire and he'd never know you spoke. In fact, I've never seen such absorption. I think I'm crazy about the little fellow but I can still live in the world while enjoying him. But Banks can't. In the baby's presence Banks' world is all baby and nothing else.

However, in spite of the attraction of babyhood, by October that fall of 1929 I was telling Sylvia something of Banks' interests at Duke in connection with his teaching career. I said that he had the proper number of students to make his course a discussion one, centered (as one might very well have predicted) around religion and science, their respective scopes, fields, and conflicts. Some of the students are from the Divinity School. One of them told Banks that he was the first professor he had had to whom he could talk over his doubts and troubles. His questions were similar to those Banks himself used to have. Now he can help this student as no one then helped him.

Then I spend a paragraph telling how we had managed to get more comfortable furniture for the living room and that I hoped he could make his students feel free to come in, because I thought that contacts with faculty were often more beneficial to them in the long run than classwork.

Earlier that year, Banks had ordered the new edition of the *Encyclopaedia Britannica* and had said that getting it would be the great event of the year and that no one could imagine his "childish anticipation." In a letter telling Sylvia about it, he said it was not too expensive, "only $119.50." This, "instead of a new car. It will delight me as much as my first pair of long pants."

By October, 1929, I mentioned that the encyclopedia came and that "Banks is certainly getting a lot of pleasure and profit out of the set. He needs it constantly in preparing for his classes."

The summer of 1929 was, it seemed, an excessively hot one, and we were living on the second floor of a two-family house. However, I said

I haven't minded the heat so much because I daren't complain since Banks has been so loudly expecting me to do so. One can't fulfill *all* of a man's expectations! It raises his opinion of his prophetic abilities too high.

Men are always a problem, but Banks has been an unusually easy one to live with this summer — working unceasingly on his lectures for the next year. Me? I'm busy rearing my child, and I too have been, in my own opinion, easy to live with.

And now I find among letters that Sylvia saved, this reference from Banks to the same situation. He says

I am literally sticking to my job these days. The seat of my trousers sticks to my chair, my arm sticks to my paper. Louie, who usually is ready to melt at the slightest provocation, is bravely getting through this heat better than I would have expected. [So is virtue rewarded!]

By April, 1930, we had both Robbie and baby Sally, who was then about two months old. Robbie, while I was incapacitated during the time of Sally's birth, became so attached to Banks that he didn't want me to do anything for him. But I've enjoyed it all. The babies are the *realest* little objectives to work for, I've had. As an occupation they seem worthwhile to me — though I have no feeling that I'm an especial success. I know Banks thinks I'm pretty mediocre and I guess I'm none the better for his opinion, which I resent a little.

By June of that year, I was deeply involved in domesticity:

Taking care of the babies is more absorbing than I supposed it would be to me. I do miss the feeling that I am anybody mentally or intellectually, but mostly I don't have time to think of that. I realize that we have come to the stage of which it may be said, "He developed but she stood still." I realize it when outsiders are present. Then I seem to leave the burden of thought and conversation almost entirely to Banks. It is partly because he takes it and partly because I give it.

We were drifting that way before the baby came, but since, I have been so sleepy much of the time that I couldn't think and so shut in that I had nothing of which to think so that now I feel pretty much of a liability socially. I don't intend to remain so, however, now that I'm getting sleep again.

Banks is the best old husband of all. He seems so understanding — if I just remember to approach him right. While I was so tired that was hard to do and he didn't know or sense the state I was in, and so a little friction developed. I guess I had forgotten that in our early acquaintance I had very well learned that he didn't "read between the lines." I should have remembered now, but didn't, that intuition from him about my feelings was something I should not expect. His heart was in the right place but the way to it was not as automatically open as I tended to assume.

Of the situation that developed, however, I wrote that the "friction is gone now that I'm better." I learned later that Mrs. McDougall gave Banks a little rundown on my physical state and explained to him that it was a general one for mothers the first months after childbirth. That was all he needed to know.

Shortly after that, we received tragic news from my home back in Ohio. My sweet little beginning-school niece, Alice, fell off a school bus and was fatally injured. On October 14, 1930, I wrote

I just had the awful telegram — awful! awful! And we're way down here where we can do nothing. But if we were there, what could we do? It's a senseless universe! Humanity is too fragile, with its feeling, emotional side, to live and expand fully in such a world! I wonder, oh I wonder what the answer is.

Later, five years later and two more babies later, in 1935, in my diary comes another little family reference on Banks. After telling how uninterested I was in my own photograph in a family group picture we had taken, compared to the way I would have felt in earlier years, I say

Banks has changed too in something of the same way. Both of us now, for instance, want gifts for *family* use rather than strictly personal ones. I think that tells a lot.

On a different theme, the record then continues

I seem no longer to be worried about keeping up mentally. Somehow the question isn't up so much. We are both deeply interested and absorbed in research, Banks all he must be, I all I can be. I am beginning some tests with children, our own and some of the neighborhood youngsters, and that interest is so spontaneous there is no question about it, but only how to get more time for it.

I find a diary entry (January 19, 1936) which says

I often think how blithely we all march along into the unknown future with its pitfalls and perils, always expecting things to be good even though we know they can't always be so. Sometime, if Banks' absence should be permanent—what a contrast it would be to this short temporary one which seems hard enough to me now. [Little did my imagination then cover the reality which now, forty-five years later, I am experiencing!]

This is the "lone-est" night I've had in a long time. Banks has been gone since a week ago Wednesday. He is on a lecture trip to Schenectady, Boston, New York. Presumably he is in Washington tonight and intending to return here tomorrow. All during the period of his absence until tonight I've been able to provide myself with some interest or occupation strong enough to prevent myself from missing him too much. But tonight it gets me.

Then I tell that six-year-old Sally had been acutely ill a few days before and that although the doctor had treated her successfully and she was now quite well again, it had been the first case of real illness "in my lucky maternal career. It serves to remind me how bad such an illness can be."

The entry then continues with a reference to my attempts to give ESP tests to some of the neighborhood children. Also mentioned is an effort I had made to test Mrs. McDougall formally; that is, with the regular ESP technique. In a natural spontaneous way, her psychic ability seemed very evident, an impression augmented by anecdotes she often told which besides being intriguing in outline lost nothing, Banks and I thought, from her animated way of telling them.

My first attempt to test her with the ESP technique was, however, too spontaneous for the results to have been recorded, except that in my memory they were fantastically high. But as naive as we all still were, then, about the spontaneous and evanescent character of the extra-sensory ability, we had not yet ceased to expect to duplicate such success. Accordingly, we were still much disappointed when, the second time around, it was not forthcoming. And that was what happened in my succeeding attempts with her, as I reported in my January, 1936, diary entry: "My last two experiments with Mrs. McDougall were not very successful."

It was not until several years later, on March 8, 1938, that I was able to resume diary writing. The intervening years had, indeed, been full of pitfalls and perils which had demanded my energies and attention. My young sister, Miriam, had suffered a severe illness which developed into pneumonia, an even more fearsome disease then than it is today, for the discovery of antibiotics for its treatment was still in the future. Following that and Sally's illness already mentioned, both the little girls — Betsy, aged 3, and Rosie, 1½ years — had also been very ill, Betsy almost mortally so. The bad colds that they contracted developed into pneumonia, as had Miriam's not long before. In the hospital with both of the children, I almost literally *forced* the authorities to allow me to stay in the children's sickroom. For a week, the doctor concurring, I was given a cot in the room with them and I was there day and night. I was able thereby not only to check up on a negligent night nurse but to get quick help the night Betsy's breathing practically stopped.

Besides all this, McDougall was in rapidly declining health with inoperable cancer. About that, I recorded in my diary

> Dr. McDougall's situation is nearly a personal tragedy of ours, only slightly removed. Banks has gone over this evening to see if there's anything he can do to help Mrs. McDougall.

Over the next period, until McDougall's death in November, 1938, Banks continued to help in every way he could. Often, as the patient's strength declined, and since the McDougalls were then living in an apartment on the East Campus of Duke University, Banks was able to help the invalid get a bit of exercise walking in the shady grove nearby. During these times, many serious conversations took place between them.

Unfortunately, the situation did not permit the recording of these talks nor of Banks' later reports of them to me. I remember mainly that, as might have been expected, the subject "after death, what?" was a major one. On that topic, McDougall was at least optimistic, as I remember Banks telling me; I'm sure that to Banks, as to all who had known this great man, this great mind in his prime, the idea that an intellect and personality such as his should be annihilated by death was unthinkable. Sally, only about eight then, told me long afterwards that her father told her then that she should try not to forget Dr. McDougall for "he's the greatest man you will ever know."

Many times over the succeeding years, when Banks and I walked in or by that grove of trees on the East Duke campus, he would comment on his memory of those walks and talks there with his great teacher and colleague.

On November 29, 1938, my record says

Dr. McDougall died last night. Even though we have known for the last few days that the end was very near, it is a shock nevertheless. We can only be relieved that it came suddenly and as painlessly as we are told. He was unconscious the last several days and apparently out of pain. But it is as if someone who really belonged to us had passed. I had hardly realized how much affection for him, as for a father, I had. And Banks more yet. He has said very little. He never talks about painful topics.

But last night when we both were wakeful and knowing that Dr. McDougall could hardly survive the night, we got to talking. Banks voiced the old, old question, the one which has actuated so much of his intellectual life and mine. He said something like, "Now that this grand old man is passing—what? Where does he go? What is the answer?"

We talked ourselves around—or Banks did—to a renewed glimpse of our fundamental objectives. It seems as if in a way we have had a considerable loss of perspective. The *details* of ESP and parapsychology have tended to obscure the far horizon toward which we are laboring. Banks commented on the fact that this fall, since last September at Columbus (Chapter 10) really, something has changed in him, perhaps something vital gone out. It seems as if he has come to care less, whether or not it means that he takes the whole research less seriously or whether he's lost interest or just become too tired. I've known it and wondered a lot about what we could do to revitalize ourselves, himself particularly.

For a few weeks, Banks has been trying to give over or give up the *Journal* to Gardner Murphy. Earlier such a thing would have been unthinkable. I think it's partly the result of being tired of the slavery it has entailed which prevented him from getting much done besides the editing. Charlie (Stuart) has been sick and even at the best, he can't accomplish it all. Anyway, Banks now feels that if he could get the *Journal* off his hands and have time for his research again, it would be a great relief.

Another change has been in the policy about publicity. He's apparently decided now that a few years of quietude when the problems of ESP don't get aired in every newspaper would be a good thing. And so, instead of "more publicity," the plan I had thought he'd have to adopt, he's chosen the "less" one. That too I think is partly the result of tiredness.

Anyway, recounting the various factors that have come in at this juncture to weigh him down it seems small wonder that the zest has gone out of his routine in parapsychology. The Columbus meeting and the strain it involved, the added red tape and safeguards beyond reason imposed on the research, the critics who say, "It may be a legitimate field but someone else but Rhine must do it," the obstacles that have kept an ESP machine from being perfected, the lack of any eager new young persons coming on, etc. — all these factors have counted against it, with at the same time little of a positive nature to off-set them.

Banks says he used to long for a cause for which he could fight through thick and thin. Now he's got a cause but isn't sure he wants to stick to it through thick and thin. "Maybe I'm that kind of a fellow."

But I can see that he isn't "that kind of a fellow." He's really the kind he thought he was, but he's tired and discouraged at this juncture and being so it's hard to glimpse again the ultimate objective of which he is not tired and the question which I know he can never quit, no matter in what guise he'll have to seek it.

And now Dr. McDougall is gone — he who was so much interested in that same question. Maybe now he knows the answer — if there is a knowable answer. Now he's gone and Banks vows anew that we *will* hunt for it. And I say we won't always be messing around with these little narrow-minded two-for-a-nickel psychologist critics. We will just somehow go ahead and pioneer. I think that's Banks forte and he does too.

have been responsible. If so, however, it was hard to see how that could have caused the sound because both ornaments were attached to a tinsel string and not directly to the branch.

After all, it was impossible to explain the happening with certainty, but I felt as if perhaps I had come closer to a genuine psychic event than I ever had before. I could just imagine Dr. McDougall doing it and his glee if he knew he had succeeded in making us take notice. At least the little sound could not possibly have been better timed than it was. And he knew the problem so well, knew our interest. If he could he surely would want to let us know — if he could.

But — Mrs. McDougall was certainly a psychic person, if any such exist. And now, many years later, parapsychologists, at least, know about psychokinesis; and from my own studies of reports of spontaneous instances of PK, I know that whatever the entire explanation of them may be, when such experiences do occur it seems to be at periods of strong emotional tension. So — was it a promise, or an example of the still unsolved mystery of PK?

Several years passed, during which Banks gradually acquired three regular-sized projects that needed to be worked on simultaneously. The first was his teaching at the university; the second, that of counselling and guiding students who needed help; and the third, his ESP research. The counselling job was extracurricular. It had come about gradually and spontaneously from the student contacts he made in the psychology courses he taught. From those courses he had drawn the subjects for ESP tests, but from the same source had come students asking help for personal problems of all kinds. All of this was in addition to his interest in psychic research.

A few of these student problems spilled over to the home situation. One of them resulted in a young faculty man's not being dismissed from the university because of his unconventional sexual life. With Banks' advice and encouragement, he eventually changed that and was married to a partner with whom he achieved a normal family life.

With three such potentially full-time lines of endeavor, it was inevitable that Banks' time was too crowded. But although each should have been a full-time job in itself, he managed for a time to carry on with all of them because they all seemed so well worth doing that it was hard to decide among them. Or rather, it was a problem to decide between two of them, for the teaching had to go on. The salary depended on that.

Then, even though it seemed that Banks' activities could not be extended further, a new situation developed in which he had to take part. Naturally enough, with his interest in psychic research becoming known and the fact that, in the past, research in the field had usually meant research with mediums, the question had come up whether he would engage in that too. But he was devoted to experimental methods in the laboratory first. He thought that the other might come in time, but first he wanted to see if he could get evidence of telepathy experimentally in normal or ordinary subjects. And so he had begun the research on the topic mainly with students from his classes.

However, the fact that research on telepathy was under way at Duke University was soon known in psychic research centers, and a widely known medium with an especially good reputation, Mrs. Eileen Garrett, offered herself for study. When speaking as a medium, her messages came through a "control," an entity purporting to be distinct from herself, and she did not understand how that could happen. She herself, as well as psychical investigators, wanted to know what kind of mental processes were involved, and specifically whether her controls were actual separate personalities, as they claimed, or constructs made in her own mind, as psychologists held. She arranged, through McDougall, to come to Durham for several weeks of study, and Banks, eager to test whether a medium of her ability could manifest ESP in the laboratory, decided to crowd in a study with this purpose. Her visit would be financed by a grant from a wealthy patron of hers, Mrs. Frances Payne Bolton, a retired congresswoman from Ohio, who also was deeply interested in the survival problem. Soon arrangements were made and Mrs. Garrett arrived.

I have never succeeded in adequately describing Mrs. Garrett. She was a new type to all of us, an extremely vivacious Irish lady. Even her red fingernails, a commonplace now, were a sensation in our unsophisticated little community then. They were especially striking against her very white skin and black dress.

Although I don't think Mrs. Garrett's main reason for coming was fulfilled by her visit, Banks gave her ESP tests in both her normal state and when in trance and her "control" was in operation. The possibility was that differences in psychic ability might be shown between the two, differences that could be interpreted as bearing on the question of their identities. However, no significant difference was found, for her test scores were the same in each situation. They were not spectacular, but in general at about the level of a good ESP student subject. The control thus seemed to be a "split-off" from her own mind.

One result of this visit for Banks and his research was that, through Mrs. Garrett, he came into contact with her donor, Mrs. Bolton. Eventually, Banks and McDougall visited Mrs. Bolton; the possibility that she would finance a larger project of research on survival was discussed, and she agreed to do so, contributing ten thousand dollars a year for three years. This served to decrease Banks' teaching load by making possible a salary for an assistant.

Naturally, Banks was much encouraged by this financial aid. His earlier years of research had been accomplished with very little financial outlay. As already mentioned, at one time, he had the small grant from the university of $400, which allowed him to fulfill several obligations such as paying Linzmayer for the time he spent staying on after graduation for further ESP tests. But the early student subjects had been volunteers. Their own interest and its satisfaction had been their only impetus and their only recompense.

However, there was a condition attached to the financial aid from Mrs. Bolton. She and Mrs. Garrett both were intensely interested in the survival problem; and that, and that only, seemed to them worthy of support. They had little appreciation of the necessarily slow way that scientific investigations must proceed, beginning with the simpler elements of a problem. In this instance, that first step would have to be to determine the status of telepathy, to find out whether or not it was an actuality. This of course meant experimental research. But these ladies were impatient for more direct mediumistic research, and only that. For a time, Banks struggled to find a way to win the financial support he needed in order to continue to expand his telepathy research, and at the same time to placate and please these prospective patrons. I doubt if his effort could ever have been called successful, but I guess it did add considerably to his persuasive abilities, not to say anxieties and preoccupations. (In the course of it, he and Mrs. Garrett became, as they called themselves, "good and friendly enemies," and exchanges between them were excellent entertainment for any listener like me.) But the financial aid depended on Mrs. Bolton's concept of research on survival.

Banks tried to make her (and all of his contributors) realize that through their support he was enabled to pursue his inquiry into the great problem about the nature and destiny of human beings in which they all were interested. To that end, and as he strongly felt, he tried to make them feel that they were partners in this grand enterprise. Copies of several letters demonstrating this are preserved. One, to Mrs. Bolton, details the status of the research which, whether or not it was appreciated by her, is very informative now in understanding the situation as he saw it then. It starts thus:

> May I tell you something of what the "partnership" has been doing and discuss with you some of the plans for the summer? I want to avoid boring you ... yet I would like you to know what is going on.

This was written in July 1934, just after the first publicity about ESP and he told her how pleasing it was that the work had received "wide acceptance." "Epoch-making," he says, seemed to be a favorite word. He mentions reviews by Dr. Waldemar Kaempffert, Dr. E.E. Free, Dr. Walter Franklin Prince, Duke professor Hornell Hart, and several popular writers, and continues

> It seems to be true ... that the world is somewhat ready for the truth about mind and its larger meaning in the universe. It will be thrilling to be a part of the system of discovery that reveals it!

Then he details a plan with Murphy to send out assistants to promulgate research. (It was one, however, that was never carried out.) Next comes a list of scientific journals that had asked him for articles or were planning to publish reviews so that, he says,

> It is not immodest to say that no work will be better advertised. And since it is for the "world," I want the world to know about it.

The plan of work for the summer, he said, was to continue research on precognition. "By this and the earlier research, it will be shown that the human mind is *not materially limited*." The proof of this is necessary, he added, before the idea of survival can be demonstrated.

The next step, he said, is to find all of the direct effects that mind can exert on matter, and for this, "mountains of proof" of psychokinesis will be necessary. In life, it is done through the brain, but without the brain (after death) the mind would be powerless to affect the material world if there were no psychokinesis.

Then he interjects that the religions of the world have recognized action such as this as "Divine Purpose, Spirit, etc." The huge amount of data on psychokinesis (Chapter 12), he says, already supports this idea that the mind can affect matter directly.

Next he mentions the already successful research showing the reality of clairvoyance ("psychometry"), and that another step he is planning is "mental forcing," preliminary to the study of spirit agency or separation of mind and body (a project that did not get carried out.) "Beyond separability," he says,

> lies the great Mt. Everest of problems, "If a man die, shall he live again?" Sometime in the years ahead, I *hope* to scale it.

He cites, then, the help he will need, including "yourself," Professor McDougall, Pratt, Stuart, Miss Pegram, Mrs. Rhine. He says that in a few years he hopes to organize an institute for parapsychology and to weld it into the permanent structure of the university. To accomplish this, with the help of Dr. McDougall and Dr. Few, he says, is the objective of his effort.

He emphasizes that he is telling her this because he considers her a partner, and not that he is trying to get financial aid. "When I begin to 'fish' for financial aid," he says, "I will do so openly and frankly."

He outlines his plans for writing reports and for research with his students, Pearce and Margaret Pegram. He says that Pratt, Stuart, the young Zirkle couple (former students), and several others, including seven of his psychology students, will be working with him; and he outlines the projects in which they are to be engaged.

> We will have to guard against overdoing it, for the sake of departmental policy and harmony, at least until we organize as an institute. Some members of the department are already sensitive.

Then, he asks if she will permit him to arrange the allocation of funds according to perceived need. He says he has engaged Pratt and Stuart for $100 each for the summer, with perhaps a $25 supplement, and the Zirkles for $200, Pearce for $100 a month, Cooper (another student) for $100–$200. He says that Pegram (then a student at a neighboring college) is working for nothing, that he is trying to get her to Duke, and if that is successful she will need $500 for the year. He also has reserved $900 for Mrs. Garrett and small sums for several others. Besides all these, he is trying to save out $500 in order possibly to get for study and testing Mrs. Leonard, the most famous English sensitive. He asks Mrs. Bolton if he could call on her sometime and if she would visit "our laboratories and meet our group of workers." (He visited her, but she never visited the laboratory).

This letter, written before the adverse public reaction that soon followed, reflected Banks' first euphoria about the accomplishments and discoveries which promised so much.

On August 3, 1936, Banks wrote Mrs. Bolton another detailed letter because of a situation in which he had thought that her protégée, Mrs. Garrett, might become involved. It was written from a former resort area north of New York City, about a house that had been reported as haunted. A reputable person whom I shall call Dr. X. had described the house in an article in the *American Magazine*. As Banks explained to Mrs. Bolton, we had lived there the summer before in order to investigate the situation quietly. The outcome he characterizes as a disappointment from one point of view, although from another it gives a certain satisfaction.

We had found the "haunted" house to be a small tenant cottage on the grounds of what, apparently, had once been a large estate. The manor house was a large one nearby, clinging to the mountainside and overlooking a vast plain to the east. This larger house had been our dwelling place that summer, and I decided that for a mother of small children it was the most spectacular, most unusual, and most utterly impractical that the mind of man had ever conceived. It consisted of a tier of rooms, five stories high, built against the mountainside. A "deranged" cookstove was in the almost "blind" basement, the dining room was on the floor above, the entrance hall on the third, where also was a sitting room with a porch and a marvelous forty-mile view over eastern New York state. The two floors above it were bedrooms. The five floors were connected by an open circular staircase against the wall, one down which a two-year-old toddler or a six-month-old baby just learning to creep could easily take a lethal fall, bouncing nicely from floor to floor, or perhaps squeeze down the central pole for an uninterrupted drop to the basement kitchen below, where much more maternal time had to be spent than in enjoying the marvelous forty-mile view two floors above.

Banks' office was in the smaller, "haunted" house. By working in it constantly, he hoped to trap the ghost and learn its secret. As he explains in this letter to Mrs. Bolton, on our first occupancy of the place the previous season, he thought he had corroborated *one* aspect of the reported hauntings effects of the several which had been reported by the previous occupant.

That one effect was a peculiar little clicking sound. He tells Mrs. Bolton that "We got some apparent order to these sounds but couldn't say whether they were purposive or not." [Later he knew they were only random.]

The test as to whether or not such a manifestation was a psychic occurrence was that if they were hauntings, they should show some kind of human or intellectual aspect, and this Banks had tested on our first summer there. I remember very well Banks' telling me how foolish he had felt when, alone in that little one-room building, he had repeatedly talked aloud to the ghost, saying, "If you have a message you want to communicate, let us establish a code, one click for yes, two for no, etc." His account to Mrs. Bolton continues

> We heard the clicks a good many times. It was because of this that we wanted to bring Mrs. Garrett up here last summer without her knowing about the situation. Our arrangement didn't work out, as you know. [The reason, I think, was that Mrs. Garrett was on some other mission and couldn't come.]

Now comes the explanation. Recently Dr. and Mrs. Pratt, up here with us for part of the season, in their cottage nearby heard the same sound and were able to trace it to a window screen. Subsequent exploration led to the discovery that certain movable screens could produce such clicks under varying moisture and temperature conditions. Dr. Pratt put some screen before the fireplace and he soon had quite a concert of clicks, essentially similar to those we had heard in the building. As it happened, the summer during which Dr. X. had been in the building there was a great deal of moisture. Last summer there was a fair amount. This summer is very dry. In many ways the evidence now fits into a screen-click theory, and Dr. X and his wife are agreed that that explains it.

A later theme in the long letter is the need for a direct outlet in publication for experimental results — "a journal under our control" — so that long waiting periods before publication could be avoided.

Then, finally, comes a reference to the reason for our being at the New York haunted house, of which Banks says

> I cannot say I am in any sense a believer in the haunting principle, but I am a believer that if there are such phenomena, they could come closer to a demonstration of spirit agency than anything else I know of in nature. Working back from them, if there are any that are genuine, we might be able to find our way to a sound conclusion more quickly than by another fifty years of mediumistic utterances, though of course I am not disposed to neglect them either. There are other ways of explaining the latter. But no one has yet been able to put up a good alternative theory of the ghost who does something objective. The problem, then, is to find out if he really does.

The letter then continues with a description of an earlier trip that Banks had made to California to study an adolescent boy, Pat M., who had made national newspaper headlines. As usual with such newspaper accounts, it had turned out to be a story that Banks had had to debunk. The boy had been reported to have "eyeless sight." The claim was that he could see in spite of blindfolding bandages over his eyes. Banks had found that what had been reported as complete blindfolding was not that and the boy still was able to see down his nose and simply had been fooling the reporters who had investigated him.

I remember how, one day after his return home, Banks had emerged blindfolded from his room, his head, it appeared, entirely swathed in a big towel, and still he was able to tell me in detail what I was doing. He was demonstrating that bandages did not prevent peepholes which probably could soon be enlarged by facial grimaces.

In his letter, he also told Mrs. Bolton that on this trip he had studied five other cases, had had discussions with colleagues, and also had visited Mr. John Coover in California. Coover was a man who had diverted to other uses the funds that had been donated to Stanford University for psychic investigations after, as Coover reported, he had found no evidence of ESP. However, Banks and also Dr. Thouless in England later analyzed his data and found that they did show such evidence. Since Coover was a mathematician, this raised a question about his sincerity that, as far as I know, was never answered.

Then, continuing his letter, Banks told Mrs. Bolton about a visit he had made to an old gentleman in Cleveland who, like her, was much interested in the question of survival and was, in fact, already convinced of it, Mr. Charles Ozanne. Banks had explained to him that only research by modern scientific methods could ever convince a skeptical world of survival. The upshot had been, he said, that Mr. Ozanne decided to leave his fortune, the savings of a careful and frugal lifetime, to survival research. Ozanne had been an educator, a high school teacher, and had amassed savings of many thousands of dollars. This promise of bequest gave Banks a great uplift. (In actuality he never got it.)

Later, in a letter in August, 1936, directly to Ozanne, Banks expressed to him appreciation for the fact that he (Ozanne) understood that the search for evidence of survival was to be a scientific one, and that the object was to

> convince others, particularly those who constitute authorities and leaders of the rest of the world.... It is this need that determines the policy of the quantitative, the mathematical, and the extremely guarded methods. We have identified and emphasized the motivational and purposive peculiarity of the survival hypothesis and now we must follow the motive— "Who would have *wanted* to send such a message?"

The letter to Ozanne then continues on the subject of finances. He explains the arrangement at the lab that assures the contributor that the money will go to the proper recipient only, and he says, then, "For your repeated offer to help from your current income, I am, if possible, even more grateful than for your decision about the inheritance."

Ozanne proved to be another person whose eagerness for research on survival made him, in time, impatient with the slow method of science; and when Banks turned to the experimental study of telepathy, rather than directly to survival, he became unhappy. Banks then advised him, in effect, to support someone who would make that direct approach, instead of the one to which Banks and the Duke Parapsychology Laboratory were devoted. He then advised the old gentleman to create a foundation of his own in whatever way he wanted. The result was the Parapsychology Foundation, an organization entirely independent of the Duke Parapsychology Laboratory. The director elected to head it, Mr. William Roll, has remained there ever since, conducting the Foundation's inquiries into survival. Although no research solution to the survival question has been announced by the Parapsychology Foundation, the fine point of distinction between the specific methods used at the Parapsychology Laboratory and the more anecdotal ones of the Parapsychology Foundation is not widely known. Clearly, not everyone wants what some view as the too-slow or too-cautious methods of experimental research. The Foundation is for those who prefer other methods. The Laboratory (now the Institute for Parapsychology) is strictly for experimental research.

Sometime in 1938, I recorded the story of an encounter we had had earlier with a lady whom we hopefully thought of as a possible donor and who ultimately told us angrily how bad we were, especially Banks. He, by then, was getting used to unpopularity of which this was one instance. That is not to say, however, that he enjoyed it; but this person's reaction was certainly more obvious than most.

Banks was unpopular among his colleagues in the psychology department, the result of a wave of notoriety that followed release of the news about the ESP research. An unwritten but universally accepted stricture on scientific procedure (to which Banks subscribed completely) is that new discoveries be reported first of all in scientific journals. Any publicity resulting therefrom should only come if and when the popular media discover and report the facts so publicized. Banks' results had not appeared in scientific publications, for they had consistently refused them. But in the eyes of his colleagues in the Duke psychology department, he had rushed out and given reports to the press — and now Duke University was being known as "the university where Rhine is." This was the basis of his unpopularity at Duke, his psychological colleagues apparently never having been convinced that he had even asked for publication in the usual psychological journals but that he had stirred up the popular reaction himself.

The lady I mentioned, Mrs. G., who became very angry at Banks, was a friend of a friend of ours from New York, one who earlier had visited the lab and contributed financially because of her interest in survival research.

Mrs. G. was also interested in the question of survival and one day just appeared at the lab, as she said, to work with us on survival. Quite untrained in any scientific way, she was more of the social type. Her chief recommendation to Banks was that she had raised money for a civic project in her home city. Naturally, hearing that, we hoped that she would do some scouting for financial aid for the lab, as the size of the staff and all its activities were severely limited by lack of funds.

But Mrs. G. made it clear to Banks immediately that she was not interested in raising money. She wanted to work in the lab and wanted Banks to give her something to do at once. She said she would "*Never, never* — and never had — solicited from individuals." It seemed that the only thing for which, by her own initial report, she had credentials, she did not want to do. But since she was as entirely innocent of and untrained in the perspectives and methods of the lab, or of scientific procedures generally, it was not easy to think of a job for her. But she settled down, came to the lab each morning, and read books from the library, waiting to be given work.

Naturally, it was not obvious how to get her in at once on any ongoing experiment even as a subject, and besides, she wanted to be an experimenter, not just a subject. Banks was too busy with his myriad duties to sit down and have another chat with her as she wanted a few days after her arrival. I supposed she must be getting something satisfying as the time passed, or she would not have stayed. I hoped that eventually she would find her place, as other volunteers occasionally had done before.

The situation regarding workers at the lab, in any event, was a bit unconventional. Although the laboratory was technically in the Duke University psychology department, it was a research organization, not a teaching one, so that regular students did not come into parapsychology since no training was offered, no courses or academic credit given. The result was that those who did work with Banks were nearly all volunteers who came because of their own interest. Sometimes they stayed and in time became satisfactory lab workers, and then Banks, as he could, would pay them nominal salaries. But generally, aside from a few old standbys like Pratt and Stuart, they soon went on to other careers. Suddenly, however, one day, Mrs. G. became very upset and angry when Banks said he really didn't have time just then for another two-hour conference with her. He had just returned from a speaking trip, was only home for a few days, then had to leave again.

He therefore asked me to invite her home to lunch so he would have time to talk things over with her and find out what he had done to offend her, and to try to explain. She came, and while still at the table read a written statement of her grievance to us. In import, it was that Banks had not cooperated with her desire to go out and raise money for us (exactly what we had been disappointed that she had not wanted to do) and she had not been treated with the respect due her qualifications.

Now she was hurt and insulted beyond repair, as we found out after an embarrassing and heated discussion in which Banks and I both tried to explain to her that we certainly had misunderstood her intentions and desires. We could get nowhere, however, and she was just as set and just as angry after all our explanations and apologies as before.

Banks had to leave at three — after he, too, had reached white heat though he had managed to control it. Neither his patience nor impatience had softened her attitude a bit. She stayed after he left, to give me a chance to clear things up if I could, and after Banks told her she had no right to leave after making charges about him and the lab, if she did not give me a chance to explain the situation.

And so I worked at that job for another hour. I told her it was not very generous of her not to accept apologies and explanations, when she wouldn't say that she didn't believe them or thought we were lying and didn't mean them — but I only got her to the point of saying that she believed *me*. Apparently, she was so mad at Banks that she did not want to be reconciled to him.

She made a lot of criticisms of the lab and Banks' relation to it. She said he was an impossible individualist and that no one could work with him, that the staff was in awe of him and only lived and moved if he let them, and that even I called him on the office phone when I went there rather than interrupt him if he was in his office with the door shut. (Her observation was correct but the interpretation of it certainly was not.)

I tried to draw her out a bit on the subject of the lab hoping that some of her criticisms might reveal some fact we ought to know and face. But the picture she painted was so totally different from the one I had in my mind that it was hard to see that both could have the same basis. She said there was no one at the lab who had any aspiration. She said everything about the place was trivial. The playful use of gum and candy bars as rewards in experiments with children had no significance for her. They were just trivialities. Even the fact that no official day of mourning was taken at McDougall's death was, to her, an indication that the place was heartless, frivolous, superficial, and aimless. And Banks was mercenary enough to try to get money from a friend of Mrs. G.'s even though she was ill. And on and on.

After she left, Banks met his assistants at lunch and asked them if they thought he was such a terrible autocrat. But he said he had no success. She would have said, I suppose, that he had them all too cowed. But she left a resume of it all as she was departing, and in it was a slight trace of amelioration of her extreme attitude. We were aware of this because she sent a copy of it to several of our patrons. Banks wrote her a letter which I thought was perfectly fine, sincere and magnanimous. I hoped it would help. I hated to have her go away so rapidly, so angry, for the misrepresentation she could make if she still felt like talking about us could be damaging.

Many years later now, I have no memory or record to show that we ever heard from her again. My main thought about her now is that she must have been a very badly spoiled only child, and although she was not the only person who worked up strong feeling against Banks, she was the most extreme in her expression of it.

During these days of excitement and tension at the lab, I was involved at home with what, for me, was still a learning experience — fulfilling the role of mother. In a diary entry of September 4, 1938, I voiced again my uneasiness about myself in this role, saying

> I wonder if I should be planning things for the children instead of the experiments, etc., occupations in which they aren't included. I do like best of all to have them all around at home as they were yesterday afternoon, Robbie trying to build a doghouse, Sally rollerskating, Betsy playing with the dogs, and Rosie in a tub of water.

> But as I know very well, I'm not good at directing their play or suggesting new occupations or diversions for them. Banks has a way of making new suggestions sound interesting but I can't copy it. My attempts just sound unnatural and the children say they don't want to do it. And so I've about decided just to be myself and let them put up with the kind of mother they drew. And therefore I've given up storytelling which was just impossible, and now they've stopped expecting it. I'm much more comfortable.

Then on July 3, 1939, I tell about my own "addiction," which fortunately was not to drugs or alcohol, but this: "I spent two hours this afternoon clearing the remaining part of the lower orchard. It's good hard work."

And then for a page or two I explain how overgrown with sedge and weeds that area behind our house (with its three-acre backyard) still is, in spite of similar inroads upon it I had made earlier.

> [A]nd all the time I wonder why I do it, and I decide the reason is only that I enjoy it — just the mere physical labor, and because the finished product looks so neat. I also tell myself that it's a good place for the children to play, although they already have space to waste. Still I know I could be hearing Betsy's music lesson, or helping Rosie out of a scrape, sewing, or cleaning the house or making a pie for supper.... I suppose it's a little like a man on a spree must feel — but can I let that fringe of weeds grow, and be a lady-mother? I'm afraid I can't.

Later, in an entry on July 4, 1939, I return to this topic:

Banks says my sense of proportion is bad, and that's the reason I make myself a slave to the yard work. He says I'm just like my father, who always undertakes more than he can do. I know he's right.... Plenty of people would prefer weeds and leisure, but I won't even say the word that would get me a power mower. [Power mowers were just coming in, and to me, unused to spending "big" money, seemed prohibitively expensive.]

On my birthday in November, 1939, when I was 48, among other topics in my diary I mentioned that Banks and I had seen the play, "Our Town," which was, in effect, the re-living in a family of one happy day; and then since my birthday had been such an entirely happy day for me, I described it and, of course, Banks' part in it.

At 4 o'clock I got the little girls ready to go downtown for my birthday celebration which Banks had planned. He came home and took us downtown, and shopped with the children while I spent that time at a nursery school meeting to which I was committed. But I joined them then and we went to see the movie, "Five Little Peppers," with afterwards the unusual treat of a family supper out. For that we went to the Oriental and had Chinese food.

The novelty of the food didn't extend far enough to make the children's enjoyment of it outlast the eating, but they did pretty well. Rosie (only about 5) forgot that she had said she didn't like it in the attempt to eat with chopsticks. Both she and Betsy managed several bites at least and Sally bravely ate her portion and Robbie did the same.

We came home the long way and as we did so sang, "Home, Sweet Home," at Banks' suggestion. Then we all hastened in to inspect the purchases, which of course ostensibly were birthday gifts the children had gotten for me. But each child had also acquired a coloring or cut-out book for himself and these were their major interests.

Rather an ordeal resulted when their father told them that they were not to look at their books tonight so it wouldn't seem like their birthday rather than mine. It was pretty hard for them to deny themselves. Rosie stayed more or less unhappy until she went to sleep. But it was a good point of discipline, I know.

Banks said we wouldn't have had the trouble if there had been the proper buildup. That need hadn't been foreseen. There had even been a bad time beforehand in getting Robbie ready to go downtown at all. He wanted to play football. It was a fine day. The boys were in the backyard and "Five Little Peppers" was "a girl's play" anyway. He couldn't see what he'd get out of it. I told him that perhaps he wouldn't get anything out of it but he ought to go if only in order not to spoil Daddy's plan. But he is still a long way from having the discipline necessary to make a gesture like that with grace.

When Banks came home and took over the problem Robbie presented in refusing to get dressed, etc., I went to the car where the little girls were waiting and got there just in time to see Rosie and Betsy having a scrap.

Sally said it was too bad for Daddy who was so happy when he got home to have trouble with Robbie first thing and now the little girls crying and scrapping too. And I explained to them how Daddy had left his work early to give all of us this treat and how bad they'd make him feel. With a real effort then they quieted down so he wouldn't know they had had any trouble.

Soon Robbie and his father appeared, Robbie looking a little perturbed but not as sulky as I expected and very soon everyone was happy.

They all enjoyed the movie.

10
Facing the Critics:
A Heresy Trial

The perils that confronted Banks in the period following the first report of his ESP research were not only those involving illnesses in his young family and the death of his great sponsor, McDougall, but he was beset also by serious professional problems, including such roadblocks as the already mentioned one of not being able to get his reports published in regular psychological journals (Chapter 7), although, curiously, critical articles about his research did find space. I remember remarking at how odd it was to see an article appear which refuted claims that had not been made in any outlet that its author would consider worthy of his recognition.

These criticisms had appeared in the spring of 1934 after the Boston Society for Psychical Research monograph *Extra-Sensory Perception* reporting the first ESP results was published. Then, to everyone's surprise and probably to Banks' most of all, this supposedly inconspicuous little report was picked up and practically advertised nationally by the *New York Times* science writer, Mr. Waldemar J. Kaempffert. He, as it happened, was a member of the American Society for Psychical Research and was alert to material on the topic of the monograph, and particularly so to this one because it was based on experimental work.

The public response to the monograph was such that Banks soon began to realize that a more generally readable account of the ESP research was needed. Accordingly, he turned to the production of a more popular version. This resulted in the book, *New Frontiers of the Mind*, which came out in 1937 and was then reviewed by the well-known reporter, Mr. E.E. Free. His review appeared in the *New York Herald Tribune* book section on Sunday, October 3, 1937. It happens to be available to me now as the Kaempffert article does not; but this review explains why *New Frontiers* was noticed and publicized.

Referring to "the mystery of telepathy," the reviewer says, "Dr. Rhine's conclusions [represent] either one of the great mistakes of scientific history or the most important piece of research done this century." He also praises the "skill in story-telling" as "almost as good as the material." Free then refers to the frequent reports from individuals of seeming telepathy, premonition, and the like, and says that science "has refused these facts orthodox standing" mainly because acceptance of them would contradict the dogma that the brain can only know about the world via the senses.

Seven years of research at Duke University, he says, have replaced the personal accounts with firm statistical evidence obtained by the use of simple experiments the results of which can be evaluated according to the theory of probability. It is shown thus, he says, that some people in such experiments can exceed the chance limit so much that "any explanation of their scores as accidental becomes ridiculous." Successful fraud in all of this, Free says, "is inconceivable." If the theory of probability is correct, then, he concludes, this work has shown a new power of some human minds to perceive "without trammels of time, space, or the senses."

A glimpse of my personal reaction to the above series of events, especially to the criticisms of it, is in my diary record of March 8, 1938, when I wrote

The ESP work is at a stage that discourages me. This past fall after the publication of *New Frontiers*, a deluge of critical articles has appeared which though in no case undermining the work, still has succeeded in demoralizing it in one way. That is, the criticisms have caused so much of Banks' attention and that of the others at the lab to go to the answering of unfounded derogatory charges that little time or spirit is left for constructive thinking.

Meanwhile, at home with our little family, I had begun to cast around for some way by which I could turn my time there to some account for parapsychology. Our four children were by 1936 about 9, 6, 3 and 2 years old, and their playmates thronged our yard in varying numbers, for I had decided that it was easier to monitor my own at home than if they were out of my range in the yards of neighbors. It was then that it occurred to me that I might salvage a bit of time for science by trying to get evidence of ESP from them.

In October, 1935, I began a first series with the technique then in use at the lab called Open Matching and with these children as willing subjects by February, 1936, had made 246 runs of the 25-card ESP deck. In this technique (just a game to the children) five "key" cards (one of each kind) were laid out, faces up on the table before the child who was being tested, the subject. The subject with a shuffled deck of ESP cards held face down would lay each card in turn by the key card he thought it would match. But in the lab that technique soon was considered vulnerable to the possibility that the subjects might get sensory cues from the backs of the cards. And so I ran a second series with the key cards covered, a technique called Blind Matching. Both methods yielded results that were "significant," which as previously explained means the chance of their occurring was no more than 100 to 1.

The specific objective of these particular tests had been to see whether the nature of the target cards (which bore single or multiple, large or small symbols, etc.) affected the rate of scoring. On this point the result showed no favoring of one order of target over another. An average score of 5.6 hits per run with a critical ratio of 7.6 was achieved, where a critical ratio of 2.5 would have been significant. And I could feel that the time spent doing these tests had been well worth the effort.

But now the value of such contributions as this (and most of the others already reported) was being undercut by the tenor of the criticisms that began to come in. To this I reacted as recorded further in the diary account earlier referred to of March, 1938:

> The need for, the pressure for, such absurd and far-fetched precautions against sensory cues has arisen that one cannot hope to do anything like

spontaneous research. Until all the required screens and witnesses are assembled, inspiration is half dead, wholly so in my case.

In my work with the children, whose ESP tests I had watched with an eagle eye, I knew that they had not guessed correctly by reading the cards from the backs or by any other kind of cue. But I could not prove it in the way these critics were demanding, even though in the second year of my tests, the key cards were kept covered and, later still, behind screens. But the idea of loading every test with the precautions now demanded was deadly to me and, I suspected, to many other would-be parapsychological researchers, too.

The effect on Banks, or one effect, at least, is easy to read in the same entry, which continues

> However, Banks seems no longer to want me to work. He appears to be so tired of the subject by the time he gets home that he doesn't want to talk about it. And so I've been unable to get from him a satisfactory serious discussion of research problems, although these more or less critical charges that continually beset him he does talk about. It's good I guess that under the circumstances he doesn't expect more of me. But I feel disappointed too, for curiously, I do have still surviving in spite of all this domesticity, quite a rudiment of scientific interest which is left with no outlet.

Later, on July 23, 1938, my record picks up in much the same vein and reflects again, in however attenuated form, the strain that Banks was continually under in the face of the critical attacks that kept coming in:

> At noon today I asked Banks to tell me what had been going on at the lab. He said he wanted to forget about it during his lunch hour. That was the reason he hadn't been talking. Of course, for the last year or two I've seen this gradual dampening of his spirits under the fire of criticism. I could understand.

> Banks gave me the outline of Kennedy's paper to read. [Kennedy was one of the vociferous critics.] It is devoted to the thesis that checking and shuffling errors could explain many of the good ESP scores; how many of these errors there might have been is left to the imagination of the reader. It's the sort of suspicion one would just like to disregard. It should not be dignified by too much notice. But it's the need to answer so many charges of equal calibre that takes the time and energy that should go to really important things.

In the interrupted March 8, 1938, diary entry, I write

Banks came home tonight and said that the upshot of his thinking and conferences with the lab staff was that we must decide now on one of two policies, either to lie down and take the criticisms or rather to let them blow over our heads while we go "into the silence," work on in oblivion trusting only to the old idea that sometime somehow truth will come into her own, or the alternative, to launch a countercampaign for recognition by publicity. The former would mean to have time and freedom for research but probably lose the means for financing it. The latter would mean to make a major objective of getting the research recognized.

I said the alternatives needed a lot of consideration before decision. But I think I already know which it must be. The Curies would have chosen the former. Most of the scientists of the past would have done so I guess. But we won't. I don't think it's because we're of grosser calibre. But it's because we work for a different objective.

I might have said explicitly then, instead of only taking it for granted, that Banks could not do it that way because the message he was getting was not for ourselves alone, or even just for the psychic researchers, but for a world that needed it so badly.

However, taking that greater objective as obvious without repetition, I continue in the same entry

However, if the second alternative is chosen it will not be without regret that the peace that the other one would have given will have to be passed up. I suspect that if I were the one making this decision, I'd take the easy one. But Banks is different. He must get the report of his work out where it will count in the world. He knows that therefore he will have to make this fight. He will loathe it and be sick to death of it. It will take his youth and his enthusiasm but he'll do it. He'll do it because he must.

Then comes a different turn of thought. The time was the summer of 1938 and although we did not know it, World War II was barely more than a year away. The foreshadowing uneasiness felt that summer by all thoughtful people was hanging heavily over us, too, as the continuing diary indicates.

We went to a movie tonight which stirred us both up about Hitler and Europe, and have just returned. No one could see it, making real the tragedy of today as it did, without being deeply affected. We were more so than by any recent experience, for the factors making up the emotional impact of the movie are not new. We know them all. This film just sort of brought them into focus.

After the feature ended, I just sat there in some sort of trance, feeling that somehow there must be a way to stop this war-maddened world. Some way! Some way! If we just think hard enough! I almost felt as if I could think of a way if I'd just think a little harder — a little harder. But before I could get down deep enough, before I could get the necessary concentration the silly comedy came on and scattered my attention just as everyday affairs always draw one from the mountaintop.

Some of the feeling persisted, however. We drove the long way home, half of it in silence. Then Banks began to talk. He said the reason for the present chaos is because there is no ultimate objective in the world. As in the movie, one person fights for his sheep, one for his valley, one for adventure, one for money, but no common objective exists.

I said I thought there is something in Spengler's idea. It seems to me this civilization has passed its zenith. Now it's on its way to blotting itself out and nothing can stop it. Things are worse now after the modern inventions and the science of the time than they were.

But Banks says no. He will hardly even let me state the idea. He won't even let me express my fears that a struggle to the death between democracy and fascism is inevitable. The times of Napoleon and the times of Hitler are just the same, I say. But people can kill each other faster now. Armies are more dangerous now that they are armed with modern inventions. Well, he says, then that's necessary. It must be best. But I object that it's a pretty barren philosophy, if we have to call the worst the best in order to have the best triumph!

Then Banks comments that men through the ages have gotten the idea of a value higher than that which individuals read into things. How have they gotten the idea? From spontaneous happenings along the same line we are studying. Those happenings, undemonstrated according to scientific standards though they be, are what in the past have given man the only fixed and ultimate goal he has ever had.

Now we come along and with ESP we think that we've gotten a tiny little bit of scientifically demonstrable evidence of the same thing. A leg of the same elephant, I say. But if we could only tell, he says, if we could *only be sure* that we aren't fooling ourselves, somehow! How can we tell this? Only by checking ourselves by every method we can find. If after this we still seem right — what's left to us but to go ahead? We have to, don't we? And we surely will, he says, with determination. He squeezes my hand. We go into the house.

And that's the reason why he'll have to launch a publicity campaign, I know. Believing in our research, it'll have to be done somehow in order to get it out where it can mean something to the world. But can we do it fast enough to change a world and avert a war? I don't see how.

Ever since we got home and while I've been writing this, Banks has been playing his accordion in the dark — all the old songs he likes so much, the same and more that he played when we were first married and before he thought he could see a way to do something about the world, when he only aspired to finding the answer for ourselves.

From all that, it is clear I think that for a nature and determination such as his, the pitfalls and perils represented by critical psychologists offer not discouragement and surrender but only impediments to overcome.

The stream of criticisms of the ESP research had not abated by the summer of 1938, as shown by each of the articles about the results of the ESP tests published in the *Journal of Parapsychology* for 1937 and 1938. The burden of these articles, along with the statements of methods, conditions, and results, included discussions as to the level of assurance that each one could claim against specific alternatives to ESP. They thus clearly indicate that the various charges of faulty procedures of the past had not fallen on deaf ears. The possibilities of spurious results that they emphasized had already been recognized and measures taken to avoid them long before any of the results had been reported; and as Banks had thought, those measures had been amply described. But in these attacks the critics ignored the descriptions of the precautions and each new critic discovered all over again the particular kind of flaw it suited him to dramatize. An example of this from the many that were made, and in this case one to which I myself responded, is reflected in a letter of mine to a Mr. Carlton Beals, a copy of which I still have. Slightly condensed, it goes like this:

January 1, 1941

Dear Mr. Beals:

I bought your book, "The Great Circle," as a Christmas gift for my husband but I am reading and enjoying it before him. I am a stay-at-home person but I go with you in imagination to the far corners of the earth and thrill with you vicariously in your countless adventures in strange and interesting places.

I've never been to Tunis and I never saw Ben-Malik-el Hilim and I could say that man Beals is a tall-tale teller. He can create any place or character he needs. I dare say if I read on beyond page 53 perhaps I'll find other persons whose existence I could question.

But if I did wouldn't I be silly? And futile? What difference would it make whether I believed you or not? You know what the truth is and you were in Tunis. It was from lack of knowledge that you made your slurring remark about "Dr. Rhine's book of clairvoyance with marked cards."

But if I don't know Tunis neither do you know ESP. If you think Dr. Rhine's experiments were done with marked cards I challenge you to come and find out or at least do not pass judgment on pain of being as silly as I would be if I should say there's no Tunis.

I wish you'd someday come here and let Dr. Rhine, my husband, show you his "marked cards."

Sincerely,

(Of course we never heard from him.)
Criticisms came in also from more eminent persons like the English professor, E.R. Dodds. Again, I do not have his letter, but only a copy of the reply that Banks sent him on January 2, 1935. The objections that Dodds made are reflected in this reply, pertinent parts of which (somewhat condensed) I'll quote so that it can be inferred what Dodds' criticisms must have been. It will also show the tenor of Banks' reply.

Many thanks for your good letter. I regret that I have delayed so long in replying. It is due to my habit of saving the good letters to the last.

I appreciate your kind words, and your critical comments as well. I am in partial agreement with your feeling that more elaborate description of conditions and precautions should have been given. I undertook the report, however, without as much understanding of reactions as I now have ... and without having had much discussion of it with critical people. My later reports will show some advance along this line, I think.

As to your first point—that I should have stated whether the cards were always kept under lock and key between experiments: at the time the book was written experiments were being conducted with these same subjects which made this point irrelevant for a final decision—for instance, the distance work, the screened card work, etc. In reporting such a mass of material with an elaborate set of experiments one has to be brief somewhere. Yet I grant that such things must be clearly stated. Perhaps you are right about this. I found it difficult to decide such questions—and I am not sure now how far my judgment was good.

On your second point, I agree fully. The crosschecking should have been reported. It just did not occur to me, because early in the work we trained our subjects against similarity of preferences, but instructed the agents to vary (the target) deliberately (though not regularly) and according to a working system peculiar to each individual. Finding this successful, the matter dropped from my attention. Accordingly, at the time of writing this it was not an important question in *my* mind. It is, however, for the reader and I should have anticipated it. In the English edition of the book, which is being arranged for, I will include results of the checks made on this point.

You are the second among the psychic research people, the only ones who have raised your third point. I take it that the general concern about *bona fides* is a result of the prevalence of deception in the general psychic research field. Here, however, we are working with the more customary academic atmosphere, with our own students and assistants, and with only the usual desire to please, which every psychologist may count on with all his subjects. I grant that I have taken the matter of trustworthiness somewhat less concernedly than I would if I were dealing with a group of mediums. However, here again we have several clear cases in which the good faith of several people, some of them of rank and standing, would have to be compromised if the work is to fall, and I regard it as not essential to have to make clear at every step just how this factor stood.

The case is something like this. I feel it important to publish all of the results to permit evaluation of the anti-coincidence value, but I think we can omit some of the conditions on such points as the honesty of the assistant if we have this point later covered by an adequate group of data. For instance, as you know, I include large blocks of unwitnessed data for what they are worth, because I consider the question of the good faith of the subject who produced them as settled by a series in which he *was* adequately witnessed. In other words, it is not important to go into the good faith matter for all series. That is at least as much of a defense as I can make, but to be quite honest, I do wish that I had been more explicit, as for instance in the example you cite on page 74. "We" there actually meant only "myself." Pratt was not present.

I read with great interest and satisfaction your review of Dr. Jung's book. This reminds me of a good letter I had from him recently, expressing a strong interest in this work. He was, I find, investigating mediums when I was scarcely out of the cradle.

A reply from Dodds on January 19, 1935, makes a point about Banks' reaction to Dodds' criticism:

> Will you allow me to say that you do take criticism better than most psychic researchers! One of the diseases of the subject I find is that everybody suspects everybody else of a desire not only to disprove his results, but also to blacken his character.

The fact that because Banks had not sufficiently foreseen the strength of the resistance to his report, he had consequently failed to stress sufficiently the tight conditions under which the results had been secured was emphasized also by an experienced psychic researcher in England, Mr. Whatley Carington, with whom Banks had been in correspondence.

Apparently, Banks had written Carington about some of the experiments on PK as they were being conducted. On January 1, 1935, Carington wrote Banks and warned him of the need, not only to guard exhaustively against leakage, practical joking, etc., but to do so in a way that would *convince others* that nothing like that could have occurred. He stressed the point that merely assuring readers that none of those "leakages" had been possible would be insufficient. He said, for instance, that reports of "mind over matter" (PK) would not be believed except by the credulous. He emphasized that, although the disbelievers would be wrong, nevertheless they would not believe. Further, he said he would not blame them, for

> the whole history of psychic research is so full of cases of apparently virtuous and respectable people indulging in the oddest deceptions for the queerest motives that the matter is simply one that cannot be taken on faith.... In the present state of human knowledge, deception — whether pathological or otherwise, well-intentioned or malevolent, witting or unwitting — is only too well-established as a *vera causa*, while this is not true of paranormal phenomena (that's why we call 'em paranormal). Consequently, the critic MUST attribute reported phenomena to the better rather than to the worse established cause — to auto or hetero

deception or error, rather than to paranormality — unless it is specifically *demonstrated* (not merely asserted) that the former factors *cannot* have been operative.

In his reply to Carington (February 26, 1935), Banks thanked him and said:

Do not hesitate in the least ever to give me all the advice or warning as frankly and as fully as you feel like. We are brothers-in-arms and this is the first service we can render each other. I do not need encouragement very badly for I have been getting plenty of that this year anyhow. [He didn't yet know how soon that situation would change.]

I feel doubly pleased when I get a good blast of criticism. It helps me to strengthen my research in the future and gives me the comfort of knowing, "Well, that's the worst now," and so I do not have so much of that uneasiness within that I may be overlooking weaknesses. I need the critiques more than anybody else. I am keenly aware of that, so lay on as heavily as the spirit moves you. I think I understand your basic sincerity.

These phenomena have turned up faster than I had planned or expected them to; that is, my subjects have given me enough to think about for years. I do not intend to do much about it — except to make sure and then to make sure all over again, and then when I publish it to publish it for what it is worth and make no claims. I think you and a few others from the SPR group who have kindly written me interesting letters, have a more definite point of view than we have here in our laboratory — at least on one point.

Our point of view could best be expressed, "Here it is and here are the conditions. This is just a beginning. We are not asking you to believe this; we are asking you to be stimulated by it into repeating it or doing something else about it by way of active research." We are all taking it in that spirit.

Some of our work, you may remember, was not witnessed at all. A young psychologist holds his cards in his own hands, records his own data. One of your Council members of the SPR blew up terribly over that and wrote me a ferocious letter for doing such research. It just goes to show that he is not familiar with the research attitude of the psychological laboratory. He is used to working with mediums. He felt that we were terribly naïve. But we are seeking to discover principles, relations, and laws. We are not trying to *convince* him.

Banks' long letter then continues on the possibility of "leakage" in the experiments, saying that he didn't want it thought that he had been *trusting* his subjects, but he thought that leakage was shown to have been satisfactorily excluded if the report he wrote *(Extra-Sensory Perception)* was taken as a whole. He then adds

> Your letter and Gardner Murphy's were the best critiques I have had, yet neither one of you touched on this point [of leakage]. I am not therefore of the opinion that any large group of thoughtful readers will be much affected by the leakage hypothesis. As we go on to the report of the later work, this becomes still less probable as an alternative.

Then, in a final paragraph and on a different topic, he adds

> As I have told you before, I think [this research] has a great future. I hope that we will get the kind of institute here that can really handle the problem on a full-time basis. We might even try to persuade you to come over for a visit to help us get started sometime within the next few years. But just now there is no immediate prospect of our getting started on this project.

Banks' dream of a separate institute, as mentioned in that letter, was one destined to go unfulfilled for many years, how many, perhaps, it was just as well that he couldn't then have guessed.

In December, 1938, Banks' assistant, Stuart, reviewed and answered all the criticisms. His article was published in the *Journal of Parapsychology*. One of the most frequently raised criticisms, Stuart said, was that the ESP cards could be read from their backs. This was one of the so-called discoveries, but the reason for it had been noted at the lab and warned against when the first commercially produced cards had been received there. Banks had explained in the *Journal* that this warping had not shown up at the proof stage of the printing of the cards but it was present in the final product. However, the cost of that printing and the low state of finances at the lab made it necessary for him to accept the cards but to warn that they should only be used behind screens, a precaution which by then was advised anyway for all serious scientific research on ESP.

The warning to this effect had, in fact, been given in the December, 1937 *Journal*: "Imperfections in the commercial reproductions of the ESP cards preclude their unscreened use for experimental purposes." Stuart then gave a resume of successful work that had been carried out by several investigators using screens and some, also, with a distance between the cards and the subjects.

Another criticism was that the positive results that were reported could have been the result of errors of recording; and to back up the claim, an experiment had been set up so loosely by Kennedy, its proponent, that such errors in his results had indeed occurred. Stuart, however, easily disposed of that criticism, since the original ESP results had been closely monitored, carefully checked and rechecked, so that no such explanation could apply.

A different possibility that also was suggested was that the agent who was "sending" in a telepathy experiment unconsciously whispered the target and the subject picked it up. But, as Stuart commented, this one was "completely irrelevant to the large body of ESP research in which the card order was unknown to the experimenter." All of that on clairvoyance, for instance, fell into this category.

Another area of much criticism had concerned the mathematical evaluations that had been used. When Banks first began to make ESP experiments, he needed immediately to know the statistical value of the results he was getting. His education in mathematics, like mine, had not gone beyond the regular B.S. college requirements. Also, the field of statistics itself in the 1930's was still in the process of development. Soon it became necessary to seek help along this line; the Duke Department of Mathematics was the authority to which he turned, and Dr. Joseph Greenwood in that department became his constant resource.

By now criticism of the statistical methods (and standards that had been used) were also coming in, but between Greenwood and Stuart, they were answered. More and more the point was clear, however, at least to Banks and the lab personnel, not that the ESP statistics were improper, but that the critical psychologists themselves did not know their statistics. One such critic had even questioned whether one hit in five was the number to be expected by chance alone in the 25-card ESP deck of five symbols of each kind. He questioned the basic statistical procedure of calculating the anti-chance value of results in terms of a probability value.

One other general line of criticism listed by Stuart questioned the conceptual basis of ESP, in plain words amounting to the critics' simply saying that there cannot be anything new under the sun. The concept of ESP is new. Therefore, no such thing can be. One of these pundits said that by modern experimentation, knowledge is gained either directly or indirectly through the senses and cannot be gained without them. Thus ESP negates centuries of sound work and is "diametrically opposed to all scientific knowledge." But Stuart argued, "Speculative theories concerning the role of space and time in ESP tests as well as in all science should be the *result*, not the basis, of experimentation."

Stuart's article then concluded with a paragraph saying

There is no doubt that critical discussions of ESP research will continue to appear in psychological journals. Their quality should improve. The time seems propitious for a really serious survey of the field. If such a survey were graced by a willingness to face the issues directly in terms of the evidence and the experimental methods available, the present difference between critical and experimental conclusions might be happily resolved.

It is not that we don't need criticism for our mistakes and information on how to correct and to avoid them. But we need it in the areas of our ignorance, not in those for which the information is as available to us as to our critics.

One little reminder of the emerging work on psychokinesis comes up at this point in my diary, just before the Columbus, Ohio "heresy trial" to be discussed below. This reminder is dated July 30, 1938: "At noon today Banks brought home to show me a pair of new dice he had had made." Psychokinesis (PK) had been the subject of experimentation for years, but the results had not been published because of the critical response the ESP work was receiving. It had seemed a better strategy to let one bitter pill (ESP) be well swallowed before bringing on another.

One possible criticism of the research with dice had been that the hollowed-out spots created unevennesses and then when the dice were thrown that those somehow contributed to the extra-chance results that had been obtained in certain experiments. But this diary entry continues about the new dice:

> In these, the spots are filled in with colored pieces of the same material. This was to avoid the possibility of unequal weights on different sides. Banks threw them and got a double six. He said, with considerable emphasis, "Louie, believe it or not, I *knew* those were going to be sixes." He picked them up and said, "I'll do it again," and then, arresting his arm in mid-motion, "But no. Now doubt comes in. All my intelligence says, 'I won't get double sixes again'."

> "Well," I said, "if somehow, either in this or regular ESP, if we could just learn how — even if only one of us could learn how — to control that mental factor that inhibits, then we surely could convince all the doubters that mind can affect these objects and we could do it in a hurry."

> "Yes," he said, "but that's like telling Ben Franklin that he could convince the doubters about electricity if he would just make a dynamo and show them."

"Well, anyway," I said as he turned to go, "I wish you'd let me try these dice. — But no. That's what I would have wished a year or two ago. But now — what's the use? Suppose I did take them and suppose I got sixes all afternoon, what good would it do? I'd have no witness and who would believe me?"

"Well, I would," he said somewhat hotly. "We've got to go ahead regardless. That's the conclusion to which I've gotten now. We've got to be the scouts. Otherwise, I certainly wouldn't have sent Peggy [one of his research students at the lab] up to the meeting in Columbus this spring. It was pioneering work she was supposed to do. Pioneers don't need to raise a crop of corn on the land they discover before they report that they've discovered it. And so, we dare scout out the territory and report what we have found — no matter who does or doesn't believe it."

Sometime in the winter of 1937, Banks told me that he had a letter from the psychologist John Kennedy (already mentioned), saying that a symposium on ESP was being planned for an afternoon at the 1938 fall meeting of the American Psychological Association, the APA. It was to be held at Columbus, Ohio. He showed me an outline of the proposed program. We discussed it and noted particularly that it was made up of papers by critics and that no paper presenting the work from a constructive or factual viewpoint was included.

As it turned out, the APA symposium on ESP, although not in the Middle Ages, was to be, nonetheless, a heresy trial. Obviously, although the times were different, human nature was much the same. To mainstream psychologists, the idea that extrasensory knowing could occur was blatant heresy. This symposium was designed to show it as such, whether the terminology of the Middle Ages was used or not. However, here I'm not going to report directly on that trial but on a situation that came up behind the scenes, so to speak, and which I experienced firsthand and of which I wrote a diary account soon after. It shows the "nutcracker" in which Banks found himself at that meeting.

When we noted that the program was to feature only the criticisms of the research, we tried to make the best of the situation and agreed that it was at least *something* that the psychologists would condescend to notice the work sufficiently to devote a period even to a consideration of the criticisms. Banks himself, instead of being asked to present his findings, was scheduled to give a fifteen-minute talk on the exclusion of sensory cues in his research. He also had a chance to select a mathematician to give a paper on the statistical evaluations made.

I said I thought the meeting should be interesting and I'd like to attend it. I thought that perhaps since it was to be held in Columbus,

Ohio, only about sixty miles from my old home at Doylestown, I could find some way to get there. I mentioned this to Banks, but no plans were made. Then, one day late that summer, I asked him if he knew which ones of the men from the lab were going to the meeting and when they would be leaving. I was trying to see how I could make arrangements to go, too; a friend had promised to keep the children.

My enthusiasm was dampened, however, by the repressed emotion with which Banks told me that he didn't know, had made no plans, and didn't want to make any until the last minute. He said he was not looking forward to the occasion with anything but distaste, but only going because he had to, and felt that it would be the kind of proceeding that he would not want any more of his friends to witness than was necessary. Of course, I felt very much dis-invited. He also made it very clear that he did not want to have the feeling that his movements there were impeded by having me along. I was surprised, and nettled, too, by the implication that I would tie him down or in any way hamper his action. I was left very much undecided whether to try to go or not.

The discussion did, however, show me more clearly than I had realized before how Banks felt about this meeting. I had not realized that he would mind facing a hostile audience from a disadvantageous position as much as he apparently did. But I thought it over and decided that if it was to be as bad as he thought, I had all the more a right if not a duty to be there, too, to get a firsthand estimate of the situation.

My sister, Miriam, no longer a little girl of ten, had for the last year or two been Banks' secretary while she was a student at Duke. But now she was transferring to the University of Colorado and, enroute, would be going to our home in Doylestown on September 1, a week before the Columbus meeting. I worked out a plan for us to drive to Doylestown. Then, leaving Miriam there, I would go back down to Columbus on the day of the meeting, quite independently of Banks and any plans he might have.

When I proposed this to Banks, he didn't say much either way, and so I carried it out. Miriam and I left Durham earlier than he and went to our parental home. Banks left Durham with Pratt and Stuart on the Monday before the meeting, and they were thus at Ohio State University where the meeting was to be held, several days preceding the Friday of the ESP symposium.

After I arrived in Doylestown, and the night before I was to leave for Columbus, I had a short note from Banks that had been written just after his arrival there, saying that he had run into some complications in regard to a paper to be read by one of several students who were to report on their own ESP research. Although this young man, Jim, was not one of Banks' students, his work reporting especially high scoring had been submitted for the symposium. It had originally been reported to the lab after it had been done in Jim's college, a small institution in Missouri. He had brought his paper to the lab in Durham in person a day or two before Banks, Pratt, and Stuart left for Columbus.

Banks' note to me said the complications were such that he had been very disturbed and unable to sleep. The trouble might or might not be serious. He said he was eager to see both me and Miriam. She had decided not to go with me to Columbus, but when she heard he wanted her, she came along and we drove down together. I asked her if she had any inkling of what the trouble about Jim's paper might be, but she had no idea. I said, "If it just isn't anything that involves personal honesty, anything else won't be so bad."

"Oh, why think of that the first thing?" she said heatedly. "You are a lot too quick to think of that," and added, "Banks is, too." Of course, she didn't realize fully what reason we actually had to "think of that, first thing." I explained that I wasn't saying that it was dishonesty, but that would be the worst possibility, and I hoped Banks was not going to have that kind of situation to face. I got her mollified, but we both were much disturbed and anxious to know what the trouble might be.

When we arrived at Columbus, we found Banks' lodging house where he had reserved rooms for us; and just as we were leaving for a walk on the university campus, he and several of the other ESP people came in. He looked tired and nervous, I thought. He said he had something to write yet, and he wanted to get a little rest before the symposium at four o'clock. It was then about three. I said we were going for a walk and so he wouldn't be disturbed by us. Those were the only words we had until, drawing me around the corner where the others wouldn't see or hear, he said, "I've only had troubles this week, Louie!"

"About Jim?"

"Yes."

"It's not dishonesty?"

"Yes. Beyond all doubt — it runs through everything!"

"Oh, Banks — !"

Then I walked down the street with Miriam. I wanted to tell her what Banks had said, but decided, no, I won't. I'll let him tell her and not risk saying something I shouldn't.

About 3:30, we went and sat in the back of the hall in which the meeting was to be held. A handful of psychologists was scattered around in it, trying to listen to a man telling something about an experiment in vision. I couldn't tell just what he was saying, and no one else looked much more intelligent than I felt.

But I was bothered by the poor acoustics of the room, and by the September heat. I noticed that the man speaking was in white, and I recalled that Banks had been wearing his heavy suit. The room was an amphitheater with no windows to open, and anyone who knew Banks' speaking habits knew that opening windows was usually the first stage of his talk. I realized that even the physical setting would be all against him. He'd have difficulty being heard — and he never could stand being hot when making a talk. I considered rushing over to his room to tell him to put on a cooler suit, but I knew that his clothing would have been the last thing on his mind when he left home and that he probably hadn't even thought to bring an extra suit. I could do nothing!

Miriam spied Jim's professor in the audience, and she suggested that we go down and ask him what the trouble was. But I thought we'd better not mention it until we got a cue from Banks. She agreed.

Soon the crowd began to gather for the four o'clock meeting on ESP, and it sounded like the trampling of a herd, and that was what it was. By four o'clock, when Banks appeared, the place was packed even to the aisles. The chairman had to clear the front row so that the speakers and stenographer could have a place to sit.

I began to get stage fright and was so nervous I had to force myself to sit still so that Dr. Bradley, a psychiatrist, sitting next to me, would not interpret me psychiatrically. I surely was glad I was not the one who was going to have to speak, and I hoped that Banks didn't feel the way I did; but, considering everything, I knew he did. Before very long, I noted with some relief that he had taken off his coat, although he was the only man there in shirtsleeves. A little later, Kennedy also took off his coat. Considering that he was the chairman, I thought it was considerate of him. Later, several other men removed their coats.

When Banks' turn came to talk, I realized that he had departed from the paper he had prepared. He was talking now from an entirely different viewpoint. I knew he was very nervous, and soon he was looking around for water. There was none. Someone went out to get some but did not return for quite a while, during which time Banks had so much difficulty in speaking that he finally stopped, turned to the water tap on the chemistry table and wet his handkerchief. Then he smiled a bit and said apologetically, "I don't know why I should be so nervous." The slight stir from the audience seemed to mean that his situation was appreciated.

The first part of his talk was devoted to a reply to the previous speaker's charge that he had used bad cards and had confused the ESP issue by having at least three different kinds of cards. Then Banks, with more than usually halting speech, with obvious nervousness, but with absolute and disarming directness, seemed to me to convince the audience very quickly of his honesty, for the previous speaker, while not actually questioning it in words, had done so in fact. But I thought that

Banks was certainly convincing on that point and was so throughout his talk, although not very clear nor even lucid always. Altogether, I thought from the point of view of structure, organization, and delivery, it was about the poorest speech I ever heard him make. Miriam and I both were uneasy when we saw that he was exceeding his time limit. However, he finished at last and I was so relieved that I never even noticed what others later mentioned, that he got more applause than any other speaker. I wondered if his sincerity didn't carry over all the stronger, because of his nervousness and lack of glibness.

By the time the papers were all presented, it was so late that some of the crowd had left. The discussion following was lively, but others, mainly Pratt and Stuart, carried it off and Banks didn't have to say much. I knew that pleased him, for he wanted it to be known that others shared the burden of responsibility now so that it would not be just "Rhine's work."

After the meeting broke up, a crowd remained, as usual; but I soon slipped out of the smoke-filled room. Outside, I happened to meet Jim's professor. He said at once that the week had been a strain and he referred to the "Jim affair," which he said had been the greatest shock to him he had had in a long time. He said there had been consistent changes in Jim's records, such as erasures and transpositions in Jim's call series, that were absolutely planned and consciously made, that could not have been mistakes or unconscious slips. It seemed pretty bad.

I could well realize the strain Banks had been under. Jim's work had been considered one of the best of those recently reported. The conditions as he had presented them were excellent and the results reassuringly significant. Banks had been intending to use the work as the centerpiece of his own talk. But now he was confronted with a situation in which not only was his own speech spoiled but even worse, the report of the work he had considered a new and strong proof of ESP was shown to be unreliable. I learned that just a day or two before Banks, Pratt, and Stuart had left Durham for Columbus, the first suggestion had arisen that Jim's records were dishonest. Many times in the past when the continually interesting and significant reports of Jim's work, as he had been doing it, had come to the lab, Banks as well as Pratt and Stuart had wondered if there could possibly be a "catch" somewhere. "It is almost too good to be true," they would say.

It had long been the case for these three lab watchdogs, Banks and his two assistants, that high scores, even though so desirable, always excited more initial suspicion than low or marginal ones. Because of this, Joe Woodruff, a member of the lab staff who had earlier been a student at Jim's college, had sometime before been sent back there to observe and help check Jim's records. Jim's professor had also witnessed some of Jim's work. No suspicion about it had ever arisen, however, so that more and more over the preceding months everyone had ceased to question Jim's good results.

Then, a few weeks before the Columbus meeting, a request had come from Gardner Murphy for as many original records of experiments as possible. He was to have the last paper at the symposium, which was to be on recordkeeping and checking methods. Jim, then, had been asked to turn over some of his original records to Murphy.

I should explain here that records like these consisted of two columns of symbols for each 25-card run. One column was a record of the target list, the symbols of which were randomly arranged and recorded elsewhere beforehand, their order taken originally from a table of random numbers. The second column was a record of the subject's calls made in his attempt to match the target list, while in ignorance of it. Then, later, when the columns were checked, the "hits" between the two, the instances in which the symbols were the same, were counted. Chance alone would be five, on the average, so any scores more or less than that would be of interest.

Since computers were still in the future, this checking was done by hand. Hence mistakes in scoring sometimes occurred, as later rechecking showed. The rechecking process had also shown that such mistakes were more likely to have lowered the original score than to have increased it, because it was easier for a checker to miss and overlook hits than to mistake unlike symbols as hits.

Since Jim had arrived at the lab with his records only a day or two before the trip to Columbus, Stuart, who was a master hand at such checking, had only had them a short time. It was long enough, however, for him to find errors on the sheets he did recheck. Instead of being the usual kind, errors involving the missing of hits by the checker, these were regularly errors that increased the score. Of course, this at once raised a suspicion in his mind.

But before Stuart and Pratt could get any further into the study of these records, it was time to leave for Columbus, and so they and Banks had the drive there with this uncertainty hanging over them. I could easily imagine the strain it must have been to Banks. They arrived at Columbus and got to work again on the records. It seemed that the further they got, the worse it grew, and before long they were all certain that Jim had actually consistently falsified his records. Since the card orders were fixed (prerecorded), in order to produce extra hits Jim had to resort to erasures and transpositions in the records of his call series.

The three men then spent most of the time, those days and nights before the meeting, trying to figure out what the trouble was with the data. Accordingly, they were not seen among the psychologists very much even though they were in Columbus. When Jim's professor arrived, they showed him what they had found, and he, too, was convinced — and shocked. He was upset because it seemed as if the fault was partly his in not detecting the fraud while Jim was under his surveillance.

And so it had gone, right up to the day of the symposium. In the papers Banks had prepared and meant to read, he had used some of Jim's work as a major reference. But naturally he could not use that paper now, but had no time — or heart — to prepare another. Consequently, he had to go to the symposium with only the few hurriedly written notes he could get together that afternoon after I left him in his room. No wonder he was nervous and worried. He had not been sleeping much and had been drinking coffee to make up for it. Even Dr. Bradley, beside me at the meeting, had whispered, "I never saw Dr. Rhine so nervous before."

So much for "behind the scenes." After the meeting, everyone who spoke to me said it had been a success, that the impression it had left with the audience certainly was not a bad one for ESP. I didn't know. I felt quite incompetent of judging then, though when I thought it over later I felt that perhaps they were right. At least, the case was no worse for the general audience than before, and I am sure the other papers helped. A mathematical one by Dr. Greville must have given added respect for the statistics that had been used. Also, Murphy's paper must have considerably weakened Kennedy's position about checking errors. Miss Martin's comments on her own work and Dr. Reese's little talk about his high-scoring subject would have lightened Banks' burden of criticism. So I guess our crowd had a right to feel good after the meeting.

Banks had planned a dinner for the ESP-ers afterwards. All of our crowd from the lab were there, plus Dr. Reese, Miss Martin, Jim's professor, Miss Bradley, Dr. Mühl, and Jim. It seemed quite a pleasant occasion.

All of us who knew about the Jim affair naturally were wondering whether he suspected that we knew about his dishonesty. But since he was shy and a newcomer to the group, he could be very quiet without betraying anything. I thought he didn't look very happy, and I wondered if he could help but notice that Banks in his talk had made not the slightest reference to him or his work. Considering that his conscience must have been guilty, I imagine he must have suspected something. But as far as I know, nothing ever appeared on the surface, nor was Jim's name ever again seen in the annals of parapsychology.

On the way home, Miriam was with us, and Banks told her that since she was a good and discreet secretary and understood the necessity of secrecy sometimes, he wanted to tell her about what had been going on at the meeting behind the scenes.

Those of us who had been involved were so sobered by the situation concerning Jim's work that we scarcely realized that the "heresy trial" had not resulted in a conviction. However, even though the discussion had involved a fairly lengthy examination of all the main criticisms that had been advanced, and even though in it both sides were represented, the verdict still remained in doubt, apparently, for in the following year reverberations of the controversy still resounded.

Even in the *Journal of Parapsychology* a year later (Volume 3, p. 195), Stuart, again reviewing recent criticisms of ESP research, said in his opening paragraph that since the 1938 article

> Critical statements regarding ESP research have continued to appear.... In the main there has been no addition to the points of criticism previously raised, but the fact that many continue to be raised indicates the need of keeping them under consideration.

It is a situation which, in my opinion, should never be forgotten by all serious parapsychologists. Perhaps it's like an old joke about people, which says, "A person convinced against his will is of the same opinion still." Only here, substitute psychologist for person, for even today it remains true that many psychologists are still of the opinion that the idea of ESP is an illusion, if nothing worse. For instance, as Duke professor of psychology Dr. Norman Guttman, who has been consistently critical of parapsychology over the years, and upon whom apparently no amount of data has the slightest effect, told a *Durham Herald* reporter, according to the account in that paper on November 29, 1981,

> If the chancellor asked me if it was in the university's best interests to sponsor work in this field, I would say no — there is no place for parapsychology at Duke. It won't pay off. How many times do you have to tell somebody that there ain't no Santa Claus?

Such a stand, taken by a Duke professor, however, is taken in spite of, or perhaps in ignorance of, the decade-long labors of a member of the Duke history department, Dr. Seymour Mauskopf, who with Dr. Michael McVaugh from the University of North Carolina at Chapel Hill in 1980 published a book entitled *The Elusive Science, the Origins of Psychical Research*. In this, like Diogenes searching for an honest man, the authors hunted for bona fide evidence of ESP and eventually concluded that "many of the significant results reported in parapsychology are real."

My acquaintance with ancient history is too scant to tell me whether Diogenes ever found his man, but parapsychologists can appreciate that outcome of this modern historical research and the fact that the research it entailed is meticulous, correct, and inclusive.

The general effect of the present-day situation of parapsychology on newcomers, students in the field, is summed up by one of them, Miss Barbara Lovetts, who attended the 1980 Summer Study program at the Institute for Parapsychology. She wrote about the problems of being a student of parapsychology, and her account was published in the 1981 *Newsletter* of the ASPR. She said, in brief, that for such a student

> There is a sense of being separated from the mainstream science and scientific thought while at the same time excitement about knowing that you are a pioneer, a revolutionary, a paradigm-buster ... involved in creating a scientific revolution.... However, this feeling tends to be subverted by various obstacles.

> Among them is parapsychology's lack of acceptance by the academic community. There are very few degree programs.... Although more and more institutions offer one or two courses in parapsychology, they are often not taught by trained professionals. Also, they are rarely given by the prestigious universities that pride themselves on their research traditions and their reputations as forums for open and liberal intellectual discussion.

She also remarks that very few scholarships are available, so that independent research projects must come out of "your own pocket" — and after all this, the reality is

> that there are virtually no jobs. Therefore ... you have to have ... firm training in some adjunct field on which to fall back....

> For a career in parapsychology, one has to be better than just good. That means studying hard, getting a good scholastic reputation ... no immediate rewards, no recognition ... and very little praise....

> But being a student of parapsychology is very exciting, challenging, and rewarding. If you are willing to make the necessary sacrifices ... refuse to let anything stand in your way ... the rewards may be in the distant future, but knowing you are a pioneer in uncharted space and that parapsychology will someday be part of everyone's science ... is satisfaction in itself.

In view of the general situation of the still continuing unacceptability of parapsychology on the general front, and as evidenced by the professor on our own nearby Duke campus, it is clear that parapsychology is still a long way from being accepted as a legitimate field of science.

As a child I listened to many accounts by my grandfather who, shortly after the Civil War, cleared a large tract of land in northern Ohio. I remember the stories of trying to plow fields in which many tree stumps were still remaining, and of the labor it took to grub them out, labor which often was impeded and complicated by the hornets' nests in those stumps.

In parapsychology still today stumps remain, and in some of them are hornets' nests. But the old home in Ohio now has none, lying as it does in a modern and productive farming area. And so it will come to be in parapsychology; in fact, it is already becoming so, as the hornets are dealt with by the methods the situation demands.

11

The War Years

After the ball was over
After the day was done
Many a heart was breaking
After the ball.*

The "heresy trial" was not a ball, yet after it was over, lines as I
remembered them from an old song heard in childhood came to mind.

*"After the Ball" — Charles K. Harris

Although Banks' heart was not breaking, I noticed a change in him. As I wrote in my diary on November 29, 1938,

> Banks commented ... that since last September at Columbus, really, something has changed in him, perhaps something vital gone out.
>
> It seems as if he has come to care less. Whether it means that he takes the whole research proposition less seriously, whether he has really lost interest or just become too tired, I don't know. At any rate, it's true. I have known it and wondered what we could do to revitalize ourselves, or himself especially.

Nothing specific to "revitalize" Banks after the encounter with the skeptics occurred, however, except the effect of time. To a person as dedicated to a topic as he was to this one, the quest had to continue as soon as, one might say, he had time to collect his energies again, and then he was ready to carry on the effort no matter what it took.

One topic to which Banks came back frequently even in our discussion the night of McDougall's death, was that of hauntings. They had been reported relatively frequently in the older literature of psychic research, and Banks felt that those reports should be examined again, and also all of the manifestations that appeared to bear on the survival question.

I had then added a general fear of ours, that such an investigation would be difficult to make because of

> the dread spectre of publicity hovering over to spoil everything. But I hope some way will open up. I'm tired of marking time while the psychological critics catch up, if they ever do.

The investigation of hauntings, as we well knew, would stimulate the curious, including, of course, the press; it would probably do so before a proper parapsychological study could even get started, and after it did, a careful on-the-scene investigation would be impossible.

A few weeks later, January 30, 1939, the story recorded in my diary goes on:

> Banks was telling me some of the things a woman who called at the office today told him about experiences she claimed that she had had. One was considerably like our Christmas tree experience in which a little bell tinkled just when Mrs. McDougall and I were talking about Dr. McDougall's last days.

It's the implication of such happenings that keep stirring us up. Banks, I know, is trying to think of some possible approach to the larger problem, survival. But it's pretty hard to find a place to take hold. I just hope that somehow we can manage it, but I feel perfectly helpless. I just settle down and keep house and make flower beds because I do know how to do these things and I can't see how to do the other.

The objective of attempting research on survival directly had long before this been abandoned as impractical. As Banks knew, it would have been like trying to reach a mountaintop without first scaling the lower reaches. In fact, the earlier research, which had shown the reality of the types of ESP and of PK, had been the result of the policy of trying first to establish the reality of the elementary factors that survival would entail.

In a diary entry of January 18, 1939, I mentioned that Banks was doing some research with child subjects to see if they could guess hidden numbers better than would be expected by chance, and I said, "He is much enthused by the results he got." Of course, he knew that just as one swallow doesn't make a summer, so a few sets of scores higher (or lower) than chance did not necessarily mean anything at all. Had these tests yielded only scores averaging at the chance level, they would soon have been given up. But these were encouraging and would lead to further testing.

Incidentally, I mentioned here too (on July 4, 1939) that we had a picnic with a neighbor's family which included a young man, John, with a disability that had only recently been diagnosed as epilepsy. Although I had met him before this happened, I was struck now by an indescribable look in his eyes, a reserve even in his smile. I recognized it, or imagined I did, as akin to the look of an old friend of mine the last time I saw her and after she knew that her cancer operation had not been successful.

It's understandable, I think, that the knowledge that one has an incurable illness should leave an indelible trace on the features. Any of us may have just as problematic a future, but since we don't definitely know it, we shut our eyes to the possibility that we may not live very long and so we can go on living. If one knew for sure of a tragedy that lay close ahead, it would spoil the spirit of normal living.

Later that summer, a somewhat similar theme came up on the occasion of a visit from Banks' sister, Myra. Myra had been ill, and her illness seemed to have puzzled her physician. My note said

Myra is here to rest and try to recuperate, and perhaps to find out something more about her physical condition. She thinks she has creeping paralysis and it looks a whole lot like it. She enters into the spirit of our lives here as well as her limited strength allows and I try to keep things quite normal. Yet in the back of my mind constantly is the thought that she may be looking into the unknown. At least, it may be a little closer and a little more consciously in her mind than is true for the rest of us. I know the same thought is with her all the time and I reflect that that would make a vast difference in one's outlook. She may outlive any one of us [she didn't], but because she is faced with the possibility of not doing so, the end we each know we face is real to her as it never is to us.

Then came the war-threatening year of 1940, and on September 24, I wrote

War news on the radio keeps interrupting everything. It takes considerable time to keep abreast of current news.

Banks is trying to work up the necessary enthusiasm and interest for another year of research at the lab, but the war has upset him too. I know he needs a change. After ten years of ESP he needs some new stimulus which the situation here doesn't supply. But he has to do the best he can without it.

The next record is not until May, 1941, when I was invited by Mrs. McDougall and Kenneth to go with them on a trip to Beaufort beach. I took the opportunity while there to make a long-deferred diary entry in which I say, "It could be titled 'ESP and the Vicissitudes of the Present.'" And then:

When last I wrote, we were still hoping there would be no war. Now for almost a year and a half there has been one in Europe and for a full year now all the victories have been with the wrong side. At least the overt ones have been. I suppose it is really the equivalent of a major victory that now at last this country is waking up. At least I hope so. If it doesn't it's hard to see where there's any hope.

As far as ESP is concerned I don't suppose it'll even be a problem again for generations unless there is ultimate victory for freedom and democracy. Last winter when the Finnish war was raging, Banks began to feel unsettled and I knew he was wishing he could ditch all his fight with the psychologists and go out and fight in an actual war, and by the time spring came he was more and more unsettled. I knew it was hard for him to keep telling himself that he would have to stay with his job and not go off and enlist somewhere like he did once before. The world outlook was so uncertain that for a while we didn't know if we'd be carrying on as usual by fall or not. Banks even wrote to several military headquarters to offer his services.

Besides the threatening world situation, the one at the lab was also discouraging, for attempts to raise money had not been successful. Funds were so low that a reduction had to be made in the little group of workers which had been assembled mainly from Banks' classes. They were individuals who had been interested in and challenged by the ESP and PK problems. Their salaries, even though modest by anyone's standards, were the main expense. The university provided space and Banks' own salary but only a token amount toward the lab budget. The result of this financial crunch now was that three persons had to be let go when their current term of employment ended.

Already in 1938 it had been difficult to find even proper secretarial help, because the ability to type was not the only requirement. Intelligence and interest in and appreciation of the problem were desirable, if not actual necessities, and all this for only a regulation salary. Banks, and Miriam too, realized this afresh when she was preparing to leave the lab and her job as Banks' secretary to continue her education elsewhere. They both tried to find a replacement for her, a person who would become devoted to the field as well as to Banks personally. Such a person probably would not be a young girl on her first job but an older woman, preferably married and settled down.

Together they interviewed several applicants and at length hired one, single and not in the throes of courtship, but soon she began to go out with a young law student and before long they were married and moved away. The next venture was more successful. Dorothy Pope, from Rhode Island, had begun to work at the lab, not as a general secretary but mainly to help with the *Journal*. She was competent and well-educated, and soon became interested and took pride in the little publication, the *Journal of Parapsychology*. Accordingly, she developed into Assistant Editor of the *Journal*, working under Banks' direction but becoming increasingly independent. She stayed at the lab for many years, retiring, as Editor, only recently in 1982.

By the fall of 1940 it was possible to begin building up a small research staff again. Among a few more or less temporary individuals, one was a promising young college graduate, Betty Humphrey, from Earlham College in Indiana. She had the necessary requirements, having been interested in ESP as an undergraduate and having undertaken ESP research in her senior year. Her research had not only given statistically significant evidence of ESP but had also shown an interesting effect that called for further research. Upon analysis she found the distribution of her subjects' hits in the ESP runs turned out not to be scattered at random down the 25 calls, but when the runs were plotted, they gave a U-shaped curve. This meant that the hits tended to occur mostly in the first and last sections of the runs, with fewer in the middle. When Betty reported this to Banks, he was at once interested and invited her to the lab. Patterning such as this was a sign of something other than chance; and the "salience" (as Banks called it), if it could be properly confirmed, would be another and perhaps even more meaningful evidence of ESP than extra-chance scores alone.

Then, looking back at old research data, they discovered similar hit patterns in them, too. It was a very encouraging find. This patterning had not been suspected by the experimenters in whose data it was now found, nor had Banks himself suspected it earlier. In his paper in the *Journal* reporting this work Banks said that the result was "an instance all too uncommon in ESP research, of a common pattern of results running through a moderately wide range of experimental groups."

The existence of "position effects" was to Banks like a new experiment that had yielded a very significant result. In the operation of a function so obscure and controversial as ESP, it was incontrovertible evidence of the existence of something more than chance, for chance alone could never produce an effect like that.

In the spring of 1941 the opportunity came for us to spend the summer in western North Carolina at Lake Junaluska, a former resort village by then nearly deserted. It offered the change of scene that even Banks himself agreed he needed. It was a vacation à la Banks Rhine, however, for he took his work along as well as his two helpers, Betty and Dorothy. The situation turned out to be ideal.

The major preoccupation of Banks and his two helpers all that summer long was the evaluation and writing up of the previous winter's experimental results, a complicated mathematical task which consumed every morning. The three of them worked so intensely that by late afternoon they would feel the necessity for a change. Then, the children off to the recreation center, we adults would set out to explore the country round about. We hiked up green valleys, conquered the surrounding mountains, explored the world from marshes to mountaintops, went swimming in the lake. So, in general, the summer was both a productive and a relaxing one, and it was with fresh enthusiasm that Banks came back to Durham in the fall. His health, his vigor, and his general attitude seemed definitely renewed.

In the fall of 1941 I recorded in some detail one of those days that any mother of four grade-school-age children might have, especially if among them was a rebellious adolescent like Robbie. One afternoon, the younger children and I were about to drive to the college to get Banks, after which we would all go swimming in Crystal Lake to get cooled off after a blistering day. I write

Robbie had declined to go on the swimming trip with us and from the top floor of the garage told me that the neighborhood boys who were swarming all around were just ready to launch an acorn fight. So I stopped to talk to them — Harold, Bobbie, W.L., Eddie, and the rest — and I found them just ready to break out like red-hot volcanoes against Robbie, whom they accused of shooting at them with a beebee gun [which probably was the truth].

It took an appreciable time to get a temporary mode of procedure worked out. I told the boys how much Robbie's father and I wanted them to play here, and Robbie to treat them right. But I asked them to go home while I was gone and let Robbie cool off. They started rather reluctantly and I drove off and picked up Betty and Edith on Watts Street and then on to the University where we met Banks. Dorothy and her twins and Gaither and his family came in their cars, and so we all got to Crystal Lake by 5 o'clock. Well, we did swim and it was a great relief after the heat. It got dark soon, a lovely sunset, and we were home about 6:30. Banks had to hurry for a 7:30 class after a quick meal on yesterday's leftovers.

Later that evening after baths and a pitcher of lemonade and after the younger children were all in bed, Robbie appeared to talk over his troubles with the boys. I tried to make him see that he couldn't stop the boys from "raiding" the barn as he said they had done by going down and raiding the cabin they had built down below the woods. But I didn't get very far with him. I explained the difference between the Old and New Testament philosophy, "an eye for an eye" versus "turn the other cheek." But — like the world in general — he couldn't apply it. At 9:30 Banks got home and he helped too for about 15 minutes when we sent Robbie to bed.

[I should break this account here to say that now, much as JB and I then may have felt uncertain about the kind of an adult such a rebellious youngster as Robbie would become, the years have proven most reassuring. The character elements that made him difficult to handle then were the forerunners of those that have made him a reliable and successful individual. With the help of a sympathetic life partner and three promising, now adult, children, he has for years held a very responsible position with General Motors as head of a foreign unit.]

Then Banks and I talked over the day and he told me about his proposed colloquium talk at the university for next Wednesday. We listened to the war news which is still indefinite between Russia and Germany. Then I wrote all this and now it's 12 P.M. Banks has gone to bed in the study because it's so hot upstairs. But I'll be all right upstairs.

And that's a day.

I wish I had made a resume of the proposed colloquium talk. It was the general psychology colloquium and Banks was going to present some of his research findings to his not very sympathetic departmental colleagues.

Even on the historical day of December 7, but before the news of the bombing came over the air, I had filled a diary entry with details of family life, events that then were closest of all to me. For instance, I find these little items about Rosie, the youngest, then about seven:

> Rosie had a little temp. and sore throat last night. She awakened in the night and couldn't get back to sleep. Her father told her to count to 100 and then she'd be asleep. Later she called, "Daddy, I've counted to most a million and I'm not asleep yet."

I had also added another item about Rosie, who had recently visited Julia H., a little friend who lived in the big white house on the hill, one of the most spacious, well kept, and impressive homes in the community. Afterwards, Rosie said to me, "Mama, don't you think it looks as if the H.'s are rich? But they're not." I asked her how she knew they were not, and she replied, "I asked Julia the day I was over there and she said they weren't." My recorded comment on that was, "It's clear that Rosie favors the direct approach."

Then on Sunday, May 10, 1942:

> Deep woods below our Club Blvd. house—I have never come quite to this spot before.... This really is an ugly old woods, mutilated by human beings, scarred by fires, and marred by woodcutters. But here where I am by this tiny stream, a little more of nature persists. Lots of fern is all about, a giant Jack-in-the-pulpit with its feet in the water, a scattering of hepaticas, some wild iris and some of the commoner and un-showy orchids. I'll come down here with a spade and rescue some of them for my wildflower collection.

> Banks is listening to the concert. We just finished hearing Winston Churchill's talk on the completion of his first two years as Prime Minister.

He summed up the past and sees in this present time that Hitler's "boot" is on the other foot. For now at least the bombing tide has turned from England back to the continent. He said the Allies would not use gas unless Hitler used it first. But I heard a report that the Germans have already used it in Russia. It would surely seem, however, as if Hitler would have little to gain by using it there if the R.A.F. could return it so certainly.

This is Mother's Day. The children have given me their little mementos. Robbie got me a big goldfish for the pool. The little girls made me booklets, Rosie's had original poetry in it. Nothing special is going on today. It has been a rare and peaceful Sunday for me.

Yet I don't want too many like this. It has been interesting to have the usual Sunday crowds [assorted individuals from the lab]. Yesterday we had the McDougalls for tea, the Pratts, Stuarts, Betty and Bill. It was a very quiet peaceful natural little occasion which I think everyone enjoyed.

But the same undercurrent was there. Bill and Kenneth, here now, will be who-knows-where in a few months. Mrs. McDougall says she's living only in the present. She says if Kenneth goes to England [he had already been called up by the government there] she'll never see him again [she didn't].

Banks and I can't decide whether to go to Junaluska again for the summer. He doesn't know whether or not he should do any more to try to get into war work.

The war is just at that unpredictable stage that may prove to be a turning point, but at present there's no way of knowing which way it will turn. Corregidor fell this week, but the English occupied Madagascar and the battle of the Coral Sea is still being counted as a major Japanese defeat. Also the Japs in Burma are meeting more Chinese resistance and the German spring offensive is still unaccomplished. So what will happen next?

And then I record a final reflection. After recalling that as a youngster at home, the eldest of my parents' flock of nine children, I always felt a bit ashamed of the crowd we made, I write

But now as a parent, my viewpoint is quite different. Now I feel that raising a family is a great experience, but it is partly because behind the children is the clear-eyed adult partner in the adventure, and his presence makes it complete. He's back of it all, in it all, over it all. I'm a lucky woman.

But yesterday a bomb exploded in Germany too late to kill Hitler. A terrible war is brewing and I can't do anything about it.

If Banks had kept a diary, it would be good to turn to it now and let it counterbalance mine, for on May 18, 1942, I find an entry which seems to illustrate in some detail my kind of problem in learning to get along with him. Considering that this was 22 years after our marriage began, it's obvious that we still — or, at least, I still — had difficulty learning the lessons involved.

I wonder why I feel so emotional so much of the time lately. It must be the war and my German disposition, though that last is nothing new. Just this one little morning let me list a few of the topics over which I have been deeply stirred.

First, I tried to tell Banks my feelings about the changes the years have brought since the old Wooster days when we were so deeply affected by the teaching of "service" we absorbed there, the ideals inculcated by Dicky [Professor Dickinson, the popular and much-loved director of the Wooster Summer School] and how now, these many years later, the general consensus of the media, etc. seems to be that such an idea is "sentimental." I wanted to remark on the fact that this change must be a reflection of a change in the world in general, and that maybe my little personal observation from our own lives touched on a big central fact which makes this nation so ripe for its present difficulties [the war raging in Europe]. I had heard the Governor on the radio Sunday School program preaching "service" about like Dicky back at Wooster might have done, but it was hard to see that such Sunday preaching now, even from a governor, had any weekday effect.

But Banks didn't listen. I was serious, but for some reason he wouldn't get my mood and I felt snubbed mentally and exasperated — almost to tears — but I managed not to express it. That was one time.

But a little later Banks came up to me so sweetly and was so nice to me and wanted to go for a walk that in my mind I forgave him. As we walked, the day was so perfect — a cool May day in North Carolina can be perfect — that it almost brought me to tears.

As we walked we discussed the problem of race prejudice recently current in the news [as it had not been, earlier]. That discussion came after we had talked momentarily to Donnie, the black man who lives in the little cabin nearby. He was so smiling and childlike — the thought of injustice to such as he almost brought the fool tears again.

And then two planes flew high overhead and Banks said they were our biggest bomber types. They made my eyes sting with unshed tears. I said, "I hate to look at them."

He said, "I don't. I think they're beautiful." Well, I understand that too. But I hope the time will come when we needn't think that a bomber is beautiful.

Then I heard Sir Norman Angell give a radio talk and he said, "Englishmen have dug with their bare hands in the rubble that was their homes to get out the bodies of their dead children...." And all the sorrows of the war rolled over me again.

These are only the most outstanding of two or three hours of emotional currents in my life as it goes at present.

Earlier, while still as Junaluska (August 15, 1941, before the United States entered the war), I had recorded something of my reaction to the world situation:

I have been listening to the peace aims arrived at a few days ago at a secret meeting of President Roosevelt and Prime Minister Winston Churchill "somewhere in the Atlantic" and as the full meaning and significance of this historic pronouncement is borne in upon me I feel with Banks, "This is the turning point."

Psychologically, this does something incalculable to the spirit. This crystallizes the good intent and latent goodwill of the people of this country into a crusade. Now we are confessedly fighting for the freedom of the future. It ought to help the people of England as it helps us to refute those who say this is another of England's imperialistic wars; even to those of us who have never believed that [although many American recruits did and it made them reluctant soldiers]. This gives us concrete grounds for hope that when victory comes the peace will not be lost like the last one was. After all, we on this side of the struggle will get farther than we did the last time and then the lesson from World War I will not be wasted, and then Woodrow Wilson will not have lived in vain, even though it takes this added measure of world suffering to realize his objectives and even though Roosevelt, not Wilson, must be the instrument applying that lesson.

But before the victory we still must have deeper suffering. This nation hasn't yet felt the weight of the reality as it must do if we win. We are still so complacent, narrow, selfish, while Hitler is so well-organized, integrated, powerful, and ruthless.

For six weeks now the country has watched breathlessly to see what would happen in Russia as the Germans invade it. To the surprise of all, doubtless even of Hitler, Russia has held the Germans off so that their boasted "victory in six weeks" has been shown to be only a boast.

Yet today, seven weeks after, the Russians have for the first time admitted serious losses, the situation there is desperate and one never knows when some sort of crack-up may come. But there may be hope that they will hold out until winter. If only we wake up fully here and take advantage of the present.

I've been sending Sylvia [my sister in England] grocery boxes this summer. One never knows what may be ahead for England. They say that the Battle of the Atlantic is still being lost. But anyway I'm glad that the heads of the two largest nations have made this momentous public statement [Roosevelt and Churchill]. It casts a ray of hope for an enlightened future for all the world. What must the poor people of France feel if they manage to hear it just now when under Darlan they are entering into full collaboration with Hitler!

On December 7, 1941, this country was irrevocably changed when Japan bombed Pearl Harbor, precipitating our entry into World War II. As it happened, that Sunday three young soldiers from nearby Fort Bragg were with us for dinner. At the table, we commented on not having heard any news that day. A week later, I described the scene in my diary:

After dinner, everybody sleepy in the living room, I went upstairs where Sally was listening to the radio. She said she heard that the Japs have bombed Pearl Harbor. I came downstairs and told the crowd, but no one took it seriously. They said Pearl Harbor was a port in the Hawaiian Islands. In a few minutes then we got the exciting news firsthand and in more detail. The boys then took it seriously, but for myself I couldn't exactly feel what it meant.

In fact, for most people the full meaning of "we are at war" had to have time to sink in. But to our young soldier guests that Sunday afternoon, comprehension was practically instantaneous. The sleepy group in our living room reacted as if an electric current had passed through them. At once they were no longer sleepy but alert — and unusually quiet. The mood stayed with them the rest of the day, until they left for camp that evening. I could understand their reaction. Until then, these young men's sojourn in the military had had a kind of make-believe quality. Now, suddenly, it was the real thing. But for me, writing a week later, it was still unreal.

> For that matter I can't say that even yet I have really felt what the war we are in now means. Maybe it's because I have no one very close who will get into it. But on purely rational grounds I've been glad things have gone this way for it surely was unavoidable that the U.S. take a more active part if the world situation is ever going to get worked out right. In fact, in a mess like this how could one want his own country to stay out? If there's a wrong to right who wants to miss the chance to help right it?
>
> We have wondered constantly this last year what could possibly happen to crystallize feeling so that we in this country would have an active part in the world situation. Attack was the one thing I didn't think of, probably, I suppose, because it was unthinkable that any nation would attack us.

My rather restrained approval of the turn of world events was not fully expressive, however, of the feelings of the male family members, as I find recorded in that same diary entry:

> When we told 13-year-old Robbie about the bombing of Pearl Harbor, he jumped up, shouting "War! War! Hot dog! Yippee!" Banks admitted he felt a little the same way.

That admission, I guess, gives the explanation of a note I recently found that Banks wrote, dated a few months later. He said,

> I got an offer of a commission in the Marine Corps [effective] May 26, 1942, which I am going to accept if my physical condition will permit.

One day soon after, as I well remember, we drove to Raleigh for his physical exam. We remarked that it probably was sort of a last ride together before the separation. We discussed both the family and lab affairs. On our minds a lot was the question of what would happen to the lab if Banks was away for an indefinite time. Those of us who were left would have to carry on the best we could. The *Journal* program was somewhat outlined for the year ahead, and we thought that with Dorothy on the job, we probably could manage for a while since Banks would still be in the background even if not physically present.

The returns from Banks' physical exam were long in coming and we felt as if we were marking time until the end of the year. When they did come, it turned out he had been rejected—on physical grounds. We thought it probably was because of his color blindness. That was a handicap he had managed to camouflage in 1919 when in spite of it he had been accepted by the Marine Corps as a volunteer. Or possibly his rejection now was because of defective hearing, which dated back to his years of service in the Marine Corps as a sharpshooter rifleman.

And now he was told that he was not needed. He was disappointed by his rejection. (I wasn't.) Banks then of course had to turn his attention back to the lab and to launch a new year of research with the necessary enthusiasm, even though there didn't seem to be much on the horizon about which to be enthusiastic.

Christmas Day at our house that December of 1941 was a bit quiet and restrained, partly because Banks and I remembered to prepare the children beforehand to make them understand that the war economy had already affected even the toy market, and that Christmas could not be as lavish as it might have been. They accepted the situation, and the day was a happy one. Rosie, at seven, the upper limit of the toy age, confessed upon questioning that she had hoped for a bicycle and a baby sister. Betsy was content with a toy stove and kitchen cabinet, as was Sally with my girlhood watch, and Robbie with a radio.

In the afternoon, two of the young soldiers who had been with us the day of the attack on Pearl Harbor drove in. I had not planned a big Christmas dinner and so I had to rush out and get additional supplies. I had a roasting chicken on hand but when at the store I tried to find another to go with it, I was unsuccessful and I had to take a hen, which turned out not to be a young one. When roasted, it refused to get tender, and so the meal was late and the children got impatient. However, the soldiers didn't, even though I felt they were sort of stranded with just our family present, since all the students who usually would have been around were gone for the holidays. But these young men seemed to be interested in everything, watching the children with their toys and listening to the radio, whether news or carols.

As they left, Tom with a trace of a tear in his eye said that we didn't know how much it meant to them to have had this family day with us. As I wrote in my diary,

That touched me deeply. It was so little to do for them, their lives so torn up and uncertain. They expect to be transferred anywhere any time now. And we know so well that boys like them by the hundreds who don't want to fight, don't want to be in a war, still do it with grace since it has to be done.

By the time I got back to diary writing it was several months later, Easter Sunday, April 6, 1942, and I called it an unbelievable, an incomprehensible day. I felt it such because of the complex emotional currents that were involved before the day ended.

The weather was unexpectedly and unusually hot for early April. But I had not anticipated that it would be so when I planned the menu. Instead of salad and sandwiches, perhaps with iced tea, which would have been appropriate, I had planned a wiener roast with baked beans and coffee down in the back yard at a campfire site that Banks had fixed up for such occasions. But everyone understood, I guess; and after all, the food was a minor item in the situation, and the fact that few wieners were roasted didn't matter. Everyone seemed to enjoy the holiday, regardless.

All the ESP-ers were there, including an exotic student of Banks' from Java, as well as Banks' former student, Joe Woodruff, on a visit from New York City, and Bill, a former lab worker who was due to depart for the Navy. Two soldiers were also there—Barry and his friend Tom from Fort Bragg. It was Barry's first visit for weeks, and we knew that very possibly it would also be his last. The occasion was joyous in spite of the weather and the farewells to come. It was a sort of last fling atmosphere in spite of the future, ominous and pressing close.

Later, at the house, came a time of still more mixed emotions as we all lolled around in the cool living room amused by our Javanese friend, when a sudden argument sprang up on the subject of England and the part it played in the world conflict. England was vastly unpopular in the training camps just then, we knew. "Just another of England's imperialistic wars," the soldiers said.

But Banks and I did not agree with that and we thought that since we had greater time and freedom for reading that they, we had a better chance to judge impartially than they. We thought that England was a bulwark against the rise of communism. The debate went on, good-natured but futile. Fortunately, no end was reached nor any friendships broken, and then the time came when the soldiers had to leave for camp. No wonder I said, in the entry recording it all,

I can't explain the net effect. This was a day one can't forget or evaluate. It brought the war home to me more vividly than ever before.

I've lived through one war already, and now all the more I can't bear to see these young men go on into that future. And I don't mean their physical safety so much either. But I just can't stand the thought of Bill in the Navy. He's such a gentle idealistic chap. And yet I want every man to help win the war. This conflict for me is unresolvable.

Equally unresolvable it was, of course, for all the young recruits like Tom and Barry in our living room that day. We never saw Tom again, nor did we ever hear how he fared in the war. But with Barry the story was different. Still in the nearby training camp, he continued to come to see us frequently until his company was transferred to England. After that, he and I carried on a sporadic correspondence. Early in 1943, the following letter came from him:

> Jan. 13, 1943
> North Africa

Hello, Everybody:

This letter is for all of you. For Betsy, Rosemary, Sally, Robbie, Louie, and the Boss. All of you have been constant companions since I first met you. When things get tough over here I invariably think of you and I feel all warm and bright inside.

Yesterday I received the book and the V-mail letter you sent me. I can't tell you how wonderful I felt when I saw all of your little notes and knew that you hadn't forgotten me. I look forward to the day when I can be with you again.

> Sincerely,
> Barry

My reply to that, a V-mail note to him in North Africa, came back to me with the notation stamped on it, "Undelivered, Killed in Action." Soon afterwards, a letter came from Barry's brother-in-law in Brooklyn who knew of our friendship. It gave details of the tragedy. On an expedition into enemy territory (North Africa), Barry had been instantly killed when a land mine exploded. The place of burial in North Africa was given. My diary gives my response to this sad event, when I said that it,

> more than anything that has happened to me for the long years since my mother died, makes me realize how inadequate after all is my philosophy — how inadequate anyone's must be to answer the question of death and what comes after.

I only know that there must be in the explanation a way for all these men like Barry, who were cheated out of the richness of life, to get something better than this world would have given them. We couldn't endure the thought that they should look back to this life with grief and disappointment because they missed so much of it. Somehow they must be going on to some more ultimate type of fulfillment. I must think that and that they do go on, and that even death cannot really break the ties with those we love.

My general frame of mind in this period was expressed in the following excerpt from my diary dated July 1, 1942 (Junaluska, N.C.):

The world is so badly off—just now the Allies are losing Egypt it seems and the Japs are gaining in China. They are probably getting ready to strike in Siberia. The Germans tonight claim to have captured Sevastopol. On the face of things at least it couldn't look much worse. When one thinks of all that will be involved before we can hope for victory, it's appalling. Personally I can't see much in the picture that should make me want to stay in this world and see it suffered out.

The background to these pessimistic thoughts is given in an account in the early part of this same diary entry telling of a personal jolt, which said

Tonight I stumbled onto the fact that I have an unexplainable lump in my breast. It's something I have been watching for ever since Mama died of breast cancer in 1920. Never before have I found anything to question, but there's certainly something there now. I told Banks and he thinks so too. Tomorrow we must get in touch with a doctor and I must have an examination—and all that.

Well, this is not going to make things different. I am interested in life and I'm interested no matter what turn it takes. Banks and I took a walk after supper tonight (and before I made this discovery) and we talked about his findings in the data that he is assembling this summer.

I always have my fundamental interests stirred again when I get to thinking about ESP and I get very impatient to find out the answers to some of the big questions. So much time must go into doing analyses and writing papers, etc. And our lifetimes at the best are so short. I want to know what life means. I'd prefer to find out while living, though I'll admit that everyone in the past with the same urge has had to die without finding that answer.

I know, of course, that the answer cannot be simple. But at least, even superficially, life is an interesting story, and no wonder one wants to have it continue. Here I have my nice little family. The little girls sat on my bed tonight after the concert they had gone to with Banks and they are a little group he and I can be proud of. When they're all young ladies, won't it be fun? I remember the few years at home when Esther, Ruth and I were still there but grown up and how we enjoyed it and Mama did too! We would all get together on someone's bed and talk.

This spring I've enjoyed the college students a lot, those who came to the house frequently, Betty, Edith and Bill. It's been hard to realize that I wasn't one of them, that I'm fifty. But why shouldn't I be the way I feel? And that's young and vigorous and sort of ageless.

Banks is so dear. He and I alone (it is a treat of course to be alone once in a while) climbed "True Love" (the most conspicuous nearby mountain) yesterday and we both enjoyed it very much—for the exercise, for the mountaintop, for each other.

The next entry, July 11, 1942, is headed "Mission Hospital, Asheville," and it goes on

Here is a thought that ought to be emphasized. Anybody's life, and certainly my own, if taken unexpectedly in cross-section, so to speak, at the 50-year stage would probably present an unfinished picture. At that stage, anybody ought to have lots of projects started but few finished.

Well, wouldn't it be a good idea for me now to begin to "round out the picture" as the news analysts say and try to get some of them finished up?

I seem to be getting a new impression of my life as I stand back or off somewhere and look at it as a unit. I never have done it before. It wasn't a unit. It was a process going on. Now considered as a unit it isn't as satisfying as I might have thought. I realize that as long as I was considering myself "in process," much of whatever satisfaction or complacency I felt about what my total accomplishment would be was based on *promises* rather than on completed projects.

Now I've been here in this hospital over a week and this morning I am up just after breakfast and expecting to live my day as I please within the shelter of this room where a nightgown can do for a dress.

It's after lunch now and I've written a letter to Naomi and tried to tell her how I feel about things. This is in effect what I wrote her:

When I came out from under the anesthetic, before I made any sign that those watching could have recognized as consciousness, I knew from the feeling of the incision and the bandages that the breast was removed and that therefore the lump had been cancerous. It didn't upset me at all as I might have supposed it would do had I ever contemplated such a thing when I was an outsider looking in. But now that I'm an insider looking out, from the first moment and ever since, at least this far, it hasn't upset me.

First, I realized that my main business right now is to get over this operation. Second, it's to make as much out of this hospital time as I can, and later to let the future take care of itself, and no matter what it brings, to get all out of everything I can, regardless.

So that's my working creed. I hope this is the word that will get passed around to my friends, any who may be worried. I don't want them to be worried.

Counting all the things that are in my favor I have a pretty good factual reason for not being worried, so it isn't just heroics, but only common sense. I do rather dread the reaction of a few good kindly people like Mrs. S. who always wanted me to sit on a chair or something because "You have four children." I'm afraid now they'd want to put me to bed.

And that was the substance of the letter, but the diary entry continues

On account of tires [rubber was scarce and needed for the war effort and tires were almost impossible to obtain and therefore driving had to be severely limited] Banks hasn't been able to be here much. With the help of Sally and with Betty and Dorothy there too, he is holding the family on course at home in Junaluska. He left here Monday forenoon and hasn't been back since, and I have been alone.

I have only one acquaintance in Asheville and consequently I've had solitude and the opportunity for self communion. Much as I like my family and friends I have enjoyed this time alone. I could read when I wanted to, write when I wanted to, and be busy with my weights and balances trying to figure out what's worthwhile after all. And now I think I've got far enough that I can go out into the world and circulate with a sort of renewed inner understanding that should be a help.

Reading back — what I mean about my not worrying about the future is mainly that I'm not worrying for fear the cancer will come back. The chances are reasonably good that it won't. But even so, I feel too that the chances are reasonably good that it will.

The not-worrying sentiment expressed there was put to test about six weeks later. I had been home again and engaged in the domestic routine, my physical activities about up to normal when another hike up True Love was planned. I decided to go along, not without a bit of inward question whether or not I was yet quite up to it.

I did go, managed to keep up, and to see again the inspiring and breathtaking view from the top. The rest of the hikers then decided it would be too tame to go back down the mountain the easy way by which we had come up, the circuitous but rather beaten path. Instead, why not go down the almost sheer cliff face on the other side? Agreed, as soon as said. I don't remember that anyone even suggested that I might not be up to it and I certainly didn't.

And so, down we started, each one for himself. I remembered that I was just six weeks past the operation that certainly would prolong my life. But for how long? As I went down that jagged cliff, and in places clung to a root or ledge until I could find a lower foot or handhold, I looked down to the bottom of it and noted that the drop to the ground below was clear. And then I thought, as momentarily I clung there, if the cancer comes back it will be a long and painful end for me. If just now I should release my grasp here, the end will be quick and painless. The children are almost independent. Sally has learned to carry on, and Banks would be close support for her. Should I do it? It would count as an accident, not as suicide.

Should I do it? If I just knew for sure that the cancer will come back — if I just knew it for sure! But I don't! And Banks would be blamed for letting me even make this hike. No, I can't. I must make the gamble that it's worthwhile to go on — and face the future, regardless.

(I've wondered since if that was just theoretical — would I really have done it? Anyway, I'm glad I didn't for nearly half my life lay before me.)

I'm not worried either way. Other methods of finishing off my mortal days are also possible, of course. But they all come to the same thing in the end, don't they? Anyway, I'm just keeping on feeling that it doesn't matter and I don't want anyone to stop me from feeling that way.

No one did, and a later entry, January 4, 1943, doesn't even mention it, but begins

> Still the stream of consciousness goes on [and for a page or more I trace it, and end on the next page by saying] ... Well, why am I writing all this stuff, I wonder?

> Banks is in bed with the flu. He's not very sick. But he's enjoying some books and, for a wonder, is contented just being inactive.

12

Psychokinesis

The summer of 1942, we were back in Junaluska and in the same big house, again with Betty and Dorothy. I explain in a diary entry on June 17:

Banks decided after his rejection by the military to gather all his energies and put them wholeheartedly into the research and to consider that to be his duty to the world.

As a consequence, this time he took along to Junaluska all the PK (psychokinesis) data that had accumulated over the years, just as he had done with the ESP data the summer before. Historically, the very existence of such a phenomenon as PK had not been even suspected in serious research circles, although the general public had long used the phrase "mind over matter." Banks himself had not taken seriously the possibility of such an effect when he first entertained the thought that ESP might be a reality. The job to be undertaken that summer in Junaluska, therefore, was to assemble, analyze, and evaluate all the experimental data on this topic. The work of doing this was very involved; but when the summer was over, the material had been sorted and arranged into a series of papers for eventual publication.

The implications of this discovery of a mental force which could affect physical systems without any physical means was momentous; Banks was eager for other researchers to test for it also, and thereby confirm and amplify the finding. But the world was disturbed and preoccupied by the outbreak of the war. The major attention of the public, therefore, was diverted far from items of scientific discovery, even on popular topics. This one, he knew, would be met with great skepticism and more likely would not get any notice at all. The decision, then, was to delay publication of it until a more propitious time should come. Something of the general uncertainty and unrest of the times and its effect on Banks is reflected in a letter he wrote to Sylvia (still in England) in February, 1943:

> Maybe the university will be taken over by the government, and I may not be teaching next year. Robbie and I may go out west to the wheat fields for the summer unless something better turns up. Robbie is a strong and well built lad. [He would have been about sixteen.] Of course we would not like dividing the family for so long, but it may be the only way of getting into something that will be of use. The experimental work is now pretty well written up and I could leave with a clear conscience.

> The PK work turns out beautifully—no loophole we are confident. The effect shows up repeatedly, and we have a secondary effect, and it's just a clincher. It is just great to realize all that it implies—the causal efficacy of mind over the physical order—in some degree at least. Of necessity it links up with ESP. But that is a long story.

> The English are now doing well in the ESP field. I hope they will take up PK, too, after the full publication of it in March. Oh, for this war to finish!

We are looking forward to reading Sir Norman Angell's next book regarding future plans for the world. Also, Culbertson may have the makings of a grand scheme. We just must have an international economic one, too, I think, though perhaps this would be too big a job for this generation.

In 1943, however, even though the world situation was no better, Banks decided that this discovery of a PK effect should be suppressed no longer, and that the accumulated papers on the topic should be published. As a result, all four of his *Journal* editorials that year dealt with this phenomenon. In March the title of his editorial was "Physical Phenomena in Parapsychology"; in June, "The Mind Has Real Force" (he did not mean just mental influence, but direct kinetic force); in September, "The Significance of the PK Effect"; and in December, "ESP and PK and the Survival Hypothesis."

In the first of these editorials, Banks explained that the research on PK had in fact dated back to 1934 and had been carried on simultaneously with that on ESP. The PK research, like that on ESP, had been initiated as the result of reports on spontaneous physical happenings mixed in with those in which ESP seemed to occur. He commented that the introduction of "physical phenomena" when "no previous departure from complete attention to the research and issues of extra-sensory perception has occurred" marked a turning point.

As he continued, an almost apologetic tone crept into his explanation for, as he said,

It is evident that a report of this nature represents a departure of major character for us. For the so-called "physical phenomena" have never attained to a state of scientific respectability within parapsychological circles, to say nothing of those of general psychological science.

But now he felt that the readership of the *Journal* should be told that systematic research had shown that, as phrased in the third editorial,

The mental system has a determinative influence which produces registerable effects without any conceivable physical intermediation. These effects reveal the stamp of intelligent purpose and do so in a way that is nonetheless physically a cause-effect phenomenon.

Because it needed extra validation, however, as well as because the times did not seem appropriate, this report had not been published with the one on ESP. But now many experiments conducted by many different people had confirmed it.

These experiments, he explained, were simple. They had involved the throwing of dice, with the subject willing them to fall according to both definite preselected and random target faces. These experiments did show a measurable effect of will power on a physical transaction. They demonstrated that it occurred to a degree well beyond that which might be the result of chance alone; and, more than that, the ESP and PK effects seemed to be related.

After the research on ESP became known, many reports of personal experiences involving ESP came to the lab, and in a great number of these a physical effect was said to have occurred. Typically, for instance, a woman in Ohio wrote that at the time her seven-year-old grandson in the hospital died, a geranium plant had fallen from the windowsill where it had stood all winter. No jar had occurred to cause the fall. She had intended to take the plant to him in the hospital that day. In a similar case, a man told of unexplainable knocks on his door at the hour his mother died.

It was because of reports like these, JB said, that his original attitude changed and he began to consider that perhaps such effects did present a problem worthy of research. He cast around for a suitable method by which to test this possibility in the laboratory and found it in the suggestion given by a young gambler who thought he could affect falling dice by his will. Banks recognized at once that, as a technique, throwing dice was quick, inexpensive, and even more important, was easily evaluated. With six-sided cubes, the chance of one specific face coming up when the die was thrown would be one in six. Immediately, then, he began to test the laws of chance, working at it both at home and at the office. Or, rather, he began to test the possibility of "breaking" those laws by getting more hits on a preselected target face than chance alone or any known physical force would explain.

At home all of us, including the children, were soon trying to see whether simply by "wishing" for a specified face when we threw the dice, we could get more 6's than chance would allow, then more 1's, etc. It was a fun experiment and soon became a household pastime which, though it added nothing to the world's scientific knowledge, at least helped to keep high the fervor of discovery in at least one scientist.

By the time the monograph, *Extra-Sensory Perception*, was published in 1934, experimental results on PK had been sufficiently encouraging that they well might have been reported, too. But, no mention of the effect of mind on matter was made in that volume. The topic was left for a still greater weight of evidence to accumulate. When the storm of criticism arose over the ESP findings, it obviously was not a suitable time to report the discovery of another obscure human ability, one that no doubt would prove to be at least as unbelievable as ESP.

As a result of all this, the data for PK had lain quietly on the shelf for years. The volume of it, however, had steadily increased, for it was an exciting and hence popular kind of research at home, at the office, and wherever else the news of it leaked out. PK had much of the appeal that has made dice-throwing the gambling technique that it is. In the lab, even without the money element that elsewhere made a vice of it, it was fun, too. Another but minor reason for delay in publication was that the distinction between using dice for research rather than for gambling might not be understood by the local public. The consensus of opinion was that it would be better to let the idea of using cards in ESP tests sink in before adding dice, as well.

In the *Journal* editorial of March, 1943, Banks said that he hoped that this first report would be the beginning of an ESP-PK period of work toward "the larger objective," that objective, of course, being to find the true nature of man. As he pointed out,

> The idea of a force like PK, strange as it may seem in the present-day context, is really a very old and generally assumed one, the one that says that the mind controls the body. This is none other than the "common sense notion — and also the traditional religious one."

> The general behavioristic trend, of course, runs counter to it and assumes that the force involved in muscular action originates and is controlled only in the physical body. But the experiments on PK show first that the mind has force, real kinetic force, and that it can also operate outside of the body.

He continued

> A type of lawfulness peculiar to mind and contrary to physics is increasingly evident in the ESP and PK researches.... But if the psyche is a force — in its own right, with laws and ways peculiarly nonphysical, the survival hypothesis has at least a logical chance. If the mind is different from the physical brain system it *could* have a different destiny, *could* perhaps be independent, separable, unique.... Here, surely, if ever, "hope sees a star" and the urge toward the inquiry into the question of survival receives valuable impetus and encouragement.

In the *Journal* of March 1944, Banks and his assistant, Betty Humphrey, published an article, the result of that second summer's work at Junaluska, which further clinched the case for the reality of the PK effect. Following the discovery of patterning of hits in the ESP data, they now went back and analyzed the PK results for hit patterns. Here, too, they found a pronounced and statistically significant tendency for the hits to be clustered mainly at the beginning and end sections of the PK experimental runs, quite similar to the effects found in the ESP runs of 25 calls. This was clearly a psychological effect. Added to the other evidence, it further suggested that PK was a reality. As they stated in the final paragraph of the report, these results "afford further evidence of the nonphysical character of the PK effect."

Looking back as I do now to this confirmation of the fact that the human personality includes not only an extrasensory ability but also an extraphysical one, I realize anew its effect on Banks' thinking, or rather on his determination that the world should know of this aspect of the nature of man. It was like a new and more potent weapon to a soldier beleaguered in an uneven battle with a stronger enemy. Now, the parapsychological results showed not only an extended ability of man to know his world, but also one by which without physical means he can affect it physically. Even though both ESP and PK were subtle, hidden, perhaps even presently beyond the reach of conscious control, their eventual full recognition (however audacious such a thought might be) could possibly be as fateful for the race as was the first recognition of radiation.

If so, however, the fact was far from being recognized. In 1947 Banks' third book, *The Reach of the Mind*, was published. It was, in effect, a popular statement of the discoveries of parapsychology up to that time. In Chapter 10 of the book, Banks discussed the problem of the acceptance of ESP and PK. He said, "Science does not in this year of 1947 accept ESP and PK as established.... No other phenomenon in all the history of science has had so little recognition for so much experimental research."

13

Nonretirement

In my diary record now comes a gap of fifteen years. Not until January 30, 1957, did I make another entry, and that one was the last of all. The reason for this lapse of diary writing was that, more and more, my time and attention were taken by affairs at the lab, especially after 1948, when I began a project of my own which I will describe in Chapter 14. But the lack of diary reminders means that now I must rely mainly on Banks' writings and on letters from various people for support and confirmation of my memories.

Even without such memory props, I can, of course, summarize the great family changes the years had brought. The children had grown up and gone off to college; three of them had married and were permanently away from home. In 1952, the youngest had finished high school. Then, since we no longer had to live conveniently near the schools, we sold our place in town and moved to a many-acred old abandoned dairy farm some ten miles away.

With our country backgrounds, we thought the change of scene should be a pleasant and wholesome one. Banks, or JB, as we all, from his littlest grandchild to his scientific colleagues, had come to call him, needed a counterinterest to interrupt his total effort and concentration at the lab. We thought that with a return to the land, perhaps he might undertake a little farming on evenings and weekends and so get the diversion he had not found at our home in town.

Again, our plans did not work out. While we both enjoyed living in the country, JB found that instead of the little farming he had intended, he couldn't divert the time and attention even that little would have taken. Instead, he did something quite different. As I wrote to Sally,

> Dad (I smile at him, but don't tell him) has found that the state will help to plant trees on cultivated farmland. It is a plan called the Farm Bank and Dad can get all of our fields forested so he won't have to do a thing to them. But first we must cut a crop of hay off the pasture in order to have it qualify as cultivated and now he's doing that. It is a job that will hold him for several evenings.

> His dogged resignation at this job is admirable — and amusing. "I'll do it if it kills me," as Dr. Lundholm used to say when he was confronted with a necessary but unwelcome task. Dad'll do it so that in the future he won't be bothered by the thought of what ought to be done to the pastures. And now, if all goes well, all of our fields will be in little pine trees. Dad is quite happy about it.

> I think he is getting more retirement-minded every day. By two years from now, he says, he'll turn everything over to Gaither. I think he should actually leave his office then too, but I don't quite say so, for I know that is not what he intends. He wants to be half retired and keep a room or two at the lab, write, and maybe direct research.

> Somehow I feel that he's getting a little tired of the struggle of keeping the lab going. I would be very glad if he'd really turn over the reins and without regret when the time comes.

My optimism about the pine trees turned out to be realistic, but the other item did not. Soon baby pines were planted on all the former pastures, but two years later, JB's retirement was still only a hope—and mine more than his. In fact, although I know we talked about it, I can't imagine now why such an idea as retirement for JB then when he was as yet barely at retirement age should have occurred to me. I knew very well that the strain involved in carrying on at the lab was telling on him, and I thought that if a vigorous and dedicated young person would appear who could possibly replace him at the lab, it would change things for him. However, no person whom JB considered such, appeared. Perhaps with a leader as strong as he, none could have been expected. It may have been a bit like the situation of a sprouting acorn under a big oak tree. In fact, the usual pattern for students who were intrigued by the subject matter was to work at the lab for a time, then return to more conventional pursuits when they graduated and were faced with the problem of finding a job.

Incidentally, the gossip that drifted back from them when they did so was that the venture into parapsychology had not helped, but only tended to queer their chances of jobs in psychology. The implication seemed to be that it showed a weak or erratic element in their character. This, of course, was no encouragement to later arrivals at the lab. And so, the combination of unpopular subject matter and lack of any promise of financial return or future job possibilities was enough to deter most young persons. Consequently, from the beginning, the few students who did venture to work at the lab were obviously less afraid than most to stray off the beaten track. As a result, they were likely to be rather individualistic and independent-minded. Often when they came to the lab they already had rather definite ideas of what they wanted to do, and consequently felt little need of supervision. But JB was in charge, and he had his own set of ideas and objectives. A clash of wills and personalities was thus often inescapable. One of these young people said to me once, after a disagreement with JB, "But, Mrs. Louie, it's not that I can't get along with people. I've always been able to get along with *you*." I could reply only, "But I've never had to *direct* you."

And so, fifteen years after JB's beginning in parapsychology, when the requirements of the job of directing the lab had become more clear-cut, no leader who could replace him had appeared. Such a person would have to have administrative ability, including some considerable aptitude for raising money, and that for a far from popular cause. Also, the person should be able to inspire, oversee, and direct research. All these requirements made it easy to understand as time went on why no replacement for JB had appeared, and why he could not retire.

The dearth of researchers existed not only at the lab but also in the field itself. The few new workers who had appeared elsewhere were mainly connected with the psychic research societies and were not doing experimental work. Consequently, the volume of published parapsychological research papers had not greatly increased during these years.

JB and I agreed that if he had developed something tangible and with commercial value, such as a new chicken feed even, it might have had immediate appeal. But his significant discovery about human nature had not "sold" well. Apparently, not many people wanted it, not even those in religion. They at least might have been expected to understand its significance, since the parapsychological results supported from the scientific side what religious persons had always believed, that human beings have a nonphysical as well as a physical aspect. I gradually figured out the attitude of religionists as the equivalent of saying, "Yes, perhaps you in parapsychology are proving what we've always believed. But with our Christian faith we neither need nor want your proof."

The general response on college campuses, however, was considerably different, at least as JB personally experienced it. When information about the discoveries of parapsychology spread in academic circles, the number of his speaking invitations, especially from student groups, increased. Apparently, his lectures in response to this interest were successful, and one such engagement led to another and to his name's being placed on college speakers lists. Usually a fee and travelling expenses were offered. But if a student group wanted to hear him but had no budget, as occasionally was the case, he would accept the engagement for travelling expenses only. The main objective, of course, was to spread information about parapsychology and its meaning for human life.

Whenever an engagement was within driving distance, I would go along. The drive to the place was usually largely a silent one on my part at least, as JB thought over the points he wanted to make on this particular occasion. Or, sometimes, he would think them over and recount them aloud, for each of his lectures was spontaneous and different. The return home, however, was always a time for discussion of the talk and the particular reaction of that audience to it.

I knew, and I suppose JB did too, that as a lecturer he was neither funny nor fluent. Usually he opened his talk with a few light words about something trivial or extraneous which caused a ripple of spontaneous amusement and, I think, tended to create a feeling of sympathy and expectation. But after that opener, he got down at once to the serious topic and then he held the attention of his young audiences.

I was always a bit surprised at the content of his messsage and his earnestness in presenting it, in spite of his slow and, as I often thought, too lengthy delivery. He usually overran his hour.

Before we moved to the country and after the children were all in school, I had regularly walked with JB to the lab in the morning and remained there all the forenoon in order to help with his correspondence. After the publication of his first two books, this correspondence had grown so heavy that he could no longer take time even for acknowledgments, much less real answers. It was then that I took over the job of trying to reply to such letters. Then, I remained at home in the afternoon in order to be there when the children came from school. But after our move to the country, the children all grown, we drove to the lab and returned together in the late afternoons. I then had more time at the lab than formerly. As I noted in that last diary entry, January 30, 1957,

> Since I have been working at the lab, JB and I come and go together. I have no doubt that my presence and interest there means just as much to him as it does to me.

This new situation gave me the opportunity to know at first hand the pressures under which JB worked, and also to appreciate afresh his motives and objectives. Even in minor things, like his being late for dinner, I now could be more understanding. Formerly, such irregularities had been irritating. And for JB I'm sure it was helpful to have this understanding at home, considering the frustration he had been experiencing with the outside world practically constantly since the period of critical responses had begun nearly a decade before. This frustration is reflected in an interview that JB had in 1953 with a reporter for the *Duke Alumni Register*. In it, he said

> Answering the criticisms [and even the unjustified ones were answered] required many redundant hours, because one answering did not suffice. The next critic raised much the same issue and the explanation had to be repeated.

> We succeeded in answering all the criticisms but when we found that this did not make any difference to most of the critics concerned, we began to realize that a profound philosophical bias was keeping the American psychologists from accepting the findings. It was the same bias that produced the behaviorist movement which a generation ago swept the *mind* clear off the slate of psychology and left only nerves, muscles, and glands.

Even as early as 1928, JB had been seeking advice and guidance from the few psychologists who were interested in psychical research. One of these, as already mentioned, was Gardner Murphy, then at Columbia University. Murphy replied to this early inquiry from JB by stating the ultimate objective for a psychical researcher and pinpointing the major difficulty of those who attempted to work in the field,

> If anybody has the skill and good luck to get a definite controllable psychical phenomenon in the laboratory so that anybody can come and see it and convince himself anytime, then I think psychical research will reach its 1492 in the world of science.

That reply, however, was not much help to JB. The difficulty of producing instances of ESP on demand was great enough to be almost prohibitive. Part of the reason, though not fully appreciated then, was that in nature ESP is a spontaneous phenomenon governed by deeply unconscious factors and influences. So Murphy was right in saying that the answer would be the 1492 of the field.

As a matter of fact, the difficulty of producing instances of ESP on demand gave critics of the field their most potent weapon against it. Naturally, a scientific objective is to produce the phenomenon on demand where such is possible. But it was not yet possible in this field. The prerequisite for achieving this ultimate objective was to have knowledge and control of all of the conditions necessary for the occurrence of the phenomenon. Learning what these were then had to be the first objective of research.

This difficulty of replication raised questions wherever psychical research was carried on. In England, no successful experiments in ESP were reported, although since there had been a longtime history of psychical research there, careful and painstaking experiments had been attempted. The experimenters could report that they had meticulously followed the specifications from across the ocean. Their complete failure to get results like those reported from Duke University therefore raised a sharp question, "Why on your side of the Atlantic but not on ours?"

One such inquiry came to JB from a professor, C.E. Joad. Although I do not have his letter, the questions he raised are clear from JB's reply, dated September 10, 1936:

> I cannot explain ... the reason why some persons fail to confirm ... others to succeed.... You realize how difficult it is to describe subtle differences in personality. How could one describe a successful poet or musician, and distinguish him from one who fails? How could one describe a

successful salesman? Personality differences are more important than technique ... Dr. Pratt worked slavishly with 125 subjects ... and found a remarkable one (only) on the 126th. Other investigators have found half a dozen good subjects with apparent ease.... In general, friendliness, easy sociability, capacity for enthusiasm seem to be most helpful.

From that, one can deduce that the necessary ingredient, in addition to all the specified tangible ones, was an intangible one. Obviously, to JB the question was, just what is that intangible something? It was a difficult question to answer; in a sense, all subsequent research has been an attempt to answer it. JB later did attempt to do this more specifically in a 1948 *Journal* article, "Conditions Favoring Success in Psi Tests." He said

For some time there have been requests from our British colleagues in parapsychology for some further enlightenment regarding the conditions conducive to success in ESP and PK tests.

He noted that it was impossible to give complete instructions until all facts could be assembled; what he could say now could only, at best, be suggestive.

First, the experimenter himself must be eager and even excited about the quest. Strong and persistent motivation to find the answer reliably was a first requirement. In effect, the experimenter must be a "good salesman" and the subject must have, or the experimenter must create in him, a strong spontaneous interest and a confident attitude free from reservations, since spontaneity is the key word. But spontaneity is evanescent; the experimenter must be extremely sensitive to the conditions that affect it.

This means, he said, that the test procedure, although artificial, must be reliably controlled in an inconspicuous way, with the first necessity being a genuine friendliness and a pleasant atmosphere. This is difficult to achieve in attempts to repeat or duplicate experiments, but even harder in replication attempts in which the experimenter must simulate novelty for the subject, even while keeping essential conditions the same. Even when test conditions seem the same, the difficulty of repetition is related to the fact that human beings are individual and changeable, "never the same again." On this account, he said, no repetition is perfect. As in the fine arts, the unconscious nature of the procedure is a limitation, but

we must push ahead ... until we reach facts that will either make control of psi possible or discourage us from further attempts toward that goal.

But "actual experimental testing in ESP and PK is not for everyone." (Experience was beginning to show that some experimenters, like some subjects, were "good" and some "bad" as far as their ability to elicit ESP was concerned.)

Besides the problem of controlling psi and therefore of eliciting evidence of it, a second problem also occupied critics and parapsychologists. This was a philosophical issue, a conflict between psychical phenomena and the Zeitgeist, between monism and dualism, which in 1945 JB said had often been expressed to him in words like these:

> I can follow through the experimental work in ESP and PK and can see that they are not subject to the same laws of space-time-mass as is the objective world of physics; but I have to "get off" when the conclusion is reached that this justifies a nonphysical order of reality. I simply cannot revert to old-fashioned dualism.

JB said that a bias against dualism was understandable since in the present time science more and more has

> unified the separate objective phenomena [into] the pattern of physics. Even in psychology, it has been found easier to steer clear of the more basic questions concerning the nature of human personality and attack instead the problems of behavior. However, in ESP and PK, with their properties of transcending physical boundaries, a clean break is shown with the physical tradition in the science of living beings. Here is something that is not of the physical universe; it is extraphysical.... If this confirmation of a second causative principle in nature brings us back to dualism, there appears to be no proper escape from it.

And yet, JB himself could not quite see how a complete dualism could exist because, after all, the two systems do interact in the personality. That fact must mean that dualism is only relative, and that by their interaction the two systems must be "rooted in a common system of energetic determinants which as yet is not known to science."

In December, 1944, the world war was still occupying everyone's attention. In an editorial in the *Journal*, JB commented on the fact that the government of this country is predicated on the common-sense idea of the nature of the human individual, the religious dualism in which mind and body are taken as more or less distinct systems. This was in opposition to the modern trend toward considering the brain rather than the mind as the real center of the individual's life.

But, he argued, government will vary depending on which of the two concepts it follows, and on this account the concept of personality is all-important in deciding the basis of government. He concludes that the evidence derived from ESP and PK experiments definitely favors the psychocentric hypothesis and does so in a way that lifts the entire issue out of the speculative realm in which it has hitherto existed. But he recognized that a conflict was inevitable because current beliefs were monistic, and the idea among scientific people, "by now a dogmatic conviction," was that the physical order of reality was the only one.

While JB then recognized that a relative dualism differed from that of the "classical mind-body hypothesis," he found no reason to suppose that such a "common psychophysical substrate" was undiscoverable. Therefore, he said, it was something for which "we should now earnestly begin to search." He then recalled an excerpt from a presidential address given the Society for Psychical Research by Professor C.D. Broad in 1935 in which Broad considered the possibility of a "substrate," some kind of extended pervasive medium necessary for all psychophysical interaction.

JB's qualifying adjective, "relative," however, it is only fair to say, apparently was seldom recognized by his critics. Among them, the charge against him that he was a dualist continued to be made, a charge that, today, is condemnatory and will probably continue to be so long as the present psychological viewpoint remains unchanged.

14

Psi Experiences

The unfavorable publicity that JB and his research received, as discussed in Chapter 10, had wide-reaching effects at home, as well as abroad. By 1948, even Sally, then a student at my old College of Wooster in Ohio, gave evidence of it in a letter home. She wrote in January of that year

> Mr. Mosel of the psychology department made a talk at Freshman Chapel about hypnotism. But he made a fatal mistake for which I'll never forgive

him. He was saying that hypnosis was not mysterious and was not tied up with unusual happenings such as mental telepathy. Then he said, and this is the part I mean, that mental telepathy has never been proved at all even if the Sunday papers do say so.

I wanted to run up afterwards and tell him a thing or two, but I didn't have the nerve. Someday I'll set him straight. Anyway, I'm not taking psych under him next semester as I had planned to.

However, a month later, in a letter to him just after an article by JB had been published, she was in quite a different mood:

You would be surprised how many kids have said something to me about your article and seemed to be interested. If I could make a good speech I could probably convert some of them.

Poor Sally, she had a streak of shyness and lack of self-confidence which probably was a direct result of her relationship to me. It was one which required years of trying for her, as well as myself, before it was overcome. Yet in a case like hers in the above episode, I'm sure her father would have said that anything she might have told her professor would probably have made little impression on him. JB's formula for such situations when any of the lab people encountered them was always the same, "Don't waste time trying to convince people. Instead, do more research." He knew that only good solid experimental data would in time, like drops of water on a rock, show a little effect.

It was something of the same line of thought that led JB in 1948 to turn more attention than before to spontaneous cases, the accounts of personal experiences that suggested a hidden and unrecognized ability to know about the world. As he said in an editorial, December 1948, these occurrences had "stimulated the earlier psychical researchers to look for experimental evidence" of the human capacities suggested by them. Of course, such personal reports were not of themselves proof of anything. But they raised questions, provided a stimulus to experimentation which could decide whether or not valid principles were involved. (Perhaps again here the reminder should be given that the virtue of the experimental method over the anecdotal is that it can yield a negative as well as a positive answer to a question. For instance, an experience might suggest telepathy but could not prove that some other explanation might not be the true one. The experimental method could reduce, if not completely remove that uncertainty.)

As JB said in this editorial, such experiences should have been kept in perspective in all parapsychological research, but the need for developing methods of experimental control had narrowed the attention given to the original manifestations. But now, he said, it was time to go back and look at them again. However, the job of collecting an adequate number of such cases and then of arranging them into a usable form and making a proper study of them would be an enormous one, too big, he said, for one laboratory to undertake! However, it came about that it was not too big for one woman to attempt, one who started with all the advantage of ignorance as to what would be involved and with motives which originally were somewhat mixed.

JB had felt for some time that such a study could give researchers a fresh outlook and so help them to maintain perspective, possibly even provide new outlooks for their research. He therefore called a meeting of the research staff and proposed to them that each one consider making a collection of spontaneous experiences for the enrichment of his own perspective. Each of the members, however, was deep in his own specific problem and none felt that he could take the time just then to begin such a study. All but me. I was not in the midst of an experiment.

And so, I began to read some of the accumulated mail in which persons had told of experiences of their own that suggested an *extra* sensory way by which upon occasion they had seemed to get information. A deluge of such letters had come quickly after JB's book *New Frontiers of the Mind* was published in 1937. (Incidentally, it was in this book that JB first used the abbreviation ESP in print.)

In these letters the writers described puzzling experiences that they had had which they thought might have been instances of ESP. But JB had no time to answer this mail. He wondered if I could take it over and at least give appreciative replies. I decided I could do so, for by then all of our children were in school and I could go to the lab with JB in the mornings, read and acknowledge the letters, and so relieve the pressure on him a bit.

By then several hundred such letters had accumulated. I began with a somewhat skeptical attitude toward the experiences described by the writers, for I expected to read in many of them of imaginary or at least exaggerated happenings reported by rather credulous persons. I remembered, too, a story I had heard in childhood which I suppose still affected me and tended to make me skeptical. The story was one from my father's boyhood. It involved a ghostly movement and clicking of the latch on the stair door of my grandfather's home. The mystery of it had been dispelled, however, when my father found that occasionally a mouse "sat" on the flat, old-fashioned latch on the stairway side of that door. It was the "ghost" that caused the erratic movement and clicking of the latch.

As I began to read the letters, however, my attitude began to change because of a common feature I found in most of them. The people and the specific details of the situations they described were different, but the episodes always included features which suggested ESP. Before long I thought I should copy off these accounts of individual experiences in order to be able later to compare and study them. I'm sure I entertained the family at home at mealtime very often, whether or not I thought they were interested, by accounts that had impressed me and which I'm sure came to puzzle them too.

The point was that so many of the episodes were essentially the same and also were rather uncommon, such as dreams that came true in detail, sudden urges and hunches that seemed "out of the blue," but yet were apropos of the specific situation involved. Besides, the writers seemed to be sane, although puzzled, and to be asking for enlightenment rather than for any kind of personal reward. In fact, as I commented in my first published account of my subsequent study of this material, *Hidden Channels of Mind* (p. 9),

> Although many individuals seemed hesitant and even a bit apologetic to be writing about a personal matter and admitting that they had had such an inexplicable experience, they said in effect, "If someone else had told me this I wouldn't have believed it." Perhaps the most frequently expressed motive for writing to tell about the occurrence was, "I hope this will help you in your researches."

My skeptical attitude decreased as it became increasingly evident that these persons were testifying to something more than just casual personal occurrences; that something more general must have been involved. It would have to be the ESP that JB had shown experimentally does occur.

We knew, of course, that collections of reports of such experiences had been made in England and on the Continent, collections of accounts that suggested telepathy or clairvoyance especially. I knew too the care and pains that had been taken to verify the truthfulness of the persons who had reported these occurrences. For instance, in the two-volume *Phantasms of the Living* published in London in 1885, the verifying testimony and affidavits that were collected by the authors took much more space than the accounts of the occurrences themselves. I knew very well that I could not go to such lengths to verify these reports of the experiences I was copying from this flood of letters. I certainly could not do that, not in the time I would have.

But then I realized that I myself had been impressed by the fact that the accounts showed so many basic similarities. In that very fact I came to feel that they were in effect verifying themselves. Soon I decided that a large number, say fifty or more accounts of the same kind of experience, for instance, a dream that came true in specific detail, could suggest a human ability to produce true dreams. If so, then I could collect such accounts and by their very numbers minimize any human tendency to prevaricate or even to exaggerate. Besides, it was hard to see any general motive that these hundreds of scattered persons could have had to falsify their accounts. I therefore decided to include in my collection, in order to make it truly representative, any kind of unusual experience that *could* have been the result of ESP. It would be of interest because ESP was now an experimentally demonstrated human ability. Therefore it should be expected to occur spontaneously in nature, and so the circle would be completed; the natural occurrences suggested the experiments that showed the reality of the ESP ability, and that ability explained the spontaneous occurrences themselves.

At this point, JB's interest supported my feeling that a study of these spontaneous experiences would be worthwhile. I became intrigued and interested almost from the first. I reasoned that if ESP was an ability that could be detected by laboratory studies, certainly it must occur in nature and it would have to be in experiences just like these. If so, then they should have testimony of their own to give, provided it could be properly noted and evaluated.

At that time 1600 cases suitable for such a study were in the collection and over the following years the number continued to increase until at 15,000 I ceased adding to the numbers, for new forms or types had long since ceased to appear. Over the following years my studies on this material resulted in five books. The general purpose of these was to inform the public of this facet of human nature, the psychic, so largely overlooked and denied in conventional psychological science.

Perhaps I should insert here something of the "training" I underwent in doing this, training in how to work with this husband of mine in a cooperative way in a field that was his, essentially, and only mine by adoption, although by then one that enlisted my deepest interest.

But although in a way it might have seemed that I would be to him a shorn lamb toward whom a bit of indulgence would be shown, I was soon convinced that that would not be the case. As I wrote Sally in a letter in 1955, a fragment of which still remains, and which concerns one of my early attempts to write something that had to pass JB's censorship,

> I had to write the PB (*Parapsychology Bulletin*) article and the third time I had to do it over I decided if it won't do now, Dad can do it himself. The

trouble is partly that Dad had his own idea of the way an idea should be phrased, and no one else could ever do it exactly that way. — Still I'm learning to work with him and I do appreciate the way he sees into and around things faster than I do. And so, on the whole it's fun.

I might have added that by the third trial, he usually had no time to read my version again, and so I could "get away with it." Anyway, as I remember, he spent less and less time on succeeding books of mine, if only because he had less time or energy to devote to them. I remember I asked him once after a tough round of criticism on one of my attempts, if he realized that he never found anything to praise, and that after all, I could use a little encouragement. That sent him to a bit of reminiscing and he said he had not realized that he never praised, though he guessed it was a fact. He thought perhaps it was the effect of his father's attitude, for he could not remember ever being praised, but always criticized by his own father. And so, I suppose, the critical attitude in his case was not only an inherent one, but also one set by environment too.

However that may be, fortunately we had a link between us, too deep and strong to be broken by differences which, after all, were superficial. And as my attempts at book writing went on, which essentially JB deeply encouraged, I finally began the fifth and last one, *The Invisible Picture*. It was at a stage in JB's life, however, when he could no longer supervise. In that one, partly because of his failing health and defective eyesight, he was no longer able to read the manuscript.

In that book (p. 257), I presented the still more or less unrecognized, even denied, psi ability as contributing to the concept of human personality an element quite at variance with today's generally behavioristic one. I wrote that the findings of psychical studies

> add up to more for humankind than this mundane life alone suggests. This life, the sensory life alone, turns out to show but half a human. The other half is shown ... to represent a different level, one as yet too much unknown. That is partly, of course, because it has been so long held to be beyond investigation — to be an area for religion, not for science.

Meanwhile, not only were reports of spontaneous instances of ESP being reported to the lab, but mixed in among them were occasionally cases in which PK instead might be the explanation for the event described. Then, too, there were instances in which, if the accounts were true, the PK force (if that is what it was) took an unusual form and not only single instances of its expression, but a series of mysterious physical occurrences were reported. Such series sometimes affected people in peculiar ways, as if an alien spirit were involved. These events had come to be known as poltergeist phenomena.

In 1958, effects that could have been of this kind in Seaford, Long Island, were widely reported in the news. Soon requests came to the lab for an inquiry into the situation. Pratt was delegated to make an investigation, which he did and later reported in his book, *Parapsychology, an Insider's View of ESP*. In an exchange of letters with Sally about this, I told her we discussed the idea of PK as the force which might have been involved. I said that even if fraud were impossible I doubted whether PK would be a very convincing explanation to the public. But I didn't think that Gaither would say it *was* an instance of PK but only that the possibility of it made the case of interest to parapsychologists.

The affair, however, became a lively point of discussion at the lab, and one that JB, always alert to prevent uncontrolled publicity and sensationalism, tried to keep under control. His effort, however, led to some disagreements at the staff meeting. As I wrote Sally, "The Coffee Hour at the lab today was the scene of unexpected fireworks, when Dad tried to package up the Seaford case. After all the publicity the case has already received, now the TV people want to make it the subject of one of their shows, but Dad said enough time and energy from the lab has already been expended on the case. After all, it's not an experimental issue. In effect, at the best it's on the level of a spontaneous case, and although this proposed show is a respectable one, we at the lab can't afford to give any more time to it, nor do we want the notoriety that would go with it." He added that Gaither's handling of it had been excellent, but that now it was time to get back again to regular lines of research.

I thought he explained why he took this stand very well, but one member of the staff exploded and I sensed the rest were with her. She said that the program was so good and Gaither's part in it so excellent, that it wasn't fair for JB to play it down. Probably this attitude reflected the feeling that had been building up among the staff that JB was trying to curb Gaither, to keep him from having his place in the sun. Instead, I knew that JB was putting on the brakes because he had to keep to the main course and prevent such publicity from running away with the serious purpose of the lab.

One morning a few days later, no longer on a serious topic, I wrote,

> Oh, Dad's stirring. I've been enjoying the fire he laid — must be sycamore — green, white blotched, but now it'll burn up while I'm getting Dad's breakfast. — But the breakfast is easy. The same, morning after morn-

ing for which I'm no end thankful. If he were one of those guys who wants a different menu from day to day, you could have him. By now, I only must drop the eggs and English muffin in a pan. Then he comes in, towel-aproned, salts and burns them to his taste. (Because of his deficient taste buds, the burning was almost literal). I'm telling you these secrets just in case you have anyone around who needs a model. Here's an (almost) model for you — me, for after JB begins his breakfast, I (who eat none) read the book on Russia (or whatever) to him, thereby benefitting both of us. It enlightens him and keeps me out of temptation.

A little later, in a letter to Sally from JB himself, he tells her

The pond, the cider [fresh sweet cider which he allowed to stand a day or two at room temperature until it began to "fizz" a bit and then held at that stage in the refrigerator, his only concession to a fermented drink], my letter to *Life* [commending the magazine for printing an article on the stand the black school children took in the early days of integration in Little Rock, Arkansas; JB's letter was printed in a prime spot in *Life* subsequently] — those are the things on which I have been most complimented. — Oh, I forgot my family.

And, as a little reminder to me now, I find a note dating back to this period after I had visited Sally in Arizona when her little girl, Laura Lee, was about two. I said

If Dad's to be waked up, he'd prefer it from a little songbird like I used to hear when in Arizona. He's a little bit touchy, however, when a dog does it or a midnight phone caller. The last time was at 4 a.m. instead of midnight and the man said, "I just had to tell you, Dr. Rhine, I've got the answer to all your problems." But Dad's sleepy rejoinder, "I don't want any answers at this time of night. Go to bed."

We knew, of course, that calls like that were from the unbalanced, but that, however, did not keep the phone from waking us at such ungodly hours.

Later, sometime in 1959, I reported to Sally

The main parapsychology news recently was a luncheon talk given by a physicist during the AAAS meetings in Washington, D.C. It was by a Dr. Raymond Bierge, retired, from the University of California, entitled, "Science, Pseudo-science, and Parapsychology." The old boy had read a lot but not digested very much and his talk was a jumble of mostly unfavorable quotes and references to witchcraft superstition and the Middle Ages with the general concession that the methods of science are now being tried on the "supernatural" and he doesn't know what to make of it. He said that he doesn't think like Price that it's fraud or pseudo-science, "but obviously, you can't investigate the supernatural." So on the whole he's just puzzled.

On the whole, we have to think that parapsychology is coming along if the physicists take this much notice. Dad has written the man to see if his piece will be published and if so where, or if he'd submit it to the *Journal*. [He didn't.]

Then, a different topic, but our ever-occurring one, comes in.

Mr. Ozanne gives him trouble. [Mr. Ozanne was trying to donate his fortune to "survival research."] ... If any more potential donors appear over the horizon, I'm about ready to pop them off with a shotgun before they get near the Lab.

JB wrote to Sally, saying

Life moves on here at the Lab with a combination of unsolvable problems and also with the day-to-day development of fresh interests. I often think that a parapsychologist must be a person who likes to hop from one bubble to another as they burst under his feet. But I think we have gained a little elevation.

And then a "homely" touch from me:

Dad has been clearing the brush across the lake. There's a good wild blackberry patch on the slope, but I've about given up on picking them, for unlike him, I get millions of chiggers in spite of his cure, sweat and a bath of yellow soap.

Husbands are all right as far as they go. But they're unlikely to go far enough, with big brains full of big thoughts, little people like wives sometimes seem to filter through the cracks quite unnoticed — so substitutes are advisable from both viewpoints. [Never got any, though.]

Dad's having trouble with Mrs. Bolton. He expected it. She and Mrs. Garrett want him to work with mediums but don't say so. He never said he would, but I guess they thought he'd have to. I think the "association" [with them] is going to fall through. We can't use research money that's got strings tied to it. This has, but they weren't specified at the start.

In July, I said that,

> Mrs. Bolton is holding up her payments. I won't let it spoil the summer, by Golly!

A little later,

> Another round with Mrs. Bolton. But luckily it's getting now so that nothing she does affects JB deeply. If it's anything positive, he accepts it as a gain, but unless it is that he's able to say it doesn't matter.

15

The Continuing Quest

As time went on, JB approached an age when he looked forward to a way to ease his burdens and began more seriously to search the horizon for a successor. More and more he wanted someone who would take over the "nuts and bolts" of running the lab and give him the freedom to do the writing he had long been wanting to do. His search finally led him in the fall of 1973 to find a young director who he thought could handle the job and thus relieve himself from the wear and tear of managing the place.

This young man, L, was at the time just completing medical school, but he had been attending research meetings at the lab since his early undergraduate days at Duke and was active in parapsychological research seemingly in all his spare time. L's interest and enthusiasm for parapsychology was such that he then interrupted his further medical training and devoted all his time to the field, often working at the lab until late at night. His quick intelligence, his grasp of the problems and ability to solve them impressed JB very much. In spite of his youth, he soon was JB's most satisfactory discussant of all the problems involved, which ranged from the purely intellectual to practical and even financial ones. Therefore, after due consideration, JB appointed L as director of the lab and with much relief and satisfaction, at age 78 gave over the reins to him.

As part of his official retirement as director, JB made a physical move of his office from the FRNM building to a location, two blocks away at 312 Watts Street, which had been donated to FRNM by Mrs. Marie Avery, a long-time benefactor much interested in parapchological research and also deeply devoted to JB. In order to make space at the main building I had already moved my office into this house, since I needed only office space and not necessarily proximity to the scene of research. Then with the advent of the new director, JB moved his office there too, selecting an upstairs room. I remained on the first floor, able thus to control the flow of traffic of individuals who might want to see JB.

One day some callers appeared at my door, a little group of three of the staff men from the lab, and a very serious-looking delegation they were. When the group was seated in my office, the spokesman said that they had a difficult but urgent message for JB. They wanted to tell it first to me and then maybe I would take it to him. They thought I would know how to break the news better than they would. I signalled them to go ahead, and I heard these words, ones that will stay with me forever:

"L is a fraud."

Then the story came out. It involved the computer with which the main building had been equipped. (In the days before computers were common, and although the cost seemed exorbitant in relation to the size of the FRNM budget, JB had been convinced that one was necessary and had made the investment.)

I heard then that these young men had had their curiosity aroused because L was so frequently seen hanging around the computer, they said, and especially at night when they thought he had no conceivable reason to be there. By then his devotion to the lab was so complete that he had installed a bunk in the attic and often slept there all night.

After a time the curiosity aroused in these men turned into suspicion and they thought they should tell JB about it. Before doing so, however, they realized they needed more than suspicion to convince JB. They then installed a second and hidden terminal to the computer and soon had evidence that the results that L had been reporting were falsified and included a sufficient number of false hits to account for the positive scores he had been reporting.

After telling me of their findings, the delegation then left with my assurance that they certainly had my own full approval and deep appreciation for what they had done, and that they would have JB's as well when he heard the account. I realized fully that this news would be the most devastating parapsychological message of all to take upstairs to JB. But I had to do it, and perhaps better I than these three young researchers who had gathered the evidence.

I went upstairs. JB was at his desk. I put my arm across his shoulder and he looked up expectantly. When I could speak, I said, "JB, bad news. L is a fraud." And then I told him what I had heard. He listened, stunned, but at once called L to come in, and I went back to my office downstairs.

Very quickly, L appeared and went upstairs to JB's office and almost immediately came down again and left the building. JB told me afterward that when confronted with the evidence, L at once admitted his fraud. The forethought that had been used in assembling that evidence not only had convinced JB that it was reliable but it also convinced L that he could not refute it. And so, no way remained for him except to resign and leave. He packed up immediately and within a few days was gone from town and from parapsychology as well.

He went back, we heard, to medical work. We could only hope that the lesson he should have learned from this experience would serve him well in his profession later, and that those who would depend on him, possibly for life itself, would not have trusted him in vain. Surely intelligence such as his should need no second lesson. But JB would long chide himself for having been too trusting, though I very well know that being too trusting is a failing of which JB's acquaintances would hardly accuse him.

In spite of the almost devastating upset to his plans and expectations that this episode was to JB, we agreed that it had been unavoidable and not one which he could have foreseen. The character weakness to which it attested was a deeply hidden one. L himself could only say about it, "I guess I just wanted to get ahead too fast."

Immediately afterwards, JB wrote the following self-explanatory letter, one which attests to his unfaltering devotion to the truth.

Durham, North Carolina 27708
June 19, 1974

To My Fellow Members of the Board
of Directors (and other friends) of the FRNM:

On the 12th I received the most distressing jolt I have had in many years. On that date we lost our gifted Director of the Institute, L. He resigned from all his official connections with the Foundation.

It all came to a head in one day, almost on the anniversary date of his coming as a full-time member and as Director. It had seemingly been a splendid year and we were all looking ahead with optimism when this grievous blow was dealt us.

One of Dr. L's co-workers had, under our system of multiple experimenter safeguarding of research procedures and results, observed irregularities that aroused his concern; he called in another and the two drew in a third. Together they added more definite checkups and accumulated unmistakable evidence of unreliable procedures conducted by Dr. L in the course of one of his recent experiments.

With the evidence in hand so final, I confronted L at once, and he admitted that in recent weeks he had resorted to improper methods of bolstering a research project he wanted especially to keep going successfully.

L's colleagues regarded this utterly foolish action as so much unlike him that he must have been "out of his head," that he must have been working too hard. There have been some signs that he had been working under phenomenal pressure.

It will of course take time to appraise the full possible uncertainty involved in the large amount of work L has done. Fortunately some main lines have already been independently confirmed in this and in other laboratories. We intend however that nothing will be left in doubt when a full examination has been made.

It may seem ironical that this blow had to hit us right after my article on experimenter reliability in the *Journal of Parapsychology* for March. I can only hope we can make a sound recovery from it and find an adequate successor.

I am proud and grateful for the alertness and good judgment of our staff in uncovering this shocking violation of our confidence, even while we trust it will not completely crush this able young worker who held such promise for the field.

Sincerely yours,
J.B. Rhine
Executive Director FRNM

But now where was JB's replacement? Well past the usual retirement age, he had to remain active in managing the lab's affairs. The rest of his efforts to find a successor need not be enumerated here, except to summarize the final satisfactory solution. In 1976 he found a mature and responsible person, one deeply interested in parapsychology, with a good strong background in psychology and in parapsychology and who finally was willing to give up a very responsible position in his own university and country, Andhra University, India, to come to be an assistant and then permanent director of the Institute for Parapsychology. Dr. Ramakrishna Rao had been trained at the University of Chicago, had long been active in parapsychology, and in 1967 had been instrumental in setting up the first parapsychology division at the university at Andhra.

As physical infirmities increasingly beset JB, he was forced to retire, but he continued to go to his Watts Street office as long as he could manage to get there. We still went daily for months after his failing eyesight made it necessary for me to drive, and even when the special high-powered lighting we had installed for him was no longer adequate. Then for a few months I read to him as he still maintained his interest as of old. I could join him then in rejoicing that the lab would carry on under Rao's leadership, on and on into the future as far as either JB or I needed to feel any responsibility.

JB's last words to me as I helped him into bed the last time of all were, "The work must go on." I am sure it will, under Dr. Rao and others who will follow in years to come. The question will last, I know; the answer is one for future generations.

After JB's death, I found a little pack of poems, clipped and gathered from various sources, in the back of a drawer in his desk. Some were handwritten stanzas from well known poems and one of these, from Kipling's "The Explorer," I think epitomizes his lifelong endeavor.

Something hidden. Go and find it. Go and look behind the ranges —
Something lost behind the ranges. Lost and waiting for you. Go!

January 1, 1983, Durham, North Carolina

Index

Compiled by Dorothy H. Pope

McDougall, Angus 191
McDougall, Kenneth 191, 234, 239
McDougall, William 121, 126, 140, 141, 194, 196, 197, 207; correspondence of, with Rhine 93, 94, 118, 137; at Duke 113, 117, 118, 123–125, 135, 141; at Harvard 93, 138, 177; illness and death of 188–189, 190–191, 193; and the Lamarckian research 137–139; and the Margery mediumship 99, 102, 103, 104; opening editorial by, in the *Journal of Parapsychology* 178–179; personality of 141; reputation of, as a psychologist 179; resistance of, to behaviorism 124; as sponsor of the *Journal of Parapsychology* 177–178; on telepathy 154; and the Thomas material 113, 114, 118, 124
McDougall, Mrs. William 124, 141, 145, 186, 188, 234, 239; and the "Christmas tree" case 191–193
McVaugh, Michael 228
Mediums 194, 195, 199, 275; *see also* Garrett, Eileen; Keene, Sally; the Margery mediumship
Mediumistic evidence 173, 195; *see also* Thomas, John F., psychical material of
Murphy, Gardner 94, 118, 119, 190, 196, 218, 226, 227, 263
Myers, F.W.H. 92, 160

New Frontiers of the Mind (J.B. Rhine) 157, 208, 209, 269

Ohio Northern University 15, 19
Ozanne, Charles E. 200, 275

Parapsychology 173
Parapsychology, An Insider's View of ESP (Pratt) 273
Parapsychology Bulletin 271
Parapsychology Laboratory, changing personnel in 202; funding of 197, 275–276
Pearce, Hubert 160, 197

Pegram, Margaret 196, 197
Phantasms of the Living 270
Phi Beta Kappa 97
Phi Lambda Upsilon 97
Plant physiology 89, 96–98, 100
Poltergeist *see* the Seaford case; Spontaneous cases, possible PK in
Pope, Dorothy 235, 236, 244, 249, 252
Position effects in PK data *see* Psychokinesis, patterning of hits…
Pratt, J. Gaither 159, 196, 197, 199, 202, 222, 225, 264; and the "Jim" records 226–227; as a possible successor to Rhine 259; and the Seaford case 273
Precognition 173–175; possible effect of PK on 173
President's Rifle Match, won by Rhine 58, 80
Prince, Walter Franklin 99, 100, 102, 103, 104, 105, 109, 143, 196
Psi *see also* Extrasensory perception, Psychokinesis; conditions favoring 264; counterhypotheses to evidence of: recording errors 219; sensory cues 210, 217–218, 221; statistical inadequacies 219, 221; unconscious whispering 219; *see also* Fraud; and the mind–body problem 265–266; unconscious nature of 269
Psychical research, criticisms of experimental work in 174, 175, 176, 178, 190, 197, 203–204, 207–211, 213–221, 228, 232, 262; first university grant for 154; and physics 172, 265, 275; professional handicaps in 260; and religion 196, 261; replicability of experimental results in 263–264
Psychical Research Foundation 201
Psychokinesis (PK) 173, 193, 196, 220; by the experimenter in selection of targets 173; decision to publish data on 253–256; patterning of hits in data of 257; and the "psychic shuffle" 173; random targets affected by 173–174; relationship of, to ESP 255
Publicity 190, 196, 197, 201, 211, 213, 232, 261, 273